CHECKING EXECUTIVE POWER

CHECKING EXECUTIVE POWER

PRESIDENTIAL IMPEACHMENT IN COMPARATIVE PERSPECTIVE

Edited by Jody C. Baumgartner and Naoko Kada

Westport, Connecticut
London

Library of Congress Cataloging-in-Publication Data

Checking executive power : presidential impeachment in comparative
   perspective / edited by Jody C. Baumgartner and Naoko Kada.
     p. cm.
   Includes bibliographical references and index.
    ISBN 0-275-97926-1 (alk. paper) — ISBN 0-275-97927-X (pbk. : alk. paper)
     1. Presidents. 2. Impeachments. 3. Comparative government. I. Baumgartner,
Jody C., 1958- II. Kada, Naoko.
JF255.C46 2003
342'.062—dc21   2003051771

British Library Cataloguing in Publication Data is available.

Library of Congress Catalog Card Number: 2003051771
ISBN: 0-275-97926-1
    0-275-97927-X (pbk.)

First published in 2003

Praeger Publishers, 88 Post Road West, Westport, CT 06881
An imprint of Greenwood Publishing Group, Inc.
www.praeger.com

Printed in the United States of America

The paper used in this book complies with the
Permanent Paper Standard issued by the National
Information Standards Organization (Z39.48–1984).

10 9 8 7 6 5 4 3 2 1

Contents

Tables and Figures

Acknowledgments

This book is the result of a collaboration that began over the Internet. In the course of electronic correspondence between the two editors regarding recent work each had done on impeachment in their respective countries of focus, the idea for producing this volume was born. The editors then contacted other contributors who they knew had worked on, or might have an interest in working on, impeachment, again via the Internet, and this book grew from there—without this medium of communication, it might not have materialized.

Most of the papers that comprise this volume were originally presented at a panel at the Midwest Political Association Annual Meeting in spring 2002. It was at that time that most of us gathered to meet and discuss the project. The generous and insightful comments by the panel chair, Dr. Michael Mezey (De Paul University), and discussant, Dr. Ryan Barilleaux (Miami University), were extremely helpful as well as very encouraging. Thanks are also due to James Sabin of Greenwood Publishing, who, through two different projects with Jody, has offered a great deal of professional assistance and encouragement.

It has been a great pleasure for Jody to work with the contributors to this volume, all of whom have brought valuable knowledge and understanding to the project, and without whom it would not have been possible. All have been a pleasure to work with, and he is grateful for the opportunity to expand his circle of friends. He would like to thank them for their patience, cooperation, and trust, and of course for their excellent contributions. Similarly, the close collaboration with Naoko has been insightful, fruitful, and a pleasure. It was her intellectual checks that kept the project on track. On a personal note, he would like to thank his wife Lei for the enormous amount of patience she displayed during the year or so we were working on this project.

Naoko would like to thank Jody for his patience and grace during the production of this book. She would also like to thank the contributors for their superb work under a very tight schedule, many of whom were old friends before, and new friends made in the process. She is ever grateful to her husband, Anthony, for his understanding and support during the sometimes quite stressful collaboration of this project.

CHAPTER 1

Introduction: Comparative Presidential Impeachment

Jody C. Baumgartner

INTRODUCTION

Presidential impeachment is the equivalent of a political earthquake. It convulses, disrupts, and in many cases, polarizes the body politic as few political events can. The rancorous debate among scholars, public intellectuals, and political commentators during the Clinton impeachment illustrates this perfectly.[1] Impeachment proceedings have the power to disrupt and destroy political careers, and that destruction is often not limited to the president. The fall of U.S. House of Representative Speakers Newt Gingrich and Bob Livingston in late 1998 during the impeachment proceedings of U.S. President William Clinton are evidence of this fact. Presidential impeachment is, in short, an extraordinary political event.

Presidential impeachment proceedings are historically rare, but the 1990s saw a wave of them that began with the impeachment and subsequent removal of Brazilian President Collor in 1992, and continued throughout the decade. In all, a total of seven presidents, from every corner of the globe, faced a serious impeachment challenge during this period. This book examines and compares these impeachment efforts.

Should we view the recent wave (if it can be called such) of impeachments with alarm? Does it indicate democratic instability, as some might think? Or, as others maintain, is it a positive sign, since as the result of impeachment proceedings (successful or otherwise), future presidents will better understand that they can and will be held accountable? Is impeachment, as still others suggest, a healthier alternative than removal of a president by military coup or assassination?

Presidential impeachment is a subject that remains shrouded in misunderstanding. What exactly does impeachment mean? For example, before Clinton's impeachment in 1998, many U.S. citizens understood "impeachment" to mean removal from office. But there are other questions about the process as well. Why do presidential systems have provisions for impeachment at all? Is impeachment, as some claim, strictly a legal proceeding, or is it something more? What explains the emergence of an impeachment attempt? When are they most likely to succeed?

The contributors to this volume have shed some light on these questions, illuminating the extraordinary process of presidential impeachment. The book casts a wide net, examining presidential impeachment in several countries in several regions of the world, with chapters devoted to impeachment attempts in the United States, Colombia, Brazil, Venezuela, Russia, the Philippines, and Madagascar. In each of these countries there has been a serious attempt to impeach a sitting president within the past decade or so.

The basic assumption of this book, and one that is addressed throughout, is that impeachment is a political, rather than a legal proceeding. In other words, this book is about the *politics* of presidential impeachment. Each case study includes a discussion of the historical and constitutional bases of the presidency, the structural balance of governmental power, constitutional and statutory provisions for impeachment, the structure of party politics in each country, and presidential popularity prior to the impeachment attempt. After discussing these contextual factors, all of which are related to the emergence of an impeachment attempt, the authors move to an examination of wrongdoing (alleged or otherwise) by the president or those associated with the president and the associated scandal, the reaction by the legislature, and how the impeachment process played out in the institutions of government. While the framework is broad, it is focused enough to allow for comparison between the cases and some general conclusions about all phases of the impeachment process and executive accountability to be drawn.

The remainder of this chapter discusses why it is important to understand presidential impeachment, and then reviews the extant literature on the subject. A general discussion of the theoretical and historical bases of impeachment and a discussion of the framework which guides our study follows. Finally, the cases are briefly introduced.

WHY STUDY PRESIDENTIAL IMPEACHMENT?

Understanding impeachment is important for several reasons. As previously noted, between 1990 and 2001 there were several presidential impeachments attempts in various countries throughout the world. While outcomes in each case varied, such frequency suggests that presidential impeachment may not be all that uncommon, particularly in newer democracies.

Presidential impeachment, as it has been adopted over the years in various countries, is similar to, but more extreme than, a vote of no-confidence in parliamentary systems. Presidential systems, with their strict separation of functions, are designed to (among other things) maximize executive stability at the expense of checking the executive. Besides impeachment, these systems have no regularized "means of removing an unpopular—and possibly feckless—chief executive."[2] Thus, although unwieldy, impeachment is the ultimate check on the power of a chief executive in a presidential system, and therefore a fundamental democratic element of these systems. By itself, this makes it worthy of study and important to understand.

Interestingly, the subject of presidential impeachment has been largely ignored by political scientists. For many years this was justified, since few stable democracies were, in any meaningful sense, "presidential." However, an increasing number of new democracies are opting for some form of presidentialism, whether in its strictly separated form (as in the U.S.) or in hybrid form (sharing executive power with a prime minister, as in France) form.[3] Therefore, it has become increasingly important to understand presidential systems and presidential power, and by extension, how presidential impeachment works. This is especially the case in newer and more fragile democracies, where executive-legislative conflict can contribute to a breakdown of the regime;[4] in these cases, impeachment constitutes a legal-constitutional alternative to less preferred or more familiar alternatives such as system breakdown, military coup, *autogolpe*, etc.[5]

THE LITERATURE

Political scientists have been strangely silent on the subject of presidential impeachment. A summary of the literature on this subject leads to three main conclusions. First, most of the existing work is descriptive, and, either explicitly or implicitly, normative (e.g., did the crime justify the punishment?). Second, most of it is the product of historians, journalists, insiders, or legal scholars. Finally, existing impeachment literature is by and large limited to studies of individual impeachment cases in the United States.

There is little book-length scholarship about presidential impeachment that can properly be considered political science. Exceptions to this include an edited volume from 1975 examining Watergate and its effects on American politics.[6] The Clinton impeachment occasioned two book-length works, one of them an edited volume that examines all aspects of the affair, and another that looks at legislative behavior through the lens of local constituencies and money.[7] There are several published papers that address various aspects of the Clinton impeachment in the U.S., including, for example, some that examine Congressional voting behavior,[8] others that examine public opinion,[9] another that deals with the use of senatorial rhetoric in the Clinton and Johnson trials,[10] and a study which suggests that impeachments are more likely in this modern era of intense partisan conflict.[11]

Historians have contributed several very good accounts of the trial and impeachment of Andrew Johnson, which, although focusing on the role of Reconstruction politics and the relationship between Johnson and Congress, are by and large descriptive.[12] Journalistic and insider narratives about the impeachment efforts directed against both Presidents Nixon and Clinton abound, and although many are compelling, and illuminate certain aspects of the politics of impeachment, they are generally descriptive, fairly narrowly focused (on a particular case), and often have a particular normative bent.[13]

There are also a number of legal texts on the subject, but as might be imagined, these take a legalistic approach to impeachment, focusing mainly on what constitutes impeachable offenses and the procedures involved in impeachment.[14] At this point it might be useful to discuss what we believe to be the deficiencies of the legal approach to understanding the politics of presidential impeachment.[15]

The legal approach first assumes, erroneously, that what constitutes an impeachable offense can be determined with some exactitude. Under this assumption, the only U.S. presidents (for example) who ever broke the law were Andrew Johnson, Richard Nixon, and Bill Clinton. There are, however, differences of opinion over whether or not any of these three men ever committed high crimes or misdemeanors. Furthermore, the legal approach tends to ignore presidents who may have broken the law but were never held accountable (for more on this, see Chapter 2). In other words, there are many presidents who may have acted outside the confines of the law but who never faced an impeachment threat.

The legal approach to the study of impeachment also assumes that partisan differences should not play a role in whether or not a president is to be impeached; this of course is a normative argument. The idea is well encapsulated in the following passage from one of the standard texts on impeachment:

The major *problem* with the impeachment process is that members of Congress are likely to feel tremendous pressure to forego investigating a president with high approval ratings or substantial popularity.[16]

The author goes on to suggest that elected officials should be willing to "undertake political risks" in the process of impeachment. In other words, the passage implies that politicians, who are constrained in their behavior in the pursuit of a variety of goals (including winning elections), can somehow be expected to act non-politically. We do not necessarily disagree with this ideal, but an understanding of impeachment that is centered around it misses the reality that while the focal point of a given impeachment may be understood in legal terms and the process is structured like a trial, impeachment is fundamentally a political process from beginning to end. Simply put, the men and women who decide the fate of presidents during impeachment proceedings are political beings.

Indeed, James Wilson, an active and prominent participant in the constitutional convention, and subsequently a Supreme Court Justice, declared that impeachments were "proceedings of a political nature . . . confined to political characters, to political crimes and misdemeanors, and to political punishments."[17] For his part, Alexander Hamilton observed (in *Federalist 65*) that the impeachment process would be denominated POLITICAL:

The prosecution of them, for this reason, will seldom fail to agitate the passions of the whole community, and to divide it into parties more or less friendly or inimical to the accused. In many cases it will connect itself with the pre-existing factions, and will enlist all their animosities, partialities, influence, and interest on one side or on the other; and in such cases there will always be the greatest danger that the decision will be regulated more by the comparative strength of the parties, than by the real demonstrations of innocence or guilt.

During the effort to impeach Associate Justice William O. Douglas of the U.S. Supreme Court in 1970, then minority floor leader Gerald R. Ford (R-MI) proffered perhaps the most evasive but at the same time realistic definition of impeachment. "An impeachable offense," he said, "is whatever a majority of the House of Representatives considers [it] to be at a given moment in history; conviction results from whatever offense or offenses two-thirds of the other body considers to be sufficiently serious to require removal of the accused from office."

Ford's seemingly obvious conclusion was based upon the Kelley Memorandum, within which the perceived intention of the founders was addressed. "If the framers had meant to remove from office only those officials who violated the criminal law," it read, "a much simpler method than impeachment could have been devised. Since impeachment is such a complex and cumbersome procedure, it must have been directed at conduct which would be outside the purview of the criminal law."[18]

In short, what stands out about the literature on presidential impeachment is that most of the work on the subject has been done by those who adopt a non-political or non-systematic approach to understanding it. Additionally, almost all of the English-language work on impeachment is restricted to the U.S.; there is a distinct lack of scholarship that deals with presidential impeachment in other countries, either individually or comparatively.[19] This book is designed to remedy that situation.

THE PRE-HISTORY OF PRESIDENTIAL IMPEACHMENT

Before discussing presidential impeachment and the factors that lead to impeachment attempts (successful or otherwise), a brief history of the concept and practice of impeachment is in order. Although many variations for presidential impeachment exist, the basic model for the procedure is found in the U.S. Constitution, which in turn drew upon the British and colonial experience with impeachment.

Impeachment, a legislative trial, was introduced in the fourteenth century in Great Britain. It was used by Parliament against public officials, and occasionally against powerful private citizens, for any variety of misdeeds when prosecution by regular courts was not considered to be practicable (if, for example, a court was susceptible to bribery or intimidation by the accused).[20] Impeachment was often used by Parliament as a tool to gain power relative to the Crown and its officials. Similar to the American version of impeachment, the House of Commons (the lower house of the legislature) decided whether to impeach (literally, "to accuse" or "to charge"[21]) an individual, and if impeached, a trial was conducted by the House of Lords (the upper house of the legislature). If convicted, the House of Lords also imposed punishment; unlike in the U.S., punishment sometimes included criminal-type sanctions (even death) as well as removing public officials from office.

In practice, the misdeeds for which an individual might be impeached could be either criminal or political in nature; in other words, unlike in the American variant of the procedure, objectionable policies were considered fair game for impeachment of a public official. Also unlike the U.S. version of the practice, the monarchy (more generally the royal family), as the highest public officials in the land, were considered beyond the purview of the impeachment powers of Parliament.

Although technically they were forbidden to do so, American colonial assemblies adopted and often used the practice of impeachment; the trial was typically conducted before governors' councils. As in Great Britain, impeachment proceedings were often motivated by political concerns and were also a way of challenging authority. The point is that the framers of the U.S. Constitution were very familiar with impeachment by the time the Constitutional Convention convened (for example, the impeachment of Warren Hastings was being conducted in Parliament while the Constitutional Convention was underway).[22]

Chapter 2 discusses the adoption of presidential impeachment provisions during the Convention. What is important to note is that virtually every presidential or semi-presidential democracy since then has adopted constitutional provisions for removal of a sitting president by way of impeachment; this fact, as well as its theoretical implications, are explored in greater detail in the final chapter.

THE FRAMEWORK FOR THIS BOOK

As previously noted, we take the position that presidential impeachment can only be understood as a political phenomenon. The word *impeachment* generally refers to a political trial to remove a public official. In this book we will usually be talking in terms of the *impeachment process*, by which we mean a process that begins with the formation of some investigative body, typically (though not always) in the legislature, to examine the alleged misdeeds of a president (or those close to him) and subsequent activity surrounding the authorization of a trial to remove the president.[23] In common usage, if a trial is authorized, the president has been formally *impeached*; in places we use the term impeached in this sense of the word as well. But the impeachment process also includes a trial, which can ultimately lead to presidential exit from office. Of course not all impeachment efforts reach this stage, a fact we discuss in more detail. The remainder of this section discusses the determinants and stages of presidential impeachment.

Factors That Condition the Process of Presidential Impeachment

We have identified five factors that we suggest condition the emergence and outcome of presidential impeachment attempts. These factors affect the likelihood that an impeachment attempt will be made and how successful it might be, and include (1) the institutional balance of power between the various branches of government; (2) the constitutional and statutory provisions for impeachment; (3) the structure of party politics; (4) presidential popularity prior to allegations of presidential wrongdoing; and (5) other factors, including the media environment, economic conditions, and international pressures.

The Institutional Balance of Power

A description of the constitutional framework of government and the institutional balance of power between the various branches of government is necessary to set the stage for a discussion of impeachment in a particular country. At least one other national institution besides the president is involved in the impeachment and removal process, so understanding the regime structure and the relationship between the various institutions of government is critical to establishing a baseline for a discussion of impeachment.

It matters, for example, if the presidency is fairly weak (i.e., has few legislative powers) vis-a-vis the legislature.[24] Here we might expect to see a greater likelihood of an impeachment attempt, if, for example, a president tried to exert influence over the legislature. Conversely, if the president is strong in relation to the legislature, impeachment may be the only constitutional-legal way for a legislature to exert any control over the executive. In Russia, for example, a strong presidency may have led to many of the various impeachment attempts against Boris Yeltsin in the 1990s; these attempts were also conditioned by conflictual relations between Yeltsin and the legislature prior to the establishment of the present regime.

If the selection process for members of the high courts (e.g., a Constitutional or Supreme Court) or the upper house of the legislature is dominated by the president, and if either (or both) are involved in the trial to remove the president, the removal attempt might theoretically have less chance of success. Importantly, the institutional balance of power varies in its effect on the impeachment process across cases. In other words, the explanatory power of this variable alone may approach insignificance, but explicating it adds needed context. Table 1-1 outlines the structure of the regime in each of the cases we examine.

Constitutional and Statutory Provisions for Impeachment

In almost all countries presidential impeachment is difficult. This is by design, since one of the motivations for settling on some form of presidentialism as opposed to strict parliamentarianism is to achieve a greater degree of executive stability. This said, in some systems, impeaching and removing a president is more difficult than in others. A discussion of the legal provisions for impeachment, both constitutional and statutory, is necessary for understanding both the emergence and course of an impeachment attempt. In particular, which institutions of government are responsible at what stage, and what size majority is required for successfully moving the process to the next phase? Although lower houses of the legislature are in most cases responsible for the actual impeachment (authorizing a trial) itself, in some countries an upper house of the legislature conducts the trial, while in others the high court(s) does so, and in some few others, either the lower house itself or both the high court(s) and the upper house are involved. Of course, more institutions involved in the process mean more potential veto points, making it theoretically more difficult for an impeachment attempt to succeed. Table 1-2 outlines the constitutional and statutory provisions for impeachment in each of the cases in our study.

The Structure of Party Politics

Presidential impeachment is played out between institutions of government that are comprised (with the exception of some presidents) of members of political parties. Unsurprisingly therefore, presidential impeachment typically has distinct partisan overtones. Thus, an overview of the shape of party politics in each country is critical to understanding presidential impeachment, particularly when discussing the organization of the legislature, the partisan composition of legislative committees, and the manner and history of judicial appointments. A focus on party politics

Table 1-1.
Regime Structures

Country (Year of Constitution)	Lower House of Legislature	Upper House of Legislature	Constitutional Court	Supreme Court
Brazil (1988)	House of Deputies; 503 members; 4-year terms	Senate; 81 members; 8-year terms	N/A	11 members; appointed for life (mandatory retirement at age 70); president nominates, Senate approves
Colombia (1991)	Chamber of Representatives; 161 members; 4-year terms	Senate; 102 members; 4-year terms	9 members; 8-year terms; appointed by Senate from list presented by president, Supreme Court, and Council of State	23 members; 8-year terms; appointed by Court itself from list presented by Judicial Council
Madagascar (1992)	Unicameral National Assembly; 150 members; 4-year terms	(N/A; a 90-member Senate, serving 4-year terms, was recently constituted, but not in session during impeachment proceedings)	9 members; 6-year terms; 3 members appointed by President, 2 by National Assembly, 1 by Senate, 3 by Superior Council of Magistrates	11 members (for cases involving members of the government Madagascar also has a 9-member High Court of Justice)
Phillippines (1986)	House of Representatives; currently 216 members; 3-year terms	Senate; 24 members; 6-year terms	N/A	15 members; appointed for life (mandatory retirement at age 70); appointed by president from list of nominees prepared by Judicial and Bar Council

(*continues*)

Table 1-1. (*continued*)
Regime Structures

Country (Year of Constitution)	Lower House of Legislature	Upper House of Legislature	Constitutional Court	Supreme Court
Russia (1993)	State Duma; 450 members; 4-year terms	Federation Council; 178 members; 4-year terms	19 members; 15-year terms; president nominates, Federation Council approves	> 100 members; president nominates, Federation Council approves
United States (1789)	House of Representatives; 435 members; 2-year terms	Senate; 100 members; 6-year terms	N/A	9 Members; life terms; president nominates, Senate approves
Venezuela (1961–1999)	House of Deputies; 201 members; 5-year terms	Senate; 46 members; 5-year terms (except for ex-presidents, who are senators for life)	N/A	15 members; 9-year terms, renewable; appointed by a majority (of those present) in joint session of Congress

Table 1-2.
Constitutional and Statutory Provisions for Impeachment

Country	Investigation (Decision Rule)	Impeachment (Decision Rule)	Trial (Decision Rule)
Brazil	Ad hoc legislative committee (> $1/_2$ members present)	Lower house of legislature ($2/_3$ members)	Upper house of legislature ($2/_3$ members)
Colombia	Legislative committee (> $1/_2$ members)	Lower house of legislature (> $1/_2$ members)	Upper house of legislature ($2/_3$ members present)
Madagascar	Lower house of legislature (not specified)	Both houses of legislature[1] ($2/_3$ members)	Constitutional Court (not specified)
Phillippines	Legislative committee (> $1/_2$ members)	Lower house of legislature ($1/_3$ members)	Upper house of legislature ($2/_3$ members)
Russia	Legislative committee	Lower house of legislature ($2/_3$ members)	Upper house of legislature ($2/_3$ members)[3]
United States	Legislative committee (> $1/_2$ members)	Lower house of legislature (> $1/_2$ members)	Upper house of legislature ($2/_3$ members present)
Venezuela	Supreme Court (> $1/_2$ members present)	Upper house of legislature (> $1/_2$ members)[2]	Supreme Court (not specified)

From Naoko Kada, *The Politics of Impeachment* (unpublished doctoral dissertation, San Diego: University of California, 2002).

[1]The upper-house Senate was not yet constituted during the 1996 impeachment proceeding.

[2]Decision made only after the judicial branch determines that the president has committed a crime.

[3]Legislative decision in both houses must be confirmed by Constitutional and Supreme Courts.

includes, for example, whether the party system has two or multiple parties, how institutionalized the party system is, the degree of discipline parties display in voting, what ties (if any) the president has to any particular party, how strong those ties might be, and why.

It matters, for example, if the country in question has a fairly well-established two-party system, where divided government is the rule (as in the U.S.); here we might expect to see the president and legislature at odds with greater frequency, and thus, a greater likelihood that an impeachment attempt will emerge. Or, if a president is elected with few or no formal ties to a political party, we might be less surprised if a legislature initiated impeachment proceedings based on a presidential scandal. If that legislative majority displays a fair amount of party cohesiveness in voting, we would similarly be less surprised if impeachment was successful. If, on the other hand, the president and a majority of the legislature were from the same, fairly disciplined party, it would be theoretically harder to impeach and remove the president, given the same scandal. These examples serve to suggest, again, that we are hard-pressed to understand presidential impeachment without first understanding its partisan foundations.

Presidential Popularity

Another factor important to understanding the emergence and outcome of a presidential impeachment attempt is presidential popularity. Simply put, it is more difficult (and politically costly) to impeach and remove a popular president than an unpopular one. Most commentators who, for example, compared the Clinton and Nixon impeachment attempts, often dwelled on the nature of the crimes involved, downplaying (perhaps conveniently) the fact that in one sense the two cases were completely different: unlike Nixon, Clinton enjoyed consistently high public approval ratings throughout the course of the impeachment scandal.

Of course presidential popularity does not by itself determine the course of an impeachment attempt, and, as with all of the factors that comprise the impeachment setting, examples counter to this rule can be found. Russian President Yeltsin, for example, was extraordinarily unpopular the last six years of his tenure, and successfully survived the 1998–99 impeachment attempt by the Russian State Duma. On the other hand, Brazilian President Collor was quite popular when his investigation began. It was only when impeachment proceedings uncovered compromising information that people began to demand his impeachment.

Nevertheless, presidential popularity does affect whether and how impeachment proceedings are conducted. Presidential popularity might affect the likelihood that a president will be subjected to formal investigation; conversely, it might change public opinion so that an ongoing investigation becomes more vigorous. In short, even though the level of presidential popularity prior to an impeachment attempt is not necessarily a good indicator of the president's fate, it should be taken into account, given its impact on the elected politicians and magistrates who decide the president's future.

Other Factors

Finally, in terms of setting, there are other factors that may facilitate or impinge upon the emergence and course of a presidential impeachment attempt. These might include a liberal media environment in which professional norms are oriented toward investigative journalism. In a setting like this (for example, the U.S.), all other things being held equal, reports of presidential wrongdoing are more likely to be transformed into a political scandal than in a country where journalists are threatened or otherwise censored by state authorities or journalistic norms do not stress investigative journalism. Adverse economic conditions might make a population more willing to support an impeachment attempt, especially if the president is perceived as being responsible for those conditions; this may have been a factor in the cases of Russian President Boris Yeltsin and several Latin American presidents. International pressure may also play a role, as it may have done, albeit counterproductively, in the impeachment attempt of Colombian President Ernesto Samper in 1996, where ordinary Colombians rallied against U.S. intervention.

Stages of Presidential Impeachment

Specifying the conditions under which an attempt might be made to impeach and remove a president sets the stage for a discussion of presidential impeachment; it falls short of fully accounting for the process itself. The impeachment process moves through several stages, and in one sense centers around a single question: can accusations of presidential wrongdoing be translated into a scandal that is "politically effective" enough to lead to and sustain an effort to impeach and remove a president?[25]

The process of presidential impeachment starts with allegations of wrongdoing against the president or those associated with the president that emanate from the legislature, a special prosecutor or investigative committee, prominent public figures, or news reports. While presidential wrongdoing is but one factor in an impeachment effort, it is typically the central focus. And, although we have downplayed the legal aspects of presidential impeachment thus far, it must be said that although exceptions exist to the rule (see especially the case of Venezuela in Chapter 7), the best chance for an impeachment attempt gaining steam and eventually being successful rests on two conditions. First, there must be good reason to believe that the president is personally involved in the wrongdoing. In other words, the closer the president is to the situation, the more likely that allegations of wrongdoing will be transformed into a political scandal. Second, the wrongdoing must constitute what is commonly considered to be a serious breach of conduct.

Although more will be said on this, a simple example here will illustrate: consider the relative ease with which a consensus was built in the impeachment attempt of President Richard Nixon compared with the controversy that surrounded the Clinton impeachment. Without trying to justify Clinton's sexual iniquities or his perjury before a grand jury, these actions clearly did not constitute wrongdoing comparable to Nixon's. In fact, it may be the case that the distinction here, in the end, is the difference between an act of serious wrongdoing on the part of the president and a legislature looking for a way to remove a president whom it finds objectionable. This is an oversimplification, of course, but it further reinforces the idea that impeachment can only be understood as a political process and in political terms.

In fact, one of the hallmarks of a presidential impeachment attempt (successful or otherwise) is the political scandal surrounding the affair. In this respect, it can be suggested that in most cases, regardless of where the allegations of presidential wrongdoing originate, the more "politically effective" the scandal is, the more likely the attempt to impeach and remove the president will be successful. In other words, most successful impeachment attempts are accompanied by a fair amount of public and elite outrage surrounding allegations of presidential wrongdoing; in simple terms, the greater the degree of outrage, the more seriously the legislature is forced to consider it.

Public and elite outrage, and thus the severity of a scandal, can be measured (if only indirectly) by opinion polls that show whether people believe the president is culpable for the alleged crimes, whether people think that the "crime" warrants impeachment and removal, and overall presidential favorability (as opposed to the typical presidential job approval polls). In addition, elite reaction can be gauged by following and interpreting how various elites are attempting to frame the issue in their public statements.

The next stage occurs when the scandal moves into the halls of government. Typically it makes its first appearance in the lower house of the legislature when one or more members call for investigation of the president's conduct. If it gains traction, what follows may, for example, involve the formation of a special committee or hearings in a pre-existing committee. It is in this stage that the impeachment attempt often takes on its character and battle lines are drawn. What follows is a struggle wherein the president tries to form and maintain a "legislative shield," (see Chapter 4) or a sympathetic legislative coalition, to counter the impeachment effort, while the forces pushing for impeachment attempt to build a successful anti-presidential coalition. Here, the partisan composition of the legislature is often a major factor.

In sum, the process of presidential impeachment is a combination of all of these factors. The setting provides a more or less fertile ground for an impeachment attempt to emerge, based specifically on the severity of presidential wrongdoing, public and elite reaction, and the subsequent partisan response in the legislature.

Once an impeachment attempt is formally started, three phases can be identified: (1) accusation and/or investigation; (2) deliberation and voting on impeachment; and, (3) the impeachment trial. In each phase there are variations on the possible outcomes.

Accusation and/or Investigation

This is the initial phase of presidential impeachment, where the scandal has gathered enough momentum that the legislature or a high court begins looking into the matter. In this phase we might see any number of indicators that a serious impeachment attempt has begun. It might be the introduction of a resolution in the legislature to impeach; in the U.S., the House of Representatives will refer the matter to one or more committees; in other cases, an investigative body will be formed or a special prosecutor may be appointed, either in the legislature or the courts. The point is that, in this phase, an impeachment effort has officially started.

Deliberation and Voting on Impeachment

In some cases the impeachment attempt dies after the initial phase. In other cases, the legislative committee or other relevant body formally recommends that the legislature as a whole or court (as the case may be) take up the question of impeachment, asking that an impeachment trial be authorized. In these cases the impeachment process has reached the second phase. If the process has reached this phase it has most likely become a major focus in the news media, when the committee (or other investigative body) has formally reported on the advisability of presidential impeachment to the whole legislature.

Impeachment Trial

If a political trial is authorized by the legislature, the president has formally been impeached. The next phase of the impeachment process is the impeachment trial itself, which may be conducted by the upper house of the legislature, a high court, or any combination thereof. It is this phase that decides whether the president will remain in office and, in some cases, if criminal charges will be brought against the president.

Outcomes of Presidential Impeachment

In this book we classify cases of presidential impeachment by outcomes. That is to say, although the phase at which the process ended may vary, there are three outcomes possible: (1) impunity, (2) survival, and (3) exit.

Impunity

Presidential impeachment attempts that are classified as cases of impunity are those in which no vote is taken to impeach the president. Although these cases may make it past the accusation and/or investigation phase to the deliberation and voting phase, they go no further. Again, no formal vote to impeach is taken, and the president typically emerges relatively unscathed. In fact, in cases that go no further than accusation and investigation, it might be that the impeachment attempt receives little attention in the press and the public is largely unaware of the effort. Examples of impunity would include the attempt to impeach U.S. President Reagan (investigated in the House and the Senate in the summer of 1987) and several of the attempts to impeach Russian President Yeltsin prior to 1999; in both cases, legislative committees examined the question, but this was as far as the process advanced.

Survival

Cases of presidential survival are those cases of presidential impeachment efforts where a vote is taken either to impeach or to remove the president and the president survives. In other words, cases of presidential survival may occur in the deliberation and voting phase or in the impeachment trial phase. If, for example, a vote is taken to impeach the president and is defeated, it is a case of presidential survival. Examples of impeachment attempts that fit into this category are those of Russian President Yeltsin in 1999, or Colombian President Samper in 1996. On the other hand, if the president is impeached (a trial has been authorized in the deliberation and voting phase) and in the trial the vote to remove the president is defeated, this is also a case of presidential survival. The trial of U.S. President Clinton in 1999 in the U.S. Senate is an example of an impeachment attempt in this category. In a case of presidential survival, the formal challenge facing the president is greater; this is what distinguishes it from a case of impunity.

Exit

If the president leaves office and does not finish his or her term, it is a case of presidential exit or removal. This is true whether the president is removed as the result of a guilty verdict in the political trial (as in the case of President Albert Zafy of Madagascar, for example), is removed by a decision of the legislature or court outside of normal constitutional and statutory impeachment procedures (as in the case of Philippine President Estrada or Venezuelan President Pérez), or if the president resigns prior to the trial taking place (for example, U.S. President Nixon in 1974). In other words, although there may be variation in how exit takes place, the result is that the president does not complete his term of office; unlike the other outcomes, it can occur during any phase of the process. Table 1-3 summarizes the phases and possible outcomes of presidential impeachment.

THE CASES IN THIS BOOK

The cases presented in this collection include examples of all three possible outcomes of the presidential impeachment process. Each author, while discussing their case within the framework of the book, has his or her own particular focus or approach.

In Chapter 2, William Perkins examines impeachment in the U.S.; included is an examination of the impeachment efforts against John Tyler,

Table 1-3.
Phases and Outcomes of Presidential Impeachment

Phase & Action	Outcomes*
Information about Presidential Wrongdoing Surfaces (pre-Impeachment Phase)	
President is not accused	Presidential impunity
President is accused	Move to investigation phase
Investigation	
Investigative body reaches no conclusion; matter dies	Presidential impunity
Investigative body concludes president is not guilty	Presidential impunity
Investigative body recommends charges be brought against president	Move to deliberation/voting stage
Deliberation and/or Voting	
Deliberative body reaches no conclusion; matter dies	Presidential impunity
Deliberative body does not authorize a trial against the president	Presidential survival
Deliberative body authorizes a trial against the president	Move to trial phase
Trial	
President is "acquitted"	Presidential survival
President is found "guilty"	Presidential exit (removal)

* Presidential exit is possible at any stage, via presidential resignation.

James Buchanan, Andrew Johnson, Herbert Hoover, Richard Nixon, and Bill Clinton, as well as the censure of Andrew Jackson. The chapter focuses on the idea that every impeachment attempt in the U.S. has occurred during a period of divided government, highlighting the proposition that impeachment is a fundamentally political, or more specifically, partisan, phenomenon.

In Chapter 3, Yuko Kasuya shifts the focus to the Philippines and the impeachment effort against Joseph Estrada that started in late 2000 and culminated in his removal from office in January 2001. A case of exit, the president was removed in an "extra-constitutional" manner inasmuch as the transfer of power from Estrada to his Vice-President Gloria Macapagal-Arroyo took place as the result of action by the Supreme Court, outside of normal impeachment procedures. It is suggested that the impeachment of Estrada was facilitated by the fact that Philippine parties are notoriously weak, and his extra-constitutional removal was driven by the social movement known as "People's Power II."

Victor Hinojosa and Aníbal Pérez-Liñán examine the scandal and impeachment inquiry of President Ernesto Samper of Colombia in Chapter 4. This was a case where impeachment was considered by the legislature as a whole, but there was no trial. In spite of enormous pressure from the U.S. before, during, and after the affair, Samper survived in large part because of the popular opinion that opposed his impeachment and the patronage powers of the Colombian president, which in turn influenced legislators to support him.

In Chapter 5, Philip Allen focuses on Madagascar, where a democratic republic was inaugurated in September 1992 and Albert Zafy won a run-off election for the presidency in February 1993. From the outset his presidency seemed doomed as he struggled against fissiparous tendencies in a recalcitrant parliament; in the end, his position proved untenable. In the summer of 1996 he faced wide-ranging impeachment charges, and the High Constitutional Court subsequently found him culpable on three articles; in September he announced his resignation. And, after a little more than a year, the new president Didier Ratsiraka faced and survived an impeachment attempt himself.

Jody Baumgartner explores the efforts made to initiate impeachment proceedings against Russian President Boris Yeltsin from 1993 through 1999 in Chapter 6, focusing in particular on the 1998–99 attempt in which the State Duma came very close to successfully impeaching him on one of the five charges that he faced. There are several examples of a president (the same president) accused and/or investigated (pre-1998) as well as a case of deliberation and voting by the legislature as a whole (1998–99). Yeltsin's survival was in large part due to the strategic calculations of deputies in voting on the five articles of impeachment. In the end, the case highlights the notion that impeachment is one of the many strategies by which a legislature can attempt to exert pressure on the executive.

In Chapter 7, Naoko Kada compares two cases from Latin America, Brazil and Venezuela; both resulted in presidential exit. In 1992, Brazilian president Fernando Collor was impeached and removed from office for allegedly benefiting from an extortion scheme run by a close friend who had been his presidential campaign treasurer. In 1993, Venezuelan president Carlos Andrés Pérez was impeached and removed from office for allegedly pocketing secret defense funds. The author explores these two cases of presidential exit and the idea that impeachment might not be an effective tool to combat executive corruption, and the implications of that for Latin America democracy.

If power was never abused presidential impeachment might not be necessary. But of course history is replete with examples of even the best-intentioned individuals taking advantage of their positions to further their own ends. Thus it is important to understand presidential impeachment, the ultimate check on the abuse of executive power, as well as how the process itself might be abused. The authors of this book bring a wealth of expertise about the countries they study and an eclectic mix of approaches to studying this subject.

In the final chapter, Naoko Kada pulls the threads together, summarizing the findings of the book. She reviews the factors driving presidential impeachment that seem to be common to all of the cases. In addition, she explores the implications of these findings, especially important for newer democracies, in greater detail, and points to what we believe to be exciting areas for future research.

CHAPTER 2

The Political Nature of Presidential Impeachment in the United States

William B. Perkins

INTRODUCTION

In 1974, during impeachment proceedings against President Richard Nixon, David Dennis, a member of the House Judiciary Committee, defended the beleaguered president. The congressman was unmoved by any legal debate over impeachment, and smugly observed that it was not the first time a "client had lied to me."[1] At the same time, Representative William L. Hungate observed that "there are some Democrats on the committee who would vote to impeach Nixon today. And there are a few Republicans," he continued, "who wouldn't vote to impeach Nixon if he were caught in a bank vault at midnight."[2] Impeachment in the United States is not, and has never been, a matter of law. It is, and always has been, a matter of politics.

There is little reason to believe—despite conventional wisdom and the focus of partisans—that presidential malfeasance has ever been the core congressional motivation behind attempts to remove a president from office. Dennis and Hungate understood this process as it exists in the U.S. The history of impeachment in the U.S., to quote Alexander Hamilton, clearly demonstrates that the process, when used, has been fueled by differences "more or less friendly or inimical to the accused."[3] Politics, not law or principle, has historically driven the American impeachment process.

The list of serious attempts by Congress to remove the president of the United States has not been limited to Andrew Johnson, Richard Nixon, and Bill Clinton—the most famous and outstanding examples. Andrew Jackson withstood an extra-constitutional attempt by the Senate in 1834. John Tyler was the first president to face an actual vote on impeachment in 1843, followed by a vote on James Buchanan in 1860. Grover Cleveland faced an attempt in 1896, and votes were conducted on Herbert Hoover in

1932 and in 1933. Three different resolutions were introduced against Harry Truman in 1952.[4] Ronald Reagan was a target in 1983 and again in 1987. So was the first George Bush in 1991.[5] Impeachment intrigue has also swirled around Woodrow Wilson, Dwight Eisenhower, and Lyndon Johnson.[6] Even George Washington was not immune to discussion of impeachment.[7] Serious talk about impeaching the president of the U.S. has, in fact, been extraordinarily common.

Research on the motivations behind impeachment have ranged from electoral concerns of members of Congress,[8] to political intrigue,[9] to matters of principle.[10] Differences between the president and Congress over the making of public policy as the motor of impeachment has received scant scholarly attention even though every historical attempt to impeach the president has had a policy connection. The question has not been addressed, perhaps, because it is so obvious. Yet there are those who would still like to believe that impeachment is a legal matter. It is not. Impeachment is all about, and has always been all about, politics and policy, not the law.

Every serious attempt to remove the president from office has been characterized by partisan differences at a time of divided government, when the president's party did not also control Congress (see Table 2-1). The most serious attempts have occured right after abrupt changes in the partisan composition of Congress or in the partisan affiliation of the president. There is a distinct connection between impeachment and the fact that different political parties control Congress and the presidency. Throughout American history no congressional majority party has ever attempted to impeach and remove a president from the same party.

THE MEANING OF IMPEACHMENT

The Constitution holds that the president may be impeached in cases involving treason, bribery, and high crimes and misdemeanors. The House of Representatives is given the constitutional power to approve such charges by a majority vote. In the event that *any* charge is approved by the House, the case then goes to the Senate as the trial body. If two-thirds of the senators present approve *any* charge, then the president is found guilty and removed from office. Anything less than a two-thirds vote by the Senate in trial means that the president remains in office.

Constitutional procedures are simple. However, there has never been any agreement upon what constitutes "high crimes and misdemeanors." There is enough divergence in British and colonial practices and the way in which impeachment was incorporated into the Constitution to merit a brief discussion of the debates surrounding the adoption of provisions regarding the impeachment of presidents during the Constitutional Convention.

Table 2-1.
Presidents, Unified/Divided Government, and Trends in Impeachment

Only Unified	Mostly Unified	Half/Half	Mostly Divided	Only Divided
Van Buren	Jackson[2]	Polk	Eisenhower[2]	Tyler[2]
W. H. Harrison[1]	Grant	Pierce	Clinton[2]	Taylor[1]
Lincoln	Wilson[2]	Buchanan[2]		Fillmore
Garfield[1]	Truman[2]	Arthur		A. Johnson[2]
McKinley		B. Harrison		Hayes
T. Roosevelt		Cleveland (2nd)[2]		Cleveland (1st)
Harding[1]		Taft		Nixon[2]
Coolidge		Hoover[2]		Ford
F. Roosevelt		G. W. Bush		Regan[2]
Kennedy[1]				G. H. W. Bush[2]
L. Johnson[2]				
Carter				

[1] Died during first term in office
[2] Threatened with impeachment

Impeachment was apparently a part of the constitutional debates from the outset; it was, for example, included in the Virginia Plan proposed early on by Edmund Randolph.[11] Most of the delegates involved in the debates on impeachment were those who had a good deal of experience with the procedure.[12] From the beginning, however, discussion concerning impeachment deviated from the British model in two respects. First, the procedure was to be used only for public officials while in office; second, the only punishment was to be removal from office. This divergence was patterned after the most widely used impeachment practices in the various states.

There seemed to be a consensus in the Convention that the impeachment (accusation) phase itself should be the responsibility of the House of Representatives; the first difference over impeachment proposals involved the appropriate venue for the trial phase. After a variety of alternatives were considered (e.g., a council of governors, state and/or national courts), the idea of conducting the trial in the Senate was settled upon. To many delegates this venue seemed to "po[se] the fewest problems" in terms of who was less likely to be corruptible during the trial.[13] Supreme Court justices, for example, having been appointed by the president, might be likely to side with the president who appointed them in cases of impeachment.

The second area of contention centered around the question of the impeachability of the president; this debate was not entirely separate from the issue of instituting the presidency, what form the office should take, for which functions the office should be responsible, and even the method of presidential selection and term of office. The debate over presidential impeachment was resolved when the delegates concluded that the alternative to presidential impeachment was impractical. In the absence of a constitutional check on presidential power, a president could cause any variety of mischief. In that event, the only recourse (removal mechanism) would necessarily include such things as assassination or revolt. Equally important, in the words of Benjamin Franklin, impeachment would provide a way for a president who was innocent to "vindica[te] his character."[14]

A third debate focused on what should constitute an impeachable offense. After it was agreed that presidents would be subject to impeachment provisions, the Convention tentatively adopted language that provided for impeachment in cases of presidential "malpractice or neglect of duty." The scope of impeachable offenses was narrowed considerably when the Committee of Eleven proposed that the grounds be restricted to "treason or bribery." It was later moved to add the term "maladministration" to the clause, but this wording was dropped when Madison pointed out that such a provision would mean that a president's tenure would be wholly contingent upon the "pleasure of the Senate." George Mason then proposed substituting "bribery and other high crimes and misdemeanors." This phrase passed in the Committee without further discussion.[15]

The final debate with respect to impeachment was over how many Senate votes would be needed to remove the president. Here again, the idea of insulating the president somewhat from momentary passions and factionalism compelled the framers to adopt the two-third majority rule; implicit in this decision was the recognition that impeachment could and might be used for political purposes. This reinforces the notion that there was a good deal of disagreement over the meaning of impeachment and what constituted an impeachable offense. On the other hand, understanding that the process would inevitably become politicized caused the framers to agree on the two-thirds removal rule. Lacking a coherent definition of impeachable crimes that might be committed by the president, they insured that the nature of the removal process would have to transcend politics. If two-thirds of the senators present could agree that the House charges met the threshold of what constituted high crimes and misdemeanors, then the likelihood that politics had driven the process would be lessened. On the other hand, if fewer than two-thirds of the senators were in agreement then the likelihood that politics would be the driving force behind the process was tacitly understood.

In fact, the difficulty of how to define an impeachable offense has never been settled, and debate surrounding various impeachment attempts throughout American history has reflected that fact. For example, during the impeachment trial of Judge Charles Swayne in 1905, the defense held that malfeasance separate from official duties is not impeachable behavior. "Excepting bribery there is no case in the parliamentary law of England which gives color to the idea that the personal misconduct of a judge, in matters outside of his administration of the law in a court of justice, was ever considered or charged to constitute a high crime or misdemeanor."[16] Benjamin F. Butler (R-MA) tried to build the case against President Andrew Johnson in purely legal terms. "We define therefore an impeachable high crime or misdemeanor," he valiantly argued, "to be one in its nature or consequences subversive of some fundamental or essential principle of government or highly prejudicial to the public interest, and this may consist of a violation of the Constitution, of law, of an official oath, or of duty, by an act committed or omitted, or, without violating a positive law, by the abuse of discretionary powers from improper motives or for any improper purpose."[17]

On the other hand, Senator Lyman Trumbull (R-IL) took issue with these assessments in 1868. "Once set the example of impeaching a President," opined Trumbull, "for what, when the excitement of the hour shall have subsided, will be regarded as insufficient cause, and no future President will be safe who happens to differ with a majority of the House and two-thirds of the Senate on any measure deemed by them important, particularly if of a political character."[18] Fellow Republican James Grimes, pointedly eschewing politics, echoed Trumbull's sentiment. "I cannot believe it to be our duty," wrote the Senator from Iowa, "to convict the President of an infraction of a law when, in our consciences, we believe the law itself to be invalid."[19]

Clarence Cannon, who served as House Parliamentarian from 1915 to 1921, recognized the difficulty in explicating politics from principle, and even trumpeted the autonomy of the accusers: "If the Constitution puts no limitation on the House of Representatives or the Senate as to what constitutes these crimes, misdemeanors, and misbehaviors, where shall we go to find the limitations? There is no law, statutory nor common law, which puts limitations on or makes definitions for the crimes, misdemeanors, and misbehaviors which subject to impeachment and conviction. . . . Outside of the language of the Constitution . . . there is no law which binds the Senate . . . except that law which is prescribed by their own conscience, and on that, and on that alone, must depend the result."[20]

In short, it is clear that given the history of British and colonial impeachment practices and debate during the Constitutional Convention, it is highly unlikely that the framers believed they were crafting a nonpolitical impeachment clause. They fully understood that politics, not principle, might color any future attempt to impeach and remove a president.[21] Debate and practice since the Convention have confirmed the fact that impeachment essentially has no meaning in law. Its meaning depends upon the political make-up of Congress, particularly the Senate, since it is that body that is charged with deciding on the question of removal. "It rests with the Senate alone," David Y. Thomas has pointedly written, "to say what are impeachable high crimes and misdemeanors."[22]

IMPEACHMENT IN AMERICAN HISTORY

Andrew Jackson's bout with impeachment is an anomaly, for it was the Senate that instigated the effort (only the House can impeach the president). On July 10, 1832, Jackson vetoed a bill written for the continuance of the Second Bank of the U.S. and then made plans to transfer federal funds to state banks, angering the soon-to-be-Whigs in Congress.[23] After wrangling with the president for more than a year, on December 26, 1833, Henry Clay (W-KY) introduced a resolution to censure Jackson; three months later a reworded resolution was passed by the Senate, censuring Jackson for assuming "authority and power not conferred by the Constitution and laws, but in derogation of both."[24] In response, Jackson protested to the Senate that he had been charged with what was, for all intents and purposes, an impeachable offense. The rift clearly demonstrates a political vendetta by Clay and his associates even if the charges were couched in legal terms. For its part, the House, under the guidance of Democrat James K. Polk's Ways and Means Committee, reacted equally politically and refused to act on the Senate's resolution and instead endorsed the president's actions.

John Tyler's first offense was that of being a Democrat-turned-Whig. Upon the death of William Henry Harrison, Tyler, also the first person to succeed to the presidency due to a presidential vacancy, upset the congressional majority Whigs when he vetoed a tariff-distribution bill in the summer of 1842. In a scathing report, a House select committee investigating the reasons for the veto, chaired by ex-president John Quincy Adams and a Tyler opponent, recommended the passage of a constitutional amendment requiring only a simple majority of both houses of Congress to override a presidential veto. Because of Tyler's behavior as a Democrat (he had in fact been booted from the Whig party in 1841) in opposing the tariff, the committee also observed that impeachment might be the proper course of action. Two Democrats on the committee, Charles J. Ingersoll (PA) and James I. Roosevelt (NY), dissented.[25]

Importantly, Tyler did not have a vice president; under existing law the next person in line to succeed him was the Whig president pro tempore of the Senate, Willie Person Mangum of North Carolina. In addition, Whig Senator Henry Clay (KY), whose presidential ambitions match no other person in American history, fanned the flames of impeachment, although he did urge caution. Despite Tyler's signature on the compromise Tariff Act of 1842, a resolution calling for a special committee to investigate the president's actions was introduced in July in the House of Representatives by

John M. Botts (WV). Five months later, on January 12, 1843, the Botts resolution was defeated 127 to 84, with only Clay and Van Buren partisans supporting it.[26] Although the Whigs held a 133 to 102 majority in the House, enough Whigs and most of the Democrats sustained the president in what was a clear partisan attempt at impeachment.[27]

In 1860, James Buchanan faced a political challenge from the new Republican House majority. Voting as a block, on March 5 the Republicans passed a resolution empowering the Judiciary Committee to investigate improper actions and activities by the president and to establish a select committee of five to look into the matter; however, only four—all Republicans—were appointed.[28] One Democratic congressman referred to the resolution as "clap-trap and humbug" as he rose in opposition.[29] However, nothing ever came of the committee's investigation. Seven years later, fellow Democrat Andrew Johnson received the full brunt of a Republican onslaught, becoming the first president to actually be impeached and to stand trial.[30] Scholars differ over whether it was Johnson, and not the Republicans, who brought on impeachment.[31] Either way, although the battle would be couched in legal-principle terms by the accusers, it took on institutional proportions between the president and Congress, as had the treatment of Jackson and Tyler before him. It also had clearly political overtones, again as Jackson and Tyler had faced.

Johnson's principal transgression had been his refusal to abide by the Tenure of Office Act when he attempted to dismiss Secretary of War Edwin M. Stanton. Thwarted by conservative Republicans in the Judiciary Committee, the House voted on February 10, 1868, to give the House Reconstruction Committee, chaired by ultra-radical Thaddeus Stevens (R-PA), jurisdiction over the charges against Johnson—blatantly and unarguably a political move. Thirteen days later, the House, upon recommendation by the Reconstruction Committee, voted 127 to 47 along partisan lines to go forward, and appointed a nine-member committee to draw up articles of impeachment.[32] Articles I–IX and XI were concerned primarily with Johnson's refusal to abide by the Tenure of Office Act, while Article X was a rambling and exceedingly political indictment of Johnson, written by Butler, charging the president with ridiculing Congress (including indictments for his use of unseemly language and loud speaking voice).[33]

Johnson, like Tyler before him, did not have a vice president. As president pro tempore of the Senate, Benjamin Wade, a Republican from Ohio, would have become president if the Senate had succeeded in convicting and removing Johnson. Attempts to convince Wade to recuse himself (he had a personal stake in the matter, and was already in the process of selecting his prospective cabinet) failed, adding still more political overtones to the already highly politicized proceedings.[34]

When the trial began on March 5, 1868, the House managers pursued a legal argument, holding that Johnson had violated the Tenure of Office

Act, as well as a contradictory argument that "impeachment was a political and not a judicial process and therefore the Senate did not have to decide whether the President had committed an indictable offense but only whether he was fit to continue in office."[35] We are "bound by no law," stated one House manager.[36] The first vote, on the comprehensive Article XI, was taken by the Senate on May 16. Ten of the 45 Republicans joined nine Democrats in voting for acquittal—enough to sustain the president by one vote.[37] Ten days later the Republican caucus decided to bring up Articles II and III, but the result was the same and the Republicans decided to give up, bringing the trial to an end. "The Senate's trial of Johnson," according to presidential scholar Michael Nelson, "was marred by serious violations of due process and inappropriate political passion."[38] Andrew Johnson would remain in office.

In 1932, during the December lame-duck session of Congress, Lewis McFadden (R-PA) introduced a resolution to impeach President Herbert Hoover for "usurping legislative powers and violating constitutional and statutory law" in connection with Hoover's declaration of a moratorium on European payment of World War I debts.[39] The House voted on the motion twice and it was tabled both times—361–8 in December 1932 and 343–11 in January 1933. Notably, McFadden's resolution for impeachment was brought by a member of the president's own party, although the opposition Democrats controlled the House.

The near impeachment of Richard Nixon was next (the House Judiciary Committee had passed three articles of importance at the time of his resignation), followed by the impeachment and trial of Bill Clinton. Both are explored in more detail later. The purpose of this discussion has been to demonstrate that, historically, impeachment in the U.S. has not been confined to Andrew Johnson, Richard Nixon, and Bill Clinton; moreover, political intrigue, always couched in legal terminology, has pervaded the process. Even the Nixon affair, although eventually found to be teeming with legal repercussions, was initially political, and continued to be so as it wore on.[40]

Impeachment Charges

One of the more telling aspects of impeachment resolutions is how few of them have charged the president with violations of common, civil, or statutory law. The overwhelming majority have been concerned primarily with constitutional, fundamental law; public policy; and an institutional struggle between the president and Congress. All have been framed as presidential malfeasance in failing to uphold the Constitution, which is why it is not surprising to find that different individuals (and members of political parties) have held contrasting interpretations of that document.

As for Jackson, the charge against him (illegal transfer of funds) is of questionable legality. The action against Tyler was a sham as well, as he simply wielded the veto pen far too often to the liking of Whigs and others with similar policy preferences. In 1860, the House Judiciary Committee went so far as to appoint a committee of five (the Covode Committee) to investigate Buchanan for "improper actions to influence passage of laws regarding states or territories" and for "abuses at certain public buildings/works." Strictly speaking, the investigation of Buchanan was not about impeachment, although the thought (and talk) was in the air.[41]

President Johnson, on the other hand, did break the law and was quite aware that he had. In dismissing Secretary of War Edwin M. Stanton he had clearly violated the Tenure of Office Act, which had been passed over his veto, and that required Senate approval for removal of cabinet officers.[42] In addition, the president had appointed General Lorenzo Thomas to replace Stanton in the interim, although the Senate was still in session, thus making the interim appointment moot. The legal dispute between Johnson and the Republicans continues to this day.[43] The fight ended up being more an institutional struggle and a debate over how far a president must go in breaking the law, based upon differences in the making of public policy, to qualify as a high crime or misdemeanor.[44]

The 1932–33 charges against President Hoover were clearly about differences in policy goals, as the president's behavior was not at all in violation of the law. As for Richard Nixon, the Watergate affair first came to light during hearings in the Senate by the Select Committee on Presidential Campaign Activities chaired by Senator Sam J. Ervin (D-NC); these hearings were arguably a political move by the Democrats aimed at discrediting the president. As Watergate simmered for more than a year, the disastrous "Saturday Night Massacre" resulted in the subsequent filing of more than 20 impeachment resolutions. On October 23, 1973, Speaker of the House Carl Albert (D-OK) determined that he would refer the resolutions to the House Judiciary Committee. Three months later, on February 6, 1974, in a 410–4 bipartisan vote, the House delegated to that committee the sole power over drawing up the articles of impeachment.[45]

When the House Judiciary Committee undertook to write articles of impeachment, six Republicans on the 38-member committee joined all 21 Democrats in charging Nixon with obstruction of justice in the investigation. Another Republican defected in the vote, charging Nixon with abuse of power, and two members of each party switched sides in voting to hold Nixon in contempt of Congress. All three articles were constitutional in nature, representing differences between the branches and an illegal expansion and usurpation of the powers of the president.

Notably, however, the committee defeated an article charging the president with illegally bombing Cambodia, a policy matter, and with illegally evading his income taxes, a personal matter. A "majority of the committee, including a number of Democrats," write Van Tassel and Finkelman, "believed that Congress could only impeach for actions against the

government and against the political system—in a sense 'public' crimes—
and that while Nixon might be guilty of the felony of tax evasion or mis-
use of government funds, these were personal or private crimes, not
crimes against the Constitution or the nation. Thus, in the view of the
committee, they were not impeachable offenses."[46] Nine of the 21 Democrats joined the 17 Republicans in agreeing that personal malfeasance—
even if found guilty—does not rise to the level of a high crime or
misdemeanor—even when the crime is a felony.[47]

During the 1998–99 impeachment struggle, counsel for President Clinton made references to the Judiciary Committee's 1974 defeat of the tax
evasion article against Nixon. For the first time in American history, however, the Judiciary Committee passed and the House itself approved two
articles of impeachment (numbers I and III) based solely upon the perceived illegal nature of the president's personal behavior.

The third article charged Clinton with obstruction of justice and misus-
ing his office in making false and misleading statements to Congress. The
nature of that charge is therefore institutional and a possible abuse of
power (which is why it was the most contentious of the two articles voted
on by the Senate in trial). Nevertheless, the charge was still related to the
investigation of the president's personal behavior.

What, then, is the threshold for illegal presidential behavior before it
rises to the level of high crimes and misdemeanors? The question may be
without answer. Presidential malfeasance is not that uncommon. For
example, Ronald Reagan's administration clearly broke the law (the
Boland Amendment) when it continued to give military aid to the Contras
in El Salvador. Harry Truman and Lyndon Johnson both carried out
"presidential" wars without first obtaining a congressional declaration—
clear violations of Article I of the Constitution. Warren Harding drank
bourbon in the White House at a time when prohibition was the law of the
land. Finally, Abraham Lincoln, probably more than any other president,
ignored the letter of the Constitution when he illegally called up an army,
blockaded southern ports, and suspended the right of habeas corpus—all
while Congress was not in session. We forgive him, of course, because he
was trying to save the Union. But, it is also worth noting that Lincoln
served during a time of unified government.

Why were none of these presidents ever impeached or even seriously
threatened with impeachment? In each case, the letter of the Constitution
was under attack. How can illegal personal behavior rise to the level of
high crimes and misdemeanors while clear violations of the Constitution
go completely unpunished? The answer, simply put, is partisanship. If the
government is unified, the president is given near-free reign; he can even
break the law, for there is little likelihood that his majority partisan
cohorts in Congress will even attempt to impeach, let alone remove, him.
If the government is divided, on the other hand, the president must be

concerned not only with toeing the legal line, but more importantly, with the extent of policy differences between himself and Congress. The president who bucks Congress too strongly on matters of policy is most at risk of being impeached.

Shifts in Inter-branch Partisanship

The Senate voted to censure Andrew Jackson because of partisan differences over the Bank of the U.S. The House cast a vote on impeachment against John Tyler because he used his veto pen too often. A serious investigation of the president took place in 1860 because James Buchanan was not doing enough to stem events like John Brown's raid and Southern secession. It was clear early on that policy differences alone, between the president and Congress, could serve as fuel for the fires of impeachment. Something else, it appears, was happening. Every instance of impeachment in American history has been attended by a recent and abrupt change in electoral outcomes or presidential succession.

The censure of Andrew Jackson is an early example. The government was unified during Jackson's first four years. In the election of 1832, however, the Senate was taken over by the Whigs. The Whigs, who had never been in power before in any branch of government, responded by seeking to impeach Jackson for his opposition to the Bank of the U.S. A decade later, the Whigs experienced their first taste of unified government only to see the death of President Harrison result in the elevation of ex-Democrat John Tyler to the presidency. Again the Whigs responded to Tyler's policy differences by seeking to impeach him. The abrupt change of senatorial control to the Whigs in 1832 explains the Jackson censure; the abrupt ascendancy of Tyler in the face of Whig majorities in Congress explains the attempt to impeach him.

In 1858 the new Republicans took control of the House of Representatives; the next year, voting unanimously as a party, they approved an investigation of President Buchanan with a thought toward impeachment. A few years later they did impeach President Johnson, following his ascension to the presidency after the death of Abraham Lincoln. It was déjà vu circa John Tyler. An abrupt change in the presidency was in direct conflict with Republican party goals. They responded by trying to remove Johnson.

In 1896, the Republicans once again attempted to remove a Democrat (President Cleveland) following their success in the 1894 off-year election. The Democrats regained a House majority in the 1930 off-year election and eventually allowed two impeachment votes to be held on President Hoover. The next major shift would not take place until 1968, when, for the first time since 1884, the party of a victorious president (Richard Nixon) did not also take control of at least one house of Congress.[48]

Perhaps the most dramatic shift in presidential versus congressional preferences took place in 1994, when the Republicans took control of Congress after two years of unified government under the Democrats and President Bill Clinton. President Eisenhower, a Republican, had faced the same shift in 1954, when he lost his Republican majority in both houses of Congress following two years of unified government. The partisan shift under Clinton, however, was more dramatic than that under Eisenhower. The Democrats had recently been in power, and Eisenhower moderated with his Democratic opponents; Clinton, on the other hand, did not follow the Eisenhower example and confronted the Republicans in Congress, long out of power, to the point of a showdown and shutdown of parts of the government in 1995. Such presidential obstinacy with opposition majorities in Congress has never boded well for the president.

Every president who has suddenly come to power and also faced a hostile opposition has courted impeachment. And nearly every president who has been in power but was subsequently faced with a hostile opposition has also met with the prospect of impeachment. Newness to power, whether presidential or congressional, and particularly when policy differences between the two are extreme, encourages eventual impeachment of the president. Although not a sufficient precondition, partisan shifts have clearly been historically necessary in cases of impeachment of the president of the U.S. (see Table 2-2).

PARTY AND PREFERENCES IN CONGRESSIONAL VOTING

Advanced methodologies cannot improve upon reporting impeachment voting by members of Congress, shown in Tables 2-3a and 2-3b.[49] Outliers do exist. Members of the president's party have sometimes voted to proceed with impeachment efforts in the House; they have sometimes voted in committee for articles of impeachment; and they have sometimes even voted in the full House for articles of impeachment to be sent to the Senate for trial. However, such voting is quite rare. In addition, although there have been only two cases, no member of the president's party has ever voted against the president in a Senate trial. Clearly, the president's partisans have overwhelmingly voted to support the president and sustain him in office; on the other hand, partisan opponents have overwhelmingly voted against him.

Congressional impeachment voting has always been characterized by the fact that the president's partisans almost unanimously support him while the opposition almost unanimously opposes him. While this may not prove *a priori* that partisanship is what brings on impeachment, this problem does not preclude such a deduction. The previous section illustrated why the process might reach the stage of actual voting. Electoral shifts and oddities in presidential succession have historically resulted in

Table 2-2.
Impeachment Votes and Major Partisan Shifts Resulting in Divided Government

Year	What Happened	Eventual Result
1832	Whigs gain control of Senate for the first time	Vote to censure Jackson taken
1841	Tyler succeeds to the presidency	Vote to impeach Tyler taken
1848	Whigs take presidency at same time Democrats take Congress	No vote to impeach Taylor or Fillmore taken
1854	Republicans take House for the first time	No vote to impeach Pierce taken
1858	Republicans retake House	Vote to impeach Buchanan taken
1865	Johnson succeeds to the presidency	Vote to impeach Johnson taken
1874	Democrats take House for first time in 16 years	No vote to impeach Grant taken
1910	Democrats take House for first time in 16 years	No vote to impeach Taft taken
1930	Democrats take House for first time in 12 years	Vote to impeach Hoover taken
1946	Republicans take both Houses of Congress for first time in 16 years	No vote to impeach Truman taken
1968	Republicans take presidency at same time Democrats take Congress	Vote to impeach Nixon taken
1994	Republicans take both houses of Congress for first time in 40 years	Vote to impeach Clinton taken

more extreme policy differences separating the president and Congress. The way members of Congress vote, therefore, is less likely to be a stand-alone event than a symptom of what got the process started in the first place.

On the question of impeachment there has never been a House vote, nor a vote by one of its committees, when the House was also controlled by the president's party. Only opposition parties have initiated, or allowed, impeachment votes to take place.[50] This fact alone speaks volumes for what is seemingly self-evident. Throughout all of American history the president's partisans in Congress have *never* initiated an impeachment attempt, and members of Congress largely vote along partisan lines in support of or opposition to the president throughout impeachment attempts. While it is difficult to measure legal motivations for the way members of Congress vote, it is not so difficult to summarize final voting behavior and whether or not partisans have lined up with the president.

Table 2-3a.
Party Breakdowns in Impeachment Voting (Jackson through Nixon)

President—Vote	For	Against
Jackson (D)—Senate (Censure)		
Democrats	4	18
Whigs	12	0
Third Parties	10	2
Total	*26*	*20*
Tyler (D)—House		
Democrats	8	85
Whigs	75	41
Third Parties	1	1
Total	*84*	*127*
Buchanan (D)—House		
Democrats	9	45
Republicans	83	0
Third Parties	25	0
Total	*117*	*45*
Johnson (D)—House		
Democrats	0	44
Republicans	125	0
Third Parties	1	3
Total	*12*	*47*
Johnson (D)—Senate		
Democrats	0	9
Republicans	35	10
Total	*35*	*19*
Hoover (R)—House (Vote 1)		
Democrats	6	181
Republicans	2	179
Third Parties	0	1
Total	*8*	*361*
Hoover (R)—House (Vote 2)		
Democrats	10	171
Republicans	1	171
Third Parties	0	1
Total	*11*	*343*
Nixon (R)—House		
Democrats	231	0
Republicans	179	4
Total	*410*	*4*

(continues)

Table 2-3a. (*continued*)
Party Breakdowns in Impeachment Voting (Jackson through Nixon)

President—Vote	For	Against
Nixon (R)—Committee (Article I)		
Democrats	21	0
Republicans	6	11
Total	*27*	*11*
Nixon (R)—Committee (Article II)		
Democrats	21	0
Republicans	7	10
Total	*28*	*10*
Nixon (R)—Committee (Article III)		
Democrats	19	2
Republicans	2	15
Total	*21*	*17*
Nixon (R)—Committee (Articles IV and V)		
Democrats	12	9
Republicans	0	17
Total	*12*	*26*

Table 2-3b.
Party Breakdowns in Impeachment Voting (Clinton)

President—Vote	For	Against
Clinton (D)—Committee		
Democrats	0	16
Republicans	21	0
Total	*21*	*16*
Clinton (D)—House		
Democrats	31	176
Republicans	227	0
Total	*258*	*176*
Clinton (D)—Committee (Articles I, III, IV)		
Democrats	0	16
Republicans	21	0
Total	*21*	*16*
Clinton (D)—Committee (Article II)		
Democrats	0	16
Republicans	20	1
Total	*20*	*17*

(continues)

Table 2-3b. (*continued*)
Party Breakdowns in Impeachment Voting (Clinton)

President—Vote	For	Against
Clinton (D)—House (Article I)		
Democrats	5	201
Republicans	223	5
Total	*228*	*206*
Clinton (D)—House (Article II)		
Democrats	5	201
Republicans	200	28
Total	*205*	*229*
Clinton (D)—House (Article III)		
Democrats	5	200
Republicans	216	12
Total	*221*	*212*
Clinton (D)—House (Article IV)		
Democrats	1	204
Republicans	147	81
Total	*148*	*285*
Clinton (D)—Senate (Article I)		
Democrats	0	45
Republicans	45	10
Total	*45*	*55*
Clinton (D)—Senate (Article III)		
Democrats	0	45
Republicans	50	5
Total	*50*	*50*

Nearly all impeachment votes have pitted at least 50 percent of one party against at least 50 percent of the other party—most have pitted at least 80 percent of one party against 80 percent of the other party (see Table 2-4). Only three of 28 votes have not met the 50 percent–50 percent threshold[51] (the two Hoover votes and the House vote to proceed against Nixon did not pit 50 percent of each party against one another).[52] Three votes, all during the Nixon hearings, involved at least 50 percent of one party against at least 50 percent of the other. However, in all three the opposition voted at a level of 100 percent. The Democrats voted as a block on Article II (which passed), while the Republicans did likewise on Articles IV and V (both of which failed); in each case, the opposition voted within the 50–60 percent range. Sixty-four percent of the Republicans

Table 2-4.
Partisanship in Twenty-eight Impeachment Votes

Party Percentages	Number	Percentage
Less than 50% vs. 50%*	3	10.7%
At least 50% vs. 50%	25	89.3
At least 80% vs. 80%	18	64.3
100% vs. 100%	6	21.4

* The parties voted overwhelmingly with one another in the House on Nixon (to proceed with impeachment) and both times in the House on Hoover (not to proceed with impeachment).

voted against united Democrats on Article I (which passed) against Nixon, 64 percent of the Whigs voted against 91 percent of the Democrats on the Tyler resolution (which failed), and 64 percent of the Republicans voted against 99 percent of the Democrats in the House vote on Article IV (which failed) against Clinton.

Significantly, nearly two-thirds of impeachment votes (18 of 28) have seen at least 80 percent of each party in opposition to one another. Fully 21 percent (6 of 28) have been perfectly partisan (both parties unanimously opposed to one another). The attempts against Andrew Johnson and Bill Clinton seem to have been clearly motivated by partisanship. The committee and House votes against Johnson saw no defections, and the Democrats continued this united strategy in the Senate trial. Although 10 Republicans defected in the Senate, thus sustaining Johnson in office, it is not clear that they were wholly motivated by legal arguments. None of the seven "martyrs" would be reelected to the Senate, at least not as Republicans. Two of them (Ross and Trumbull), in fact, became Democrats! One (Fessenden) died and one (Grimes) had a debilitating stroke in 1869. Henderson left the Republican Party but returned 16 years later, while Fowler and Van Winkle retired at the end of their terms. And Dixon, Doolittle, and Norton had always voted more in line with the Democrats. According to Van Tassel and Finkelman,

it is not clear what Johnson['s] acquittal meant. Some senators may have voted against conviction because they did not believe Johnson had actually violated the law. . . . But, the most important reason for the acquittal was political. The seven Republicans who voted to acquit Johnson agreed with William M. Evarts, the conservative Republican lawyer hired to defend the president, who argued that "the present situation" was better than "the change proposed." In effect Evarts argued that however bad Johnson was, the situation of the nation would be worse if he was removed from office and replaced by the next-in-line for the presidency, the president pro-tempore of the Senate Wade.[53]

Four of the six perfectly partisan votes took place during the Clinton episode. The first was the House Judiciary Committee's vote for a formal investigation; the other three also involved that body in voting for Articles I, III, and IV of impeachment, while the vote on Article II saw only one Republican defect. Of the twelve votes taken on Clinton

- Four were 100 percent vs. 100 percent;
- Two were 90 percent vs. 100 percent;
- Two were 80 percent vs. 100 percent;
- Two were 90 percent vs. 90 percent;
- One was 80 percent vs. 90 percent;
- And, one was 60 percent vs. 90 percent.[54]

If one accepts this method of measuring partisanship, then the impeachment effort against Clinton clearly qualifies as perhaps the very definition of partisan politics.

As for Clinton's acquittal, it can again be argued that the president survived because senators decided his behavior did not meet the legal requirements of high crimes and misdemeanors. In contrast to the Johnson acquittal, however, when Republicans had the votes for removal even if the Democrats voted as a block (which they did), there was no chance of removing Clinton if the Democrats were to vote as a block (which they did). The 45 Democrats clearly had different legal opinions than did at least 45 of the Republicans. Senator Arlen Specter's (R-PA) dramatic vote of "not proven" pointed up the possibility that the law was more important than politics.

The *Washington Post* observed, however, that the Republicans failed "because four New England moderates and one from Pennsylvania joined with the 45 Senate Democrats to produce a 50–50 vote" that was partly attributable to the fact that "three of the moderates—Senators John Chafee (RI), James M. Jeffords (VT), and Olympia J. Snowe (ME)—were up for reelection . . . in states where Clinton enjoy[ed] substantial popularity." The *Post* concluded: "In contrast to the battle in the House, where GOP moderates were pressured by the GOP leadership to support impeachment simply to 'keep the process going,' moderates in the Senate felt no such pressure. There was no chance for the necessary 67 votes to convict Clinton, and so the Senate moderates, in effect, were given a pass by their leadership."[55] Republicans charged the Democrats with being partisan because of their block voting in the two Senate votes, apparently forgetting that they, too, had voted as a block five times during the process, including the first two votes that got the process started.

A Defector Thesis

Party identification largely explains impeachment voting behavior (see Table 2-5), but party identification is also closely related to ideological preferences. Democrats tend to be more liberal while Republicans tend to be more conservative. When it comes to presidential impeachment, Democrats in Congress nearly always support a Democratic president while Republicans in Congress nearly always oppose him. Republicans in Congress nearly always support a Republican president while Democrats in Congress nearly always oppose him. But do liberal members of

Table 2-5.
Preference Scores and Defectors, Non-defectors in the Johnson, Nixon, and Clinton Impeachments

	Mean of Party	Highest Defector	Number Who Should Have Defected	Number Who Defected	Difference
Johnson					
Senate					
Republicans	.291	.153	12	10	2
Nixon					
Committee					
Republicans (AI)	.198	.289	12	6	6
Committee					
Republicans (AII)	.198	.289	12	7	5
Committee					
Republicans (AIII)	.198	.169	8	2	6
Committee					
Democrats (AIII)	−.352	.070	2	2	0
Committee					
Democrats (AIV)	−.352	−.493	15	6	6
Committee					
Democrats (AV)	−.352	−.577	19	9	10
Clinton					
Committee					
Republicans (II)	.740	.758	14	1	13
Senate					
Republicans (1)	.666	.764	37	10	27
Senate					
Republicans (2)	.666	.378	5	5	0

Source: http://voteview.uh.edu/default_nomdata.htm

Congress *always* support a Democratic president (as conservatives oppose him) and do conservative members of Congress *always* support a Republican president (as liberals oppose him)?

One way to disentangle party from preferences is to assess the ideology scores of the party defectors, defined as those members who do not vote with the majority of their party. The procedure is to locate the highest DW-NOMINATE score of a defector within a party and then identify all those to the left (in Republican cases) and all those to the right of that score (in Democratic cases).[56] For example, if the highest score for a Republican defector is .200, then all those under .200 should also defect if preference is the motivation. Anyone under .200 who did not defect chose to remain with the party. By the same token, if the highest score for a Democratic defector is –.500, then all those under should also defect if preference is the motivation. Anyone under –.500 who did not defect chose to remain with the party. Table 2-5 assesses the number of defectors and those who should have been expected to defect in the Johnson Senate, Nixon House Judiciary Committee, and Clinton House Judiciary Committee and Senate votes.

According to this defector thesis, more legislators should have left their party and voted otherwise in eight of the 10 votes. Only one outcome would have been different—the House Judiciary Committee's vote on Article II against Clinton. One Republican defected, although his preference score indicates that thirteen others should have. Instead of a 21–16 vote in favor of the article, it would have been voted down 30–7. Nevertheless, this method indicates that several members clearly voted more in line with their party than ideological preferences would predict.

The most interesting votes are the two involving Clinton and the Senate. In the first vote, instead of being 45–55 it should have been 18–82. Twenty-seven Republicans apparently went against their preferences and stayed with their party. On the other hand, the second vote was a perfect display of preference voting. According to the *Washington Post* article, the five most moderate Republicans were exactly the ones who defected. The Senate median was right where Republicans Susan M. Collins (ME), who voted for acquittal, and Spencer Abraham (MI), who voted for conviction, sat on the ideological spectrum. Thus, in contrast to the above finding that the vote was likely partisan, it seems it was also based at least partially on preference. In other words, senators voted to acquit Clinton of obstruction of justice the same way they would vote on economic regulation and social-welfare programs.

Reelection and Impeachment Voting

Reelection concerns may not have motivated voting behavior despite the *Post*'s assessment and despite member preferences (see Table 2-6).[57] When a reelection motivational variable is added to a Logit model (measured by Clinton's performance in the 1996 election) the Clinton popularity factor holds no explanatory power. Maine had given Clinton a 21 percent margin in 1996 but Collins was not even up for reelection in 2000. On the other hand, Abraham was up for reelection in 2000, but voted for Clinton's removal even though Michigan had voted for Clinton by a 14 percent margin over Robert Dole. Mike Dewine (preference = .490) and William Roth (preference = .500) both voted for removal although Clinton's margin in Dewine's Ohio had been seven percent and in Roth's Delaware it had been 15 percent. John Warner (preference = .510) of Virginia, however, voted for acquittal in the first vote even though his state had gone to Dole (by two percent).[58]

Rod Grams, Roth, and Abraham were all up for reelection in 2000 in states that went heavily for Clinton in 1996. Tim Hutchinson and Bob Smith would not face reelection until 2002. In states that also voted for Clinton by a more than 10 percent margin, Peter Fitzgerald (IL), Judd Gregg (NH), and Charles Grassley (IA) would not face reelection until 2004. Chaffee, Gorton, Jeffords, Warner, Grams, Roth, Abraham, Hutchinson, Fitzgerald, and Grassley all had Democratic counterparts who voted for acquittal—in line with Clinton's popularity per the 1996 election.

Table 2-6.
Defection, Reelection, and the 1996 Election: First Senate Clinton Vote

Up for Reelection in 2000

Defectors	% Clinton 1996 Win	Non-defectors*	% Clinton 1996 Win
Chaffee (RI)	+33	Grams (MN)	+16
Gorton (WA)	+13	Roth (DE)	+15
Jeffords (VT)	+22	Abraham (MI)	+14
Snowe (ME)	+21		

Up for Reelection in 2002

Defectors	% Clinton 1996 Win	Non-defectors*	% Clinton 1996 Win
Collins (ME)	+21	Hutchinson (AR)	+17
Stevens (AK)	–18	Smith (NH)	+10
Thompson (TN)	+02		
Warner (VA)	–02		

*Republicans in states where Clinton won by more than a 10% margin in 1996

Also of interest is why Senators Arlen Specter (PA; Clinton, + 9 percent), Fred Thompson (TN; Clinton, + 2 percent), Richard Shelby (AL; Clinton, –7 percent), and Stevens (AK; Clinton, –18 percent) defected while their Republican cohorts (Rick Santorum, William Frist, Jeff Sessions, and Frank Murkowski) did not. On the other side of the aisle, Byron Dorgan voted for acquittal although his state, North Dakota, had gone to Dole by seven percent in 1996. Dorgan was not up for reelection until 2004, but his Democratic counterpart, Kent Conrad, was up for reelection in 2000. The most intriguing vote, however, is that of Democrat Bob Kerry, who stood for reelection in 2000 and whose state, Nebraska, had gone to Dole by a 19 percent margin in 1996 (second only to Utah in voting against Clinton). According to the results of the 1996 election, if anybody on the Democratic side had reason to defect it would have been Kerry.[59]

Evidence for reelection vote motivation is weak. Logit models (controlling for party) including variables for reelection in 2000, the Clinton vote in 1996, and the interaction between the two proved insignificant.[60] Kerry, Conrad, and Dorgan on the Democratic side, and Grams, Roth, Abraham, Hutchinson, Smith, Santorum, Frist, Sessions, and Murkowski on the Republican side, surely voted the party line. No doubt others did as well. Individual Republican defectors, on the other hand, probably did consider the legality of the charges against Clinton. However, the forgoing discussion and tests provide support for the partisanship, as opposed to the preference or legal theses, in explaining impeachment voting. The evidence indicates that the strength of preexisting factions determines impeachment outcomes. Again, Alexander Hamilton predicted that this would be the case.

SUMMARY

Richard A. Posner has written that it is "not certain that Nixon himself should have been impeached" because "the gravity of Nixon's misconduct could be thought mitigated by considerations of the national interest," a most interesting argument given the fact that Nixon actually did break the law.[61] President Ford must have had his own concerns when he pardoned his former boss. By inference, according to Posner, under certain conditions presidential misconduct is acceptable. And impeachment should be limited to considerations of whether or not the president has been negligent in performing his official duties. But impeachment has never been about congressional concerns over negligence in performing official duties. It seems to have been characterized, instead, by congressional concerns over negligence in carrying out the wishes of congressional majorities.

Reality is probably best exemplified by observing the involvement of two members of Congress who took part in both the Nixon and Clinton impeachment efforts. In 1974, John Conyers (D-MI) and Trent Lott (R-MS) were both members of the House Judiciary Committee. At that time Conyers voted *for* all five articles of impeachment against Nixon, including Article V charging Nixon with felony tax evasion. For his part, Lott voted *against* all five articles. Twenty-five years later the tables were turned. Still a member of the House Judiciary Committee, in 1998 Conyers voted *against* all four impeachment articles against Clinton, including Articles I and II, which directly addressed the president's personal behavior. Lott, now the Senate Majority Leader, voted *for* the two articles (I and III) that made it to the Senate. "It has all been decided," Lott had lamented in 1974. "We are just going through an exercise. Right now I doubt whether it will be expeditious or fair. . . . All we can do is try to see that what is done is done fairly."[62] Conyers probably shared these sentiments about the partisan nature of the proceedings 25 years later.

Impeaching the president is exclusively a phenomenon of a divided government. Presidential misbehavior during times of unified government has never been seriously challenged by Congress. On the other hand, one strand that appears to run through the initiation of articles of impeachment and especially their further progress is the personal dislike members of Congress have for a particular president. Henry Clay detested both Andrew Jackson and John Tyler although he lacked the votes necessary to remove either of them. James Buchanan was reviled by Republicans for his hands-off policy toward the southern states and imminent secession. And in 1932–33 nobody liked Hoover, although it made no sense to actually remove him.

It is arguable, in fact, that the three most personally hated presidents (by members of Congress) have been Andrew Johnson, Richard Nixon, and Bill Clinton. Johnson, after all, had been a Democrat with the unfortunate task of succeeding the assassinated Lincoln. When it became apparent that he wished to follow Lincoln's lenient reconstruction policies, most Republicans turned against him. As the impeachment process dragged on the battle became more and more a personal as well as an institutional struggle.[63] The hatred many Democrats had for Richard Nixon is legend, dating back to the 1950s. And Bill Clinton got off on the wrong foot in 1992 when allegations of his promiscuity surfaced, when he denied having inhaled while smoking marijuana, and when it was discovered that he had finessed his way out of serving in Vietnam. Personal animosity toward the president is clearly part of the impeachment story.

Another part of the story is the shifting of partisan tides and fortunes. The theory is not perfect, and is illustrated quite well in the case of President Taft, who was not impeached following the takeover of the House by the Democrats in the mid-term elections of 1910; Democrats had been out of power since 1895. Millard Fillmore faced a hostile Congress when he took over for Zachary Taylor in 1849, and Franklin Pierce met with the first Republican House in 1855. Nevertheless, the confluence of sudden

electoral shifts in partisanship, personal animosity, and policy differences
are all tinder for the impeachment fire. "There should no longer be any
doubt about the fundamental nature of impeachment," writes Walter
Ehrlich. "It is a political, not a criminal, procedure, to remove government
officials who commit either non-criminal or criminal wrongs."[64]

Serious attempts to impeach the president have occurred exclusively
when the government has been divided. Impeachment attempts have also
tended to occur following abrupt shifts in presidential-congressional partisanship. All attempts have been characterized by extreme policy differences between Congress and the president. There is no reason to believe
that impeachment has ever been based upon fundamental, constitutional
law. Presidents are not impeached because they break the law—several of
them have but have never had to face the congressional music. Presidents
face impeachment only when an opposition majority party in Congress
gets too fed up with outstanding policy differences. Charging the president with legal malfeasance is the vehicle it sometimes uses in its attempt
to bring the president back into policy harmony.

CHAPTER 3

Weak Institutions and Strong Movements: The Case of President Estrada's Impeachment and Removal in the Philippines

Yuko Kasuya

INTRODUCTION

In November 2000, for the first time in Philippine history, the House of Representatives impeached the President of the Republic, Joseph Estrada. The Senate impeachment trial that followed, however, ended in a rather unexpected manner. During the third week of the trial, on January 16, 2001, the Senator-judges decided not to open an envelope that allegedly contained damning evidence about Estrada's illegal financial transactions. Disgusted by this decision, people started gathering on the streets in and around Manila within a few hours, demanding Estrada's resignation; the number of demonstrators continued to grow in succeeding days. Concluding that Estrada could no longer govern the country in light of the massive street unrest, at noon on January 20, the Supreme Court Chief Justice administered the oath of presidential office to Vice President Gloria Macapagal-Arroyo. A few hours later, Estrada and his family hurriedly left the presidential palace. In the end, Estrada was removed from office, not because of the conviction by the impeachment court, but by street upheaval. The events of January 16 to 20 is dubbed "People Power II," since it was the second time in the Philippines that street protest forced a change in government, the first one being the "People Power Revolution" of 1986 that ousted dictator Ferdinand Marcos. Estrada's impeachment, in the terminology employed in this book, is a case of presidential exit, specifically, extra-constitutional presidential exit.

Why did the impeachment of President Estrada unfold the way it did? The manner of Estrada's removal raised many questions, including the constitutionality of the succession process, the legitimacy of the new government, and even the quality of democracy in the Philippines.[1] These issues, in turn, had a negative effect on the Arroyo government's stability. Immediately after People Power II, numerous rumors of *coup d'etat* spread. Four months later, in May 2001, an anti-government riot staged by Estrada supporters broke out, only quelled after Arroyo decreed a state of emergency. Most would agree, in light of this, that a popular uprising is an unsatisfactory manner in which to change governments, and this should be avoided in the future.[2] However, there is little consensus regarding what lessons need to be learned. While there are numerous journalistic accounts of Estrada's fall, most remain largely descriptive; few provide analyses that focus on structural factors.[3] Because of this, I highlight the structural, rather than the contingent, factors that explain the impeachment and removal of Estrada.

This chapter argues that the impeachment process in the Philippines was due to the combination of weak institutions and strong movements. First, the weakness of institutions, especially that of political parties, allowed some members of the president's party to defect, which in turn allowed the opposition to obtain the required number in the House of Representatives to impeach Estrada. In particular, my analysis suggests that the effectiveness of party discipline within the president's party depended on individual legislators' evaluation of the importance of presidential patronage. Second, a strong popular movement by the urban middle class worked as the primary catalyst for the Supreme Court's decision to install Arroyo (which meant Estrada's *de facto* removal from office). I analyze the three factors that facilitated its strength: (1) the majority of the middle class did not favor Estrada as president; (2) a movement leadership successfully encouraged the middle class to join street mobilization; and, (3) the open and accessible media provided information that provoked and helped the middle class organize and mobilize to protest.

The chapter is organized as follows: first, the background to Estrada's impeachment is presented by a discussion of impeachment rules in the Philippines and the nature of the charges against Estrada. The second section first discusses how the weakness of party discipline contributed to the passage of Articles of Impeachment in the House of Representatives and then analyzes why some legislators were less disciplined than others. The third section illustrates the role played by the strong popular movement in the process of Estrada's removal, followed by the analysis of factors that facilitated its robustness. The conclusion summarizes the chapter and discusses the implications of its findings.

BACKGROUND

Two types of background information are relevant to Estrada's impeachment case. The first is a summary of the impeachment rules under the current Philippine Constitution, and the second is Estrada's dismal performance as president, which constituted the grounds for his impeachment.

Impeachment Rule in the Philippines

Current impeachment provisions in the Philippines combine a relatively low threshold for impeaching with a slightly higher requirement for removing a president. The 1987 Constitution stipulates that the House of Representatives has the exclusive power to initiate all cases of impeachment. A verified complaint or resolution of impeachment filed by at least one-third of the members of the House constitutes the Article of Impeachment, and trial by the Senate follows. To convict requires two-thirds of the members of the Senate. Table 1-2 (in the Introduction to this volume) reveals that the one-third requirement for impeaching the chief executive is the lowest among the cases in this book (and, in fact, one of the lowest in the world). As for conviction, most countries require two-thirds support of the trial body, as does the Philippines.

The impeachment threshold was set relatively low in the Philippines because the framers of the 1987 Constitution had explicitly wished to "relax impeachment as a ground for the removal of the President".[4] In the previous democratic constitution of 1935, two-thirds of all House members' support was required to impeach a president.[5] My review of the Commissioners' discussion during the 1986 Constitutional Convention reveals that 15 years of authoritarian experience under Marcos encouraged the Commissioners to create a less stringent rule in order to remove a president once he had lost the mandate of the people. During the Convention plenary session, an original draft that provided a one-half requirement was further reduced to one-third.[6]

It is interesting to note that Estrada would not have been impeached if the 1987 Constitution retained the two-third-requirement rule employed under the 1935 Constitution. As I will discuss in more detail below, there were 87 members who supported the impeachment of Estrada in the 220-member House. The support of 87 members was more than one-third of the members but far below two-thirds; this number would not have been enough to impeach under the previous rules. Conversely, if the one-third rule had been used in the 1935 Constitution, Estrada would not have been the first Philippine President to be impeached. In the case of President Diosdado Macapagal (1961 to 1965), 42 members of the opposition party from the 104-member House endorsed his impeachment,[7] well above the one-third requirement.

Gravity of the Charges

Joseph Estrada assumed the post of President of the Philippines in May 1998. He won with a large margin, about 40 percent of the total votes cast, while the second runner up, Jose de Venecia, received only 15 percent. However, from the beginning of his term Estrada was plagued by a plethora of scandals that gradually eroded his popular support. In 1999, for example, he was accused of intervening in the Securities and Exchange Commission's investigation into a stock fraud on behalf of a friend. He was also blamed for aiding a company owned by a friend in securing an exclusive franchise for an online bingo operation. Many other scandals surfaced as well, including those that revolved around reports of Estrada and his family's new and unexplained wealth, his mistresses and their mansions, and the "midnight cabinet" composed of his drinking and gambling friends working as the center of government decision-making.

The most damning scandal, the so-called "*Juetenggate*" scandal, made the news on October 4, 2000. The Governor of Ilocos Sur province, Luis "Chavit" Singson, a longtime friend of Estrada, publicly accused the president of receiving millions of pesos from the *Jueteng* syndicate, which ran illegal numbers games. Singson also revealed that Estrada received roughly 70 million pesos (1.4 million U.S. dollars) from him, gathered from the excise tax levied on cigarettes and originally intended for the province of Ilocos Sur.

The seriousness of this scandal can be seen by the sequence of events that followed. The economy immediately reacted with the fall of the peso against the dollar and with a plunge in business and consumer confidence.[8] Less than a week after the exposé, Vice President Gloria Macapagal-Arroyo resigned from Estrada's Cabinet as the Secretary of Social Welfare. Arroyo's *Lakas* party (*Lakas NUCD-UMDP*, the largest opposition party, comprised of the National Union of Christian Democrats and the United Muslim Democrats of the Philippines) had been asking her to resign from the Estrada cabinet for some time, but she remained undecided until the scandal broke. At the same time, various influential figures and groups began publicly calling for Estrada's resignation. Manila's Archbishop Jaime Cardinal Sin issued a statement on behalf of the Presbyteral Council of the Archdiocese of Manila asking Estrada to resign. Another respected religious institution, the Catholic Bishops Conference of the Philippines, issued a similar statement. Former President Corazon Aquino publicly asked Estrada to consider resignation. A group of business associations released a joint statement condemning Estrada for the *Juetenggate* scandal and other misconduct.[9] The clamor for Estrada's resignation, which had started as early as March 2000 by some leftist groups, increased dramatically as the result of the *Juetenggate* scandal; it also broadened the social base of those demanding his resignation. In Metro Manila (as the capital region is known)[10] and other large cities around the country, numerous street rallies of various sizes condemning the president were organized.

The filing of the impeachment complaint occurred in the midst of the social, political, and economic turmoil that followed the *Juetenggate* scandal. On October 18, three House representatives, together with 24 civic groups, filed a 150-page Complaint of Impeachment in the House of Representatives.[11] The complaint accused Estrada of (1) bribery, (2) graft and corruption, (3) betrayal of public trust, and (4) culpable violation of the Constitution—all of the four grounds for impeachment listed in the 1987 Constitution.

In sum, two important preconditions are necessary to understand Estrada's impeachment case. First, the Constitution provided a comparatively lower threshold for impeachment than the previous democratic Constitution and as compared to most other presidential regimes. Impeaching a Philippine president is, in other words, relatively easy, all other things being equal. Second, the charges against Estrada were serious enough that major social institutions—religious, business, and civic groups—called for his resignation.

Next I analyze how and why the defection of Estrada's partisans in the House of Representatives contributed to his eventual impeachment.

WEAK PARTIES AND THE PASSAGE OF IMPEACHMENT IN THE HOUSE

The Impeachment Process in the House

When the Complaint of Impeachment was filed at the House of Representatives, many expected the initiative to fail, given that Estrada's allies dominated the chamber. Initially, only 40 members signed the Resolution of Endorsement that supported the impeachment complaint. To send the case to the Senate, at least 73 endorsers were needed from the 220-member House. As seen in Table 3-1, Estrada's allies were numerous enough to block the initiative. The president's party, the Struggle of Filipino Mass (*Lapiang ng Masang Pilipino*, hereafter LAMP), had 148 members. Although six LAMP members had already endorsed the Complaint at the time of filing, the overwhelming majority remained Estrada supporters. In addition, the Liberal Party, which numbered 13 members, had a legislative coalition agreement with LAMP. In total, at the time the Impeachment Complaint was filed, 155 of Estrada's allies did not endorse it, which was more than enough to kill it.

Conversely, the opposition block lacked the necessary votes. Opposition to Estrada's LAMP was mainly made up of *Lakas* and the Nationalist Party (*Partido Nacionalista*), which had a coalition agreement with *Lakas*. *Lakas* had 39 members in the House, and 25 of them initially endorsed the complaint. Fourteen *Lakas* members refused to follow the party line and endorse impeachment at the time of filing. The Nationalist Party was also opposed to Estrada, but it had only one member in the chamber. Other minor parties did not have clear party positions about the impeachment issue. Finally, in addition to the members elected via district mandates, there were 14 House members who were elected from party lists (where the number of seats in the House are allocated in proportion to votes obtained as a party).[12] Seven of these party-list representatives initially endorsed the impeachment; the remainder did not. Thus, the opposition needed an additional 33 endorsers, but their prospects initially looked dim.

Within three weeks of the filing of the Complaint, however, the opposition was able to obtain enough endorsements to impeach Estrada. This was primarily due to the defection of some Estrada allies; some *Lakas* members reportedly worked very hard to persuade reluctant House members to change their minds.[13] New endorsers included House Speaker Manuel Villar, who was until that point a staunch supporter of the Estrada administration and a member of his party. Villar's defection allegedly encouraged other House members to follow.[14] Because the opposition was able to persuade an additional 47 members to sign the Resolution of Endorsement, the total number of endorsers rose to 87, more than the one-third required. Table 3-1 lists the partisan breakdown

Table 3-1.
Change in the Number of Impeachment Endorsers by Party

Party	Composition of House (11/1999)	Initial Endorsers (10/2000)	Later Endorsers	Final Endorsers (11/2000)
Estrada Allies				
LAMP	148	6	34	40
Liberal Party	13	0	7	7
Subtotal	*161*	*6*	*41*	*47*
Anti-Estrada Allies				
LAKAS	39	25	4	29
Nationalist Party	1	1	0	1
Subtotal	*40*	*26*	*4*	*30*
Others				
Aksyon	1	0	0	0
Ompia	1	0	0	0
Reporma	1	1	0	1
Independent	2	0	0	0
Party List	14	7	3	10
Subtotal	*19*	*8*	*3*	*11*
Grand Total	*220*	*40*	*48*	*88*

Source: Compiled by author based on the list of party affiliation status as of 1999 prepared by the Makati Business Club and the list of endorsers of the Complaint of Impeachment prepared by the Library of the House of Representatives.

of new endorsers: 34 from LAMP, seven from the Liberal Party, four from *Lakas*, and 3 party-list representatives. In short, the required number of endorsers was achieved mainly because many LAMP members deserted Estrada.

On November 6, the House Committee on Justice, which had to decide whether the impeachment initiative be referred to the plenary session, met for the first time to deliberate on the filed Complaint. During the meeting its members unanimously approved the motion to send the Complaint of Impeachment to the House plenary for further action, based on the fact that the Resolution of Endorsement was signed by the required number of House members. This was sufficient to initiate impeachment proceedings under the Rules of Impeachment of the House of the Representatives.[15]

One week later, the House sent the Complaint of Impeachment to the Senate as the Articles of Impeachment without a plenary roll call vote. At the very beginning of the plenary session on November 13, Speaker Manuel Villar, who announced his resignation from LAMP on the same day, simply declared that the House was sending the Committee Report as Articles of Impeachment to the Senate for trial without any discussion or roll call voting. This became the official decision of the House.[16]

This description of the House impeachment process suggests that weak party discipline among LAMP members, manifested in the defection of some LAMP members from the party line, helped the opposition gain enough supporters to impeach the president. Next I discuss why some LAMP members defected and others did not.

Patronage, Past and Future

Party fragility has been a chronic feature of Philippine parties since independence.[17] The reason for weak party discipline, in short, is that national party leaders do not have effective instruments to sanction, either positively or negatively, their members. During election campaigns, most parties provide only marginal benefits for their nominees, do not have loyal supporters, can offer only meager financial help, and do not have the organizational resources to help candidates with their campaigns—nor do party leaders have much influence over members' legislative career advancement. To become a House Speaker, it is widely understood among Filipino legislators that what matters most is the support of the president, not one's ranking within the party.[18] Furthermore, the assignment of committee chairmanships, which go only to majority party members,[19] is determined in negotiation between the Speaker and individual legislators; the decisions do not involve party leadership. Thus, party leaders have few resources, either at the electoral or the legislative level, to pressure members to follow the party line.

Nevertheless, when the national party leader is the president, as was the case of Estrada and LAMP, the story is different. The president does have instruments to influence party members by virtue of occupying the presidency. His main tool is the control of funding for legislators' pork barrel projects. In the Philippine setting, one of the most effective means to win House elections is to bring as many government-financed projects to their district as possible. In this regard, the Philippine president can exercise considerable influence through the process of budget execution, and thus can use his power over spending to bargain with party members. This is why many political observers initially thought that impeachment would not succeed in the House, and indeed, Estrada initially exercised this tool in an effort to hold the party line. Local media reported that in an attempt to dissuade legislators from endorsing the impeachment complaint, Estrada called meetings with House members and generously distributed certificates of cash release for their pet projects.[20]

Therefore, the question is why presidential patronage was effective in persuading some legislators and not others in Estrada's impeachment case. In other words, why did some LAMP members defect while others did not? It is sensible to think that to some extent, legislators' personal conviction about the impeachment case played a role. Yet, were there any non-idiosyncratic and structural factors influencing legislators' decisions on impeachment?

Scholars who have studied the behavior of U.S. legislators in general, and in the case of the impeachment of President Clinton in particular, have shown that constituency pressure is likely to influence legislators' behavior. As argued by Mayhew,[21] the primary goal of representatives is their reelection, and for this reason they will act on behalf of their constituents' interests. A number of empirical studies on the U.S. Congress found that district-level preference affected representatives' voting behavior in general, and did so in the case of the Clinton impeachment as well.[22]

Does this theory apply in the case of Estrada's impeachment? In previous studies I have found that constituency pressure played only a marginal role.[23] In regression analysis, the level of constituency support for Estrada was not a statistically significant variable to explain LAMP members' decision when other potential factors were controlled for. In other words, all other things being equal, some legislators supported impeachment although their districts were pro-Estrada, or they did not support impeachment even when their districts were anti-Estrada. The finding that Filipino legislators are relatively autonomous from district pressure in terms of their legislative activities may not be surprising to those familiar with Philippine politics. It is widely understood that House members can stay in power as long as they provide patronage to their districts, and that their performance in the legislative arena is of little concern to voters. Thus, it is conceivable that LAMP members made decisions regarding

Estrada's impeachment without paying serious attention to their district's preference on the matter.

Instead, what turned out to be statistically significant was members' evaluation about the importance of presidential patronage. More specifically, empirical analysis supports the claim that those who received less patronage from Estrada in the past, and those who valued future presidential patronage less, were more likely to endorse the impeachment of their party leader. I elaborate on these points next.

First, I found that LAMP members who switched their party affiliation to LAMP after the 1998 election were more likely to endorse impeachment than those who were already LAMP members in 1998, because new switchers received little or no campaign contributions from Estrada during the 1998 election campaign. It is customary in Philippine elections for a presidential candidate to make financial contributions to House candidates who campaign for him in exchange for their support. In 1998, Estrada ran as the presidential candidate of the Fight of Nationalistic Filipino Mass (*Labang ng Makabayang Masang Pilipino* or LAMMP); the name was later changed to LAMP. Among the 148 House members who affiliated with LAMP at the time of the impeachment move, only 65 fielded their candidacy under the LAMMP label and campaigned for Estrada.[24] The other 83 members joined LAMP *after* the 1998 election; they ran under different party labels during the election and campaigned for presidential candidates other than Estrada, and thus received few campaign contributions from him. As Table 3-2 shows, the group of new switchers to LAMP were twice as likely to endorse impeachment than the group of original

Table 3-2.
Legislators' Impeachment Endorsement Ratio by Party

Category	Number in Category	Number Endorsed	Percentage Endorsed
LAMP Originals	65	9	13.8%
LAMP "Switchers"	83	30	36.1
Lakas	39	29	74.3
Others	33	19	57.6
Total	220	87	—

Source: Compiled by author based on (1) The Commission on Elections Report of the 1998 Election, (2) the list of party affiliation status as of 1999 prepared by the Makati Business Club, and (3) the list of impeachment endorsers prepared by the Library of the House of Representatives, the Philippines.

LAMP members. This new-member versus original-member variation was a statistically significant independent variable in my regression models.[25]

Second, I found that those who faced their term limitation were more likely to endorse impeachment than continuing members, because departing members would value future presidential patronage less than continuing members. Under the 1987 Philippine Constitution, House members cannot serve for more than three consecutive terms. As previously discussed, providing patronage to one's district is one of the most important factors of a House member's reelection, and the president has a great deal of control over this. In this environment, departing LAMP members would not value future presidential patronage highly simply because they could not run for office again, while continuing LAMP members needed to rely heavily on future presidential patronage for their reelection.[26] Table 3-3 shows that departing members of LAMP were twice as likely to endorse impeachment as continuing members. My regression analysis also supported this claim.[27]

In sum, the effectiveness of presidential patronage depended on legislators' evaluation of past and future patronage. LAMP members who valued Estrada's patronage less (new switchers to LAMP and departing members) were more likely to endorse the impeachment of their party leader. In the end, the ties that bound LAMP members were very fragile despite the widespread belief that Estrada's control of legislators' patronage would be an effective tool in dissuading LAMP members from defection.

Table 3-3.
Ratio of Impeachment Endorsers by Term Limit Classification

Category	Number in Category	Number Endorsed	Percentage Endorsed
LAMP			
Departing	31	13	41.9%
Non-departing	117	26	22.2
Lakas			
Departing	11	8	72.7
Non-departing	28	21	75.0
Other			
Departing	2	2	100.0
Non-departing	31	17	54.8
Total	220	87	—

Source: Directory of 11th House of Representatives, the Phillippines; also see Table 3-2.

Next I discuss the factors which led to middle-class mobilization into People Power II, namely middle-class disapproval of Estrada, political leadership promoting the uprising, and effective channels of communication.

STRONG MOVEMENTS

The Collapse of Constitutional Procedure

After the House passed the Articles of Impeachment, the impeachment trial started on the Senate floor on December 7, 2000. Senators became judges and the Supreme Court Chief Justice acted as the presiding officer. Table 3-4 shows the party composition of the Senate at the time of the impeachment trial. When Estrada entered office, he could count 15 of 22 senators as allies.[28] About the time that the House passed the impeachment resolution, four LAMP senators announced the withdrawal of their support from Estrada; thus, his allies decreased to 11 by the time the trial started.[29] Still, Estrada's allies had a large enough number to acquit him; to convict, the opposition needed to muster two-thirds support, or 15 votes.

January 16, 2001, marked the collapse of constitutionally defined impeachment procedures; it was also the beginning of People Power II. On that day, by a vote of 11–10, the senator-judges ruled against opening

Table 3-4.
Partisan Composition of the Filipino Senate

	Composition as of September 2000	Composition at Opening of Trial
Estrada Allies		
LAMP	14	10
People's Reform Party	1	1
Subtotal	*15*	*11*
Opposition		
Lakas	5	5
Akyson	1	1
Liberal Party	1	1
Resigned from LAMP	0	4
Subtotal	*7*	*11*
Total	*22*	*22*

the envelope that allegedly contained evidence that Estrada had three billion pesos in a secret bank account under the alias "Jose Velarde."[30] The Senate decision ignited people's anger as the senator-judges concealed the seemingly important evidence. Within a few hours after the ruling on January 16, thousands had assembled at the Epifanio de los Santos Avenue (EDSA) Shrine, the memorial site of the 1986 People Power Revolution. The next day, the Impeachment Court was suspended indefinitely, as the prosecution team[31] collectively submitted their letter of resignation; thus, there were no prosecutors to continue the trial. Meanwhile, the pouring of people to and along the EDSA highway continued; it was estimated that the crowd around the EDSA Shrine numbered as many as 250,000 people on January 17.[32]

On January 19, Estrada lost the support of the military and police forces, a serious setback. Secretary of National Defense Orlando Mercado, Armed Forces of the Philippines Chief Commander Angelo Reyes, and the Philippine National Police Chief Panfilo Lacson each announced that they were withdrawing their support from the Estrada government. The enormity of street unrest compelled the military and police forces to unanimously defect.[33] Meanwhile, street demonstrations demanding Estrada's resignation continued in various parts of Metro Manila as well as in other major cities across the country.

Around noon on January 20, at the EDSA Shrine (in the presence of thousands of protesters), Supreme Court Chief Justice Hiralion Davide administered the presidential oath of office to Vice President Arroyo, making her the 14th President of the Philippines. At this point, Estrada had not yet formally resigned. Davide had earlier offered to install Arroyo as the new president under condition of Estrada's resignation, but was prompted to swear her in earlier because, in the judgment of the Supreme Court, doing so was the only way to prevent bloodshed among street protesters.[34] This fear was based on the fact that on the morning of January 20, some protester groups were planning to march from the EDSA Shrine to the presidential palace to stage a demonstration; Court justices feared a possible conflict between the protesters and Estrada's supporters. This concern led them to unanimously agree to conduct the swearing-in ceremony immediately. In the meantime, behind-the-scenes negotiation for a graceful exit for Estrada were going on between his advisors and Arroyo's protégés.[35] At 2:30 P.M., judging that the tide could not be reversed, Estrada and his family hurriedly left the presidential palace.[36]

This chronology suggests that the immensity of street mobilization was key to the removal of Estrada and the installation of Arroyo as new president. It is interesting to note the composition of the movement. In the main, protesters were middle-class Filipinos residing in the Metro Manila area, which comprises about 13 percent of the total national population. According to a nationwide survey, 11 percent of Metro Manila respondents answered that they personally participated in a rally from January 16 to 20; in contrast, only about two percent of those who lived in other parts of the country did so.[37] The same survey also reveals that among Metro Manila residents, it was mainly upper- and middle-class Filipinos who participated; about 14 percent of upper- and middle-class respondents joined street rallies, while roughly 2 percent of lower-class Filipinos did. Given that the upper-class population is approximately ten times smaller than that of the middle class in Metro Manila,[38] it can be said that People Power II was primarily an urban middle-class movement. What, then, facilitated the middle class to turn to the streets during the days of People Power II?

FACTORS THAT FACILITATED STRONG MOVEMENTS

The "Class" Divide

The first factor that facilitated middle-class mobilization was disapproval of Estrada. To begin with, the middle class did not support Estrada for president in the 1998 election. Many in the upper and middle classes had a negative opinion of him, based on his reputation for womanizing, laid-back working style, and lack of intellectual capacity; the lower class who supported his pro-poor stands did not care about these traits. As revealed in a pre-election survey, the middle-class voters' preferred presidential candidates in the 1998 election were Joseph Lim and Raul Roco, not Estrada.[39] Exit poll survey results show that about 95 percent of the total Estrada vote came from the lower class.[40]

Moreover, in the course of the Senate trial, Estrada tried to frame the impeachment issue as class conflict between the rich and the poor, thereby aggravating his relationship with the middle class. He repeatedly stated publicly that the rich were out to remove him and that he needed the support from the poor. On several occasions he met with the assembly of slum dwellers, promising to provide them with additional services (such as land titles) in return for their continued support.[41]

In view of these circumstances, in a survey conducted about the time of the impeachment trial, it is not surprising that a majority of the middle class expressed the opinion that Estrada should be removed from office. On the question of whether Estrada should resign, the net agreement ratio (percentage agreeing minus the percentage disagreeing) for the upper and middle class was plus two percent; the ratio for the lower classes was minus 20 percent.[42] This suggests that at least a slender majority of middle-class Filipinos wanted Estrada to resign around the time of the infamous Senate decision, while the majority of poor Filipinos did not.[43]

Despite middle-class disapproval of Estrada, it is important to note that these people did not prefer to express their demands through street demonstration. Survey results reveal that before People Power II, the majority of the middle-class population was not in favor of deciding the course of an impeachment trial by a street uprising. In a nationwide survey conducted in early January 2001, less than 30 percent of total respondents were in favor of removing Estrada by street force, while roughly 50 percent disagreed (the rest were undecided).[44] In addition, before the Senate decision, the middle class had a higher expected acceptance rate of the Senate's decision (either acquittal or conviction) than the lower class. About 66 percent of upper- and middle-class respondents agreed that they would accept whatever decisions the senator-judges made; the score was lower for the lower classes (about 55 percent).[45] But middle-class dislike of Estrada alone does not explain their mobilization. Other, more immediate factors that provoked their street uprising need to be taken into account.

The Leadership That Called for Street Protest

I maintain that the second factor that facilitated the middle-class uprising was the presence of leadership that conditioned people before People Power II actually started to turn to the streets as a means of expressing their political demands. Many accounts suggest that the outpouring of people to the EDSA highway during People Power II occurred spontaneously, with neither planning nor clear leadership.[46] This does not mean, however, that the role of leadership was unimportant. Various groups took the lead in organizing street protests months before People Power II. Thus, by the time of the Senate decision on the second envelope, middle-class Filipinos were conditioned to street protest as a mode of political expression, either as observers or participants. Moreover, since leaders of this anti-Estrada movement anticipated his eventual acquittal by the Senate, they publicly indicated that his removal by popular uprising was one possible and acceptable scenario, thus further conditioning people with the notion of an extra-constitutional political change. I argue that leadership calls for street protest were one of the immediate causes for the emergence of the robust middle-class mobilization that constituted People Power II.

Three leadership groups were actively involved with street mobilization prior to People Power II, namely the Catholic church, leftist groups, and various business associations. First, Catholic church leaders played a pivotal role in organizing a broad segment of society for street mobilization.[47] Because of Estrada's "immoral" traits, it was well known that the Catholic church hierarchy disliked him well before he was elected president; for his part, Estrada distanced himself from the church after his election.[48] After the church hierarchy took a unified position that favored Estrada's resignation (after the Singson exposé), it organized demonstrations at various locations. These were usually called "prayer rallies," and were often held at religious sites. As Filipinos are predominantly Catholic, the Catholic church's active involvement in the resign-Estrada movement gave people a sense of moral righteousness in joining street protests. The church also promoted the idea of ousting the president by street protests. Just a week before People Power II, on January 10, the Presbyteral Council of Manila issued a statement that supported "peaceful and non-violent mass actions as expressions of indignation and protest,"[49] in effect an endorsement for people to turn to the streets in the event of Estrada's acquittal. Moreover, once people gathered at EDSA during People Power II, church leaders encouraged them to stay on the streets "until evil is conquered by good."[50]

Second, leftist groups aggressively organized anti-Estrada rallies before People Power II that involved the participation of their members as well as ordinary citizens. Since the beginning of Estrada's term, they were opposed to the president based on what they perceived as his anti-nationalistic, pro-Marcos stance; however, their opposition was often divided due to ideological differences. There were three main leftist groups involved in the movement—the Estrada Resign Movement, the Court of Citizen's Authority and Democracy (*Sandigang ng Lakas et Democrasya ng Sambayanan*, or SANLAKAS), and the Citizen's Congress of the Philippines (*Kongreso ng Mamamayang Pilipino*) II. Each represented different ideological positions within the Philippine left, and they separately organized demonstrations on many occasions.[51]

Third, the country's major business associations took a leadership role in the anti-Estrada movement, since their interests—the national economy—were at stake. The earliest and most vocal involvement came from the Makati Business Club, whose membership consisted mainly of large corporations from around the country. Other associations joined the call for Estrada's resignation after the Singson exposé, and eventually most business associations that favored Estrada's resignation organized street protests in collaboration with leftist groups and the church.[52]

It appears that the experience of the 1986 People Power Revolution enhanced these groups' efforts in calling for Estrada's resignation by street mobilization. The successful experience of ousting Marcos by street forces seems to have made the groups think that doing the same in Estrada's case was feasible. Individually, however, the 1986 People Power experience affected these groups differently. The leadership of the church and business associations, on the one hand, had been credited for the success of the 1986 upheaval. Their political weight has since increased, and their political involvement is now considered to be legitimate by many, although they remain primarily non-political institutions. On the other hand, leftist leaders were eager not to miss the boat this time. In 1986 the groups that formed the Estrada Resign Movement and SANLAKAS boycotted the snap presidential election and the street protest that followed. Eventually, they failed to be included in the new Aquino administration, although they had worked very hard in the anti-Marcos movements. This time they wanted to make sure they could claim credit for helping oust an unpopular government and thus gain some influence in the new regime.[53]

The Media That Provided Information

The third factor that facilitated middle-class mobilization is the existence of media that provided open and ample information. In particular, television and text messaging on cellular telephones played important roles. Live television broadcasting of the impeachment trial, especially the Senate's decision on the second envelope, first provoked middle-class anger; then cellular telephone messages organized protestors to go to the EDSA Shrine.

Television broadcasting played a role in provoking middle-class anger against the Senate's decision. Independent television stations such as ABS-CBN and GMA-7 broadcast the impeachment trial daily, unedited and unfiltered; this programming enjoyed very high ratings, particularly among upper- and middle-class Filipinos (most of whom have televisions in their homes). At the time of the Senate's decision on the second envelope, according to a nationwide survey, 88 percent of upper- and middle-class respondents were watching the scene unfold on television, while the percentage was much lower for the lower classes (about 40 percent).[54] In the same survey, the overwhelming majority (about 90 percent) of Metro Manila middle-class Filipinos evaluated the Senate decision as unjust.[55]

Text messaging through cellular telephones worked as a medium of organization for middle-class Filipinos who were outraged about the Senate decision. Cellular telephones have become increasingly popular among upper- and middle-class Filipinos in recent years, particularly the text messaging function. Statistics show that almost all upper- and middle-class Metro Manila residents owned a cell phone in 2000.[56] Merely hours after the Senate's decision on January 16, those who had cellular telephones began to receive text messages inviting them to go to the EDSA Shrine to protest.[57] One of the two major local cellular phone companies, Smart Communications, reported that during the four days of People Power II (January 16 to January 20), about 200 million messages were transmitted within the Philippines, a volume larger than all of Europe's transmission volume for one year.[58] The other major company, Globe Telecom, disclosed that it handled about 90 million messages a day between January 16 and 20, against an average volume of 71 million for the month of January.[59] According to a survey of Metro Manila residents, about 30 percent among the upper and middle class and 10 percent among the lower (zero among the lowest) class category received these invitation messages through their telephones.[60] This corresponds fairly well to the ratio of actual street participation: 30 percent of upper and middle class, eight percent of the lower class, and five percent of the lowest class,[61] suggesting that many of those who were at EDSA during People Power II were informed about the gathering by text messaging. The evidence seems to indicate that text messaging technology played an important role in facilitating the middle-class' rapid and spontaneous gathering on the night of January 16 (and during succeeding days) that led to Estrada's fall.

The use of these mediums of communication was a new experience in the history of street mobilization in the Philippines. In the case of People Power I, President Marcos was, to a large extent, successful in controlling the local mass media in his favor. He closed down vocal anti-Marcos newspapers and magazines, and existing media channels were under the surveillance of the government.[62] In the Philippines of the new millennium, sources of information have not only increased, but have also become freer from government control than before. Besides television and cellular telephones, people's political information sources include radio, newspapers, weekly journals, and the Internet; in this respect the Philippines has seen the same information and communications revolution that other developed and developing states have. The government owns a few of these channels, but the rest remain largely free from its influence.[63]

To summarize, I suggest that the combination of three factors facilitated the robustness of middle-class uprising during People Power II. First, many in the middle class did not support the Estrada presidency. Second, leadership groups such as the church, the left, and business associations guided the middle class to the streets in an effort to oust Estrada. Third, there was an open and accessible medium of communication that provided information to the middle class about the impeachment trial (television) and about the call for street mobilization (text messaging).

CONCLUSION

This chapter examined the question of why President Estrada was removed from office in the manner in which he was. In other words, why was he impeached in the first place, and why was he ousted from office by an extra-constitutional Supreme Court decision and not the Senate impeachment court? I argued that this was due to the combination of weak institutions and strong movements. First, weak party discipline contributed to the success of impeachment in the House by allowing many legislators from Estrada's party to defect to the opposition. Second, the strength of street mobilization in Metro Manila compelled the Supreme Court to install Gloria Macapagal-Arroyo as the new president, which was a *de facto* removal of Estrada from office.

The chapter also analyzed the causes of these weak institutions and strong movements. With regard to weak party discipline within Estrada's party, I suggested that legislators' evaluation of the importance of presidential patronage influenced their decision about whether to defect to the opposition. LAMP members who switched their party affiliation to LAMP after the 1998 election were more likely to endorse impeachment than those who were already LAMP members in 1998, because new switchers received little by way of campaign contributions from Estrada during the 1998 election. In addition, LAMP members who faced their term limitation were more likely to endorse impeachment than continuing members, since departing members presumably valued future presidential patronage less than continuing members.

As for the middle-class mobilization, I suggested three factors that facilitated its emergence and explains its robustness. First, the middle class did not prefer Estrada as president in the first place. Second, there was a set of leadership groups that urged people to turn to the streets. While the middle class were not inclined to replace Estrada by street protests (despite their disapproval of the president), leaders from the Catholic church, the left, and business associations provided guidance and encouragement for street protests. Third, there were accessible media that provided information to people as the impeachment proceedings continued. Live television coverage of the Senate trial provoked people's anger by showing the scene of the Senate decision to effectively halt the trial, and text messaging through cellular telephones organized the outraged middle class to go to the EDSA Shrine.

Based on this analysis, some lessons for the future can be suggested. First, future Philippine presidents should be aware that they can be easily impeached if the grounds for impeachment are very serious (as was the case for Estrada). The threshold for impeachment in the House is relatively low; the support of only one-third of House members can impeach a president. The case of Estrada's impeachment showed that the president could not firmly count on his party's support regardless of the number of his allies due to the weakness of party discipline. As weak party discipline is likely to continue in Philippine politics, impeaching a president may not be so difficult when charges about wrongdoings are as serious as was the case for Estrada.

Second, whether or not unseating another president by popular uprising will occur is likely to depend on the nature of political leadership. The three factors which led to robust middle-class mobilization in this case were (1) middle-class dislike of the president, (2) leadership, and (3) free and accessible media. Among them, I noted that middle-class dislike of Estrada was latent, in the sense that the majority of the middle class did not favor unseating him by street mobilization before People Power II began. As for the existence of a free and accessible media, this is likely to continue in the future. Therefore, whether the latent interest of the middle class—or of any other segment of population for that matter—is converted into actual collective action will depend on the nature of guidance by the leadership groups. If leaders of the church and other social institutions actively urge people to turn to the streets, another regime change by street forces may not be an unlikely scenario. If another People Power movement is to be avoided (as many would prefer), it is political leadership that needs to exercise prudence.

CHAPTER 4

Presidential Impeachment and the Politics of Survival: The Case of Colombia

Victor J. Hinojosa and Aníbal Pérez-Liñán

INTRODUCTION

In this chapter we examine Colombia's experience with presidential impeachment and the ability of Ernesto Samper to survive allegations that his 1994 presidential campaign was funded by narcotics interests. The Samper impeachment attempt was a case of presidential survival. After a brief background on Colombian politics, we discuss the allegations against the president and then introduce an element unique to the Colombian case: international pressure for the president's removal. Next we analyze public opinion data, tracing popular support for the president as the scandal evolved. Finally, we examine Samper's use of pork-barrel spending in the creation of a legislative shield that prevented his removal from office. We hope to provide more insights into what historian David Bushnell has famously called Latin America's "most understudied" and "least understood" country.[1]

BACKGROUND

In order to overcome a dramatic period of political turmoil known as *la Violencia* (the Violence) and reestablish civilian rule after the dictatorship of General Gustavo Rojas Pinilla (1953–57), in 1958 Conservatives and Liberals—the two traditional parties that had dominated Colombian politics since the early nineteenth century—signed an agreement known as the National Front. The National Front guaranteed alternating presidential power every four years (starting with a Liberal president for the 1958–62 term), parity in the distribution of seats in Congress and the Cabinet, and veto power for both congressional parties—which in practice led them to delegate power to the executive branch. The Front ruled Colombia for sixteen years (1958–74), but some of the agreements extended until 1978 and its political legacies persist even today.[2]

Paradoxically, one of the legacies of the National Front was the weakness of political parties. With 50 percent of the congressional seats guaranteed to each party by the constitutional agreement, electoral contests focused on intra-party competition for the available seats. At the same time, others outside the traditional parties—Communists, independents, followers of Rojas Pinilla—were forced to run under Conservative or Liberal labels (sometimes both) or to form guerrilla movements in protest. Third parties were allowed (with little success) after 1970 and even encouraged by a constitutional reform in 1991, but the weakness of party structures worsened over time. By the time Ernesto Samper took office in 1994, Colombian electoral laws—a highly proportional system in which every party continued to run several competing tickets—had created a perverse electoral structure that linked factional bosses and local voters through decentralized, clientelistic networks. Parties had broken into a large number of "micro-enterprises," all presenting candidates under the same label but relying on the selective distribution of pork and patronage to thrive.[3]

A second characteristic of Colombian politics has been the concentration of legal powers on the executive—the guarantor, according to the spirit of the 1886 Constitution, of national unity. The 1991 Constitution reduced the voting quota required for Congress to override a presidential veto, but it preserved the president's decree powers and his exclusive right to introduce major economic bills in Congress, creating what Matthew Shugart and Scott Mainwaring have called a "proactive" executive. This combination of a legally strong president and organizationally weak congressional parties has been described by John Carey and Matthew Shugart as the "inefficient secret" of Colombian presidentialism.[4]

The Colombian Constitutions of 1886 and 1991 followed the American model of impeachment, establishing that the lower house authorizes the trial by simple majority and the Senate removes the president from office with two-thirds of the votes (if a judicial trial ensues, the Supreme Court must handle the case). Historically, the institutional environment has not been particularly favorable to congressional oversight. In 1949, when the Liberal opposition in Congress threatened to initiate an impeachment process, Conservative President Mariano Ospina shut down the legislature and ruled by decree for several months, initiating a decline towards dictatorship that led to Rojas Pinilla's coup in 1953. Between 1958 and 1974, the National Front arrangement prevented any major executive-legislative confrontation (although President Alberto Lleras Restrepo wrestled with Congress to promote constitutional reform in 1968). In 1963, the House of Representatives established the Committee of Investigation and Accusations, but its statutes were not approved until seven years later. Only in the late 1970s and the 1980s were Presidents Alfonso López Michelsen, César Turbay, and Belisario Betancur the subjects of some investigations; no accusation ever reached the floor of the House, and the Accusations Committee was popularly nicknamed the "Absolutions Committee."[5]

Two other aspects complicated the Colombian political landscape during this period: the re-emergence of political violence since the late 1960s, and the expansion of the narcotics business since the 1970s. In 1964 the first of what would be several leftist guerilla movements emerged: the Revolutionary Armed Forces of Colombia (*Fuerzas Armadas Revolucionarias de Colombia*, or FARC) and the National Liberation Army (*Ejército de Liberación National*, or ELN). These and other armed guerilla groups carried on anti-state campaigns in areas where the state had traditionally been weak, often in the exact areas of Liberal-Conservative conflict during *La Violencia*.[6] While some groups signed peace agreements with the government and entered the political system (for instance, the group Movement April 19, or M-19, founded in 1972 and named for the date of the 1970 election when they allege Rojas Pinilla was denied the presidency through electoral fraud, disbanded militarily, and ran a candidate for president in 1990), the FARC and ELN remain armed opponents of the state.

Colombia's political violence escalated in the mid-1980s with the emergence of a third significant armed actor: paramilitary groups. The paramilitaries sprang up independently and simultaneously across Colombia. The groups had different origins and supporters: some were supported by large land owners tired of paying the FARC *vacuna* ("vaccine") who decided they could protect themselves more efficiently by other means: others were aligned with narcotics interests, including the group Death to the Kidnappers (*Muerte a los Secuestradores*), which was aligned with the Medellín drug cartel. The groups had a common enemy, however: the guerillas.

In addition to the development of paramilitary groups and the intensification of the armed conflict, narcotics interests have played an increasingly important role in Colombian politics. From the mid-1970s through the mid-1990s, Colombia's drug trafficking was controlled by large networks often referred to as "cartels." The Medellín cartel, headed by Pablo Escobar, and the Cali Cartel, headed by brothers Miguel and Gilberto Rodríguez Orejuela, emerged as the two most powerful groups. The groups had very different political strategies. Pablo Escobar first attempted to enter the political scene as a legitimate actor, running for a seat in the Chamber of Deputies and winning. When the Chamber refused to allow him to take his seat, Escobar changed tactics, choosing instead a violent war against the state, a war that ended definitively with his death in a shoot-out with police in December 1993.[7]

With Escobar's death, control of Colombia's narcotics industry shifted firmly to the Cali cartel. Their political strategy was very different, preferring, as Crandall has written, "bribes rather than bombs."[8] The scandal that erupted in Colombia and threatened President Samper with possible impeachment reveals just how far-reaching their political influence had become. Indeed, the allegations were that Cali influence had spread deep into the Liberal party and had financed the electoral campaign of the president himself.

THE ALLEGATIONS

The 1994 presidential campaign was the first under the new Constitution. One of the provisions of the 1991 Constitution was the establishment of a run-off election for the presidency should no candidate garner a majority of the votes in the first round. After the first round of voting in 1994, neither Liberal candidate Ernesto Samper nor his Conservative opponent Andrés Pastrana had enough votes to win. This caught the Samper campaign off guard: it was under-funded and unprepared for an additional month of campaigning. The scandal that enveloped Colombia for the next two years centered on allegations that the Samper campaign had turned to the Cali drug cartel for the funds it needed.

In the days leading up to the final vote, the Pastrana campaign received tape recordings of a conversation wherein Cali drug cartel chief Miguel Rodríguez Orejuela bragged to an associate that he had placed some three billion Colombian pesos (then approximately 3.5 million U.S. dollars) into the Samper campaign.[9] Fearing that releasing the tapes would appear to be a political move, the Pastrana campaign turned to two sources: outgoing Colombian President César Gaviria (from Samper's Liberal Party) and U.S. Ambassador Morris Busby. While the Gaviria government was able to authenticate the tapes in the days before the election, they refused to release them. Similarly, the U.S. feared being seen as unduly seeking to influence the election and refused to release the tapes. Samper narrowly defeated Pastrana on June 19, 1994.

Days after the election of Samper, the U.S. Drug Enforcement Administration's agent-in-charge in Bogotá, Joe Toft, irate at the corruption of the Samper campaign and his own embassy's failure to act, leaked the tapes to the Colombian press.[10] Thus erupted the first part of the scandal: the "narco-cassettes," which appeared to link the Samper campaign to the Cali cartel. It is significant to note, however, that the tapes provided no evidence of direct links to Samper himself nor any evidence that he was aware of the illicit financing. Because of this lack of a direct connection, Samper was able to weather this initial storm quite well, as public opinion data demonstrate.

The more difficult crisis emerged in late 1995 when Colombian Prosecutor General Alfonso Valdivieso initiated the "Proceso 8000" investigations (named after the case number), in which he alleged wide-ranging corruption of the Liberal Party. This scandal would affect many members of the Samper campaign's inner circle, leading to the arrest and imprisonment of former campaign treasurer Santiago Medina and campaign manager (and later Minister of Defense) Fernando Botero. The scandal touched Samper personally after these two officials confessed and turned in evidence against him. Botero's confession was particularly embarrassing as, in an interview from prison, he alleged that the president did have knowledge of the illicit financing.

This is what led to the investigation of Samper in the Chamber of Deputies. There were in fact two critical votes on the president. The first (which was earlier in the process and is the less important of the two) occurred in December 1995 when the Committee of Investigation and Accusations voted (14–1) that there was insufficient evidence to proceed with an impeachment inquiry. In February 1996, Samper was formally accused by the Prosecutor General's office, and in June the full Chamber of Deputies voted on whether to approve the report from the Committee of Investigation and Accusations that concluded that the president was innocent. In a vote of 111–43, the Chamber acquitted the president, preventing any further congressional and, in effect, judicial, action.

INTERNATIONAL REACTION

Presidential scandals and impeachments are quintessentially domestic political issues. The Colombian impeachment story is unique in that much of the push for removal of the Colombian president came from an international source: the United States. Drug control was formally declared an issue of national security for the U.S. in 1986 by President Ronald Reagan [11] and has long been the top U.S. priority in its relationship with Colombia. On this critical issue, Ernesto Samper was extraordinarily weak.

It is important to note that U.S. suspicions of Samper's drug ties far predated the release of the narco-cassettes. Early in his career, Samper was president of the National Association of Financial Institutions, and at their 1979 annual meeting, he suggested the legalization of cannabis, arguing as Alvaro Camacho has written, "for the need to control an informal and subterranean economy that does not generate taxes while contributing to generalized corruption."[12] These statements were not forgotten by U.S. officials, and some in the Clinton administration termed candidate Samper "Mr. Legalization."[13] Further, the U.S. suspected that Samper had taken bribes from narcotics traffickers when he managed Alfonso López Michelsen's 1982 presidential campaign, and was aware that when Gilberto Rodríguez Orejuela (of the Cali cartel) was arrested in Spain in 1984, Samper's private (unpublished) telephone number was found in his address book.[14]

The narco-cassettes seemed to confirm the administration's worst fears about Samper. Both governments attempted to smooth over bilateral relations in the beginning, although the U.S. did use the tapes as leverage, pressing Samper for more and more cooperation on narcotics matters in order to prove that he was clean. One former State Department official described the situation this way: "You (Samper) say you didn't take money from the Narcos. Ok. Prove it. Cooperate with us as if you hadn't."[15] A former Defense Department official spoke of the increased leverage the U.S. had with Samper and its ability to continually demand more and more cooperation.[16] In 1995 the U.S. gave Colombia a "national interest waiver" in its annual certification of whether major narcotics producing/trafficking countries are "cooperating fully" in the war on drugs. While this national interest waiver was in fact a decertification (that is, Colombia was found not to be cooperating fully), it entailed a sort of free pass allowing Colombia to avoid the mandated consequences. Colombia's drug control efforts in 1995 were impressive: between June and August, six of the top seven officials in the Cali organization were captured, including Gilberto and Miguel Rodríguez Orejuela.[17]

Yet when the Proceso 8000 phase of the scandal broke, U.S. goals shifted to the removal of Samper and the U.S. began to take harsher measures against him, hoping for his resignation or removal by impeachment.[18] In 1996 Colombia was decertified for lack of complete cooperation on narcotics matters and was not given the national interest waiver, despite the arrest of the Cali leaders. This denied Colombia all but counter-narcotics U.S. aid and required the U.S. to vote against Colombia in international lending forums. The decertification also gave the U.S. the option of imposing economic sanctions (which it did not do). On June 2, 1996, U.S. Attorney General Janet Reno presented a formal request for the extradition of the Cali cartel leaders (despite the prohibition of the extradition of Colombian nationals in the 1991 Colombian Constitution).[19] U.S. reaction to Samper's acquittal by the Chamber of Deputies was exceptionally harsh: the U.S. revoked President Samper's U.S. travel visa and essentially ended contact between the two administrations. Relations between the U.S. and Colombia did not improve until 1998 when the U.S., in anticipation of Colombia's upcoming presidential election, once again granted Colombia a national interest waiver in the certification decision.[20]

DOMESTIC REACTION

To what extent were these accusations—and the international pressures that they unleashed—able to erode public support for the administration? The conventional wisdom is, not much. Samper himself has argued that "throughout the crisis, the polls showed steady support at 42 percent. As time went by and people realized that, in spite of the predictions made by the government's enemies, the administration would not fall, not only I wasn't weakened but people in the streets started to believe that I had political super-powers—which of course I lacked."[21]

We next assess the domestic impact of the crisis by examining public opinion data between 1994 and 1998. Figure 4-1 compares two measures of Samper's popularity throughout his term. The first measure is the percentage of Colombians who ranked Samper's performance in office as "excellent" or "good" (based on surveys conducted by Gallup in the four largest cities); we refer to this indicator as the president's approval rate. The second measure is the percentage of Colombians who said that they had a "favorable opinion" of Samper (based on surveys conducted by Napoleón Franco y Asociados for the administration using national samples and occasional urban samples); we refer to this indicator as Samper's favorability index. The two measures depict a similar trend ($r = 0.93$): somewhat stable popularity rates during the first months in office, followed by a decline after the accusations took shape but without any major collapse in the administration's image. At the same time, the comparison

Figure 4-1.
Popularity Rates for Ernesto Samper, August 1994–July 1998

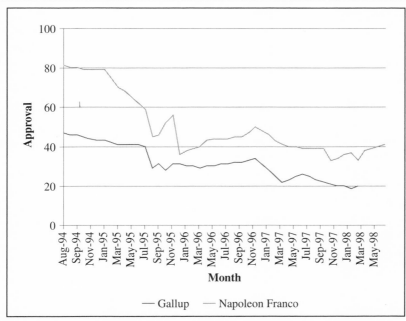

Sources: Gallup Colombia (approval rates in four largest cities), Napoleón Franco y Asociados (favorability measured for national and urban samples). Missing observations were interpolated.

of the two indicators is quite suggestive: approval rates are on average 19 percent points below favorability scores. It seems that Samper's personal image was better than his image as chief executive, and that his support among urban dwellers (captured by Gallup) was consistently lower than among the rural voters included in Napoleón Franco's national samples. Samper would end his term with a modest urban approval rate of 20 percent but a respectable favorability score of 41 percent.

Figure 4-1 also allows us to trace four phases of the Samper crisis. The first period extended from the president's inauguration in August 1994, to the arrest of his campaign treasurer in late July 1995. This quiet time before the storm included the "honeymoon" of the first hundred days in office and the launching of the Social Leap program, Samper's social policy initiative. According to the National Administrative Department for Statistics, the average inflation rate during the first 11 months of the administration was 1.7 percent, while the unemployment rate reached an estimated average of 8.2 percent. Although inflation would not turn out to be a major source of concern for the administration, unemployment would rise during the following years and constitute a barrier for any "social leap."

During this period, the political storm loomed on the horizon. In April 1995, the office of the prosecutor general (*Fiscalía*) opened the Proceso 8000 investigation into the illegal financing of political campaigns. The process immediately involved several members of Congress, Samper's comptroller general, and his campaign treasurer, Santiago Medina. As explained previously, the administration sought to preserve its public standing by launching a head-on attack on the drug cartels and, after several victories, succeeded in arresting the head of the Cali Cartel on June 9. In part because of this, the average Gallup approval rate in urban centers remained at 43 percent, and the Napoleón Franco surveys registered mean favorability rates of 76 percent.

The second period began in late July 1995, when Santiago Medina was arrested and acknowledged that the campaign had received donations from the Cali Cartel. His testimony triggered what Samper described in his memoirs as an "endless rollercoaster."[22] The president immediately addressed the Colombian people in a televised speech, accepting the possibility that the drug dealers had infiltrated his campaign without his consent or knowledge. His Minister of Defense and former campaign manager, Fernando Botero, resigned from his post and was arrested a few days later. To worsen things, *Semana* magazine published the transcripts of a friendly telephone conversation held between the then presidential candidate Samper and a woman related to the drug trafficking business. Rumors about a possible military coup in November began to unfold in the following weeks.[23] In an attempt to protect the president, the Accusations Committee of the House of Representatives refused to initiate an investigation based on Medina's testimony. Between July and December, the average inflation rate was anchored below one percent per month, but unemployment rose to nine percent. With tense political and uncertain economic conditions, the average approval rate for the administration dropped to 33 percent, and Samper's favorability declined to 53 percent.

The crisis entered its third stage in late January 1996, when Samper's campaign manager Fernando Botero declared in a TV interview that "Samper knew" about the scheme. Samper called for an extraordinary session of Congress and asked its members to reopen the investigation of his case. In March, the U.S. decertified Colombia. During this period inflation reached an average 2.4 percent, unemployment climbed to 10.3 percent, and average presidential approval rates between January and May dropped to 30 percent. In turn, favorability reached an average 39 percent, showing some signs of recovery by the end of the period.

The final stage of the crisis began with the decision of the House of Representatives to acquit Samper in June 1996 and lasted until the end of his term in August 1998. The congressional vote did not mean a full end to the administration's woes, but it meant that the threat of an impeachment was over. During this final period, the average approval rate reached 26 percent and the average favorability rate was 41 percent. After the president was absolved, there was a slight trend toward the recovery of his image until December 1996 (when approval and favorability peaked at 34 percent and 50 percent, respectively), but presidential popularity slowly declined afterwards as unemployment rose from around 11 percent in December 1996 to 16 percent in July 1998.

How relevant were each of these episodes in shaping the evolution of public support for President Samper? Table 4-1 displays two time-series models addressing this question, one for Gallup's approval rates and the other for Franco's favorability data. We have included a set of dummy variables to account for the "honeymoon" during the first three months in office, the permanent damage created by Medina's declarations after June 1995, the impact of Botero's declarations after January 1996, and the congressional decision to acquit Samper in June 1996. The models also control for levels of inflation and unemployment (data from the National Administrative Department for Statistics), presidential popularity during the previous month, and, in the case of Napoleón Franco's data, for the use of urban-only samples as opposed to national samples.

The two models suggest that Medina's testimony imposed substantial political cost to the administration (between three and nine percentage points), and that this decline in public support was unrelated to the natural erosion one might expect after the first hundred days in office. Even though Botero had greater standing in Samper's administration, his testimony apparently was less of a surprise and had a smaller impact among Colombians. When urban citizens were asked about Samper's performance in

Table 4-1.
Models of Presidential Popularity (OLS)

	Approval (Gallup)		Favorability (Franco)	
Predictor	Coefficient	Std. E.	Coefficient	Std. E
Honeymoon	− 0.0444	(1.765)	2.774	(2.991)
Medina's declarations	−3.120 **	(1.484)	− 9.075 ***	(3.125)
Botero's declarations	1.336	(1.605)	− 4.719 *	(2.687)
After June 1996	− 1.608	(1.548)	0.110	(2.265)
Inflation	− 0.589	(0.480)	− 0.373	(0.757)
Unemployment	0.171	(0.729)	0.145	(0.590)
Lagged DV	0.851 ***	(0.111)	0.521 ***	(0.116)
Urban samples			− 3.337 **	(1.568)
Constant	5.572	(9.972)	34.514 ***	(11.641)
Adjusted R²	.930		.940	
Durbin-Watson	2.31		1.490	
T (Months)	43		47	

Note: Unstandardized regression coefficients (standard errors). Missing data were interpolated.
* Significant at .1 level; ** at .05 level; *** at .01 level.

office, the shock produced by Botero's interview was virtually undistin-
guishable from the rest of the crisis. But Samper's personal image at the
national level declined approximately five percent as a result of his minister's accusation.

THE LEGISLATIVE SHIELD

On June 12, 1996, the Colombian Chamber of Representatives voted
111–43 to absolve the president and prohibit future investigations. This
decisive vote foreclosed the possibility of an impeachment, and definitively shielded Samper from removal. The composition of the Chamber
was 59 percent Liberal, 31 percent Conservative, and 10 percent for the
remaining parties (none of which controlled more than two seats). In the
remainder of this section, we refer to all non-Liberal legislators as the
"opposition" although, as Table 4-2 illustrates, the Conservatives were
divided on the Samper issue and the smaller parties adopted different
alignments. Predictably, the Liberals for the most part closed ranks to protect Samper (89 percent of them voted to absolve the president). But more
surprisingly, 44 percent of the Conservative Party and 63 percent of the
members of the smaller parties supported the president as well. Had the
opposition voted cohesively in favor of the accusations, together with the

Table 4-2.
Vote Acquitting Samper in the Colombian House (June 12, 1996)

Party	Yeas	Nays	Total	% Yeas by Party
Liberal	80	10	90	88.9%
Conservative	21	27	48	43.8
Others	10	6	16	62.5
Total	111	43	154	72.1

Liberals who defected, the Samper administration would have been only three votes away from defeat.

Why were opposition legislators willing to shield President Samper? The explanation that first comes to mind is the relatively high approval rates enjoyed by the president. It was difficult for opposition leaders to launch a frontal attack on the executive when public opinion—in particular the popular sectors and people in the rural areas—had not clearly withdrawn their support of the president. Although this variable helps us understand the reluctance of the median legislator to support impeachment, it is not very helpful in explaining why some legislators voted in favor of the accusations and others did not; in particular, it does not explain why so many *opposition* deputies—who presumably represented a greater proportion of anti-Samper voters—voted the way that they did.

We now explore a complementary explanation: the use of pork-barrel spending in order to build a legislative coalition by the executive. It was argued at the time that the Samper administration was using government grants in order to deliver funds to the districts of friendly members of congress. For instance, a citizen commission created to monitor the evolution of the crisis claimed in its final report that some members of the investigative committee of the lower house had seen the allocation of funds for their electoral bailiwicks increased as much as 55.7 percent during the 1995 fiscal year.[24]

The main tool presumably used by the executive to distribute funds was the *Fondos de Cofinanciación* (Co-Financing Funds). The Funds had been created in 1992 to support local development initiatives. At the same time, the 1991 constitutional reform had deprived Congress of its main way of financing clientelistic projects, the system of *auxilios parlamentarios* (legislative aid) that allowed members to earmark grants for local institutions from a common pool controlled by the budget committee. In this context, politicians soon realized that the Co-Financing Funds could be used as a new way to direct resources for pet projects in their districts.[25]

Between 1995 and 1998, the typical member of the House of Representatives received 3.9 billion pesos (approximately 3.4 million U.S. dollars) in co-financing grants.[26] The average Liberal received 4.5 billion and the average Conservative, 3.4. Those members who ultimately supported Samper against the impeachment charges received on average 4.1 billion pesos, while those who opposed the president received 3.4.[27]

We developed a statistical model to analyze the influence of these budget allocations in the formation of the legislative shield against impeachment. Pork is measured as the annual investment in regional projects sponsored by specific representatives (in billions of Colombian pesos). The dependent variable is a dichotomous indicator showing whether each congressional member supported the motion to absolve Samper on June 12, 1996. We have also included two control variables: party membership (whether the legislator was a Liberal or a member of any other party), and the percentage of votes for Samper in the representative's department during the first round of the 1994 presidential election.[28]

Two questions are relevant in this analysis. First, is pork used to build coalitions or to buy congressional votes? In other words, if legislators respond, do they do so out of loyalty to the executive or based on expectations of future financial support for their districts? The first situation would mean that the president must invest heavily in coalition-building early during his term, while the second situation would mean that he can buy off legislators in exchange for promises of support when he confronts the threat of impeachment. Yuko Kasuya (this volume) addresses this problem in the context of Philippine politics. In order to deal with this issue, we created two separate measures for the investment allocated to each legislator before the impeachment vote (1995–96) and afterwards (1997–98).

A second question is whether pork-barrel spending has the same influence on the members of the president's party and the opposition. It may be the case that investment is useful to preserve the loyalty of friendly representatives, but it is useless in gaining support among public opponents. Or, in a system with high incentives to cultivate the personal vote, it is also possible that opposition politicians, with little control over government patronage, are anxious to obtain resources for their local machines. In order to trace these effects, we created interaction terms to indicate whether the 1995–96 and the 1997–98 grants had been allocated to members of the opposition.[29]

Table 4-3 presents the results of the logistic regression model. Statistical analysis cannot prove that the Samper administration *intended* to use the Co-Financing Funds in order to obstruct the impeachment process. It does, however, show that opposition legislators reacted favorably to early coalition-building efforts but did not vote anticipating future streams of revenue. This finding is somewhat consistent with that of Yuko Kasuya,

Table 4-3.
Model Predicting the Vote in the Colombian House of Representatives (June 12, 1996)

Predictor	Coefficient	Std. E.
Member of the opposition	– 3.424 **	(0.722)
Investment 1995–96 (billions)	– 0.823 *	(0.360)
Investment 1995–96 for opposition	1.401 *	(0.620)
Investment 1997–98 (billions)	0.473	(0.327)
Investment 1997–98 for opposition	– 0.447	(0.491)
Samper's vote in member's district	0.010	(0.040)
Constant	2.147	(1.930)
Nagelkerke R²	.360	
N	152 ***	

Note: Logistic regression coefficients (standard errors). * Significant at .05 level; ** at .01 level; *** investment data for two Congress members is missing.

who identifies a similar pattern of loyalty among Philippine legislators *in the ruling party.*

Our findings for the ruling Liberals, however, differ from Kasuya's conclusions about the Philippine's Struggle of Filipino Mass (*Lapiang ng Masang Pilipino*, or LAMP) party. The coefficients in Table 4-3 suggest that the funds were ultimately instrumental in building support among opposition members, but they were useless in gaining the support of dissident Liberals. In fact, it seems that any special efforts to attract party dissidents may have been counter-productive, since those Liberals who disproportionately benefitted from pork remained more likely to vote against Samper. We suspect that the reason for this result is that some Liberals who occupied key positions in Congress—and were therefore well-positioned to demand funds—belonged to the *Gavirista* wing of the party (followers of former President César Gaviria), which had a distant relationship with the *Samperismo.*[30]

This model is able to predict the behavior of 75 percent of the individual Congress members, and its capability to map the behavior of the typical legislator within each party is quite accurate. Table 4-4 compares the average expected probability of voting against impeachment and the actual proportion of representatives who supported Samper among Liberals and non-Liberals (the average level of investment in the representatives' districts is reported for comparative purposes). The prediction of the model for every group is less than one percent away from the observed distribution of votes.

Table 4-4.
Predicted Probability of Supporting the President, by Party (Based on Table 4.2)

Party	Average Investments 1995-96[1]	Mean predicted probability[2]	Proportion voting vs. impeachment on 6/12/96
Liberals	1.78	0.887	0.889
Opposition	1.35	0.496	0.484
Total	*1.59*	*0.718*	*0.721*

[1] In billions of Colombian pesos.
[2] Average of model predictions for all members in a given category.

CONCLUSIONS

From a comparative point of view, the Samper crisis in Colombia represents an interesting case because it ultimately constitutes an episode of non-impeachment, or, in the language of this book, a pure form of presidential survival. According to the ideal-typical sequence of the impeachment process outlined in the introductory chapter, President Samper: (1) confronted credible allegations of official misconduct which eventually (2) became a scandal and (3) led to an investigation in the Congress. But the lower house (4) never authorized the trial, and thus (5) the president survived in office. This outcome was unexpected and frustrating for many political actors in Colombia (and abroad), but consistent with the Colombian tradition of strong presidentialism, a decentralized party system that allowed the president to build cross-party coalitions, and relatively high levels of presidential approval.

Samper was able to survive this scandal for a number of reasons. First, no smoking gun was ever produced which conclusively linked the president with the illicit financing of his campaign. While the evidence of the illicit financing is overwhelming and the president almost certainly had to have known or remained intentionally unaware of the sources of contributions (indeed, many Colombians likened the scenario to having an elephant in one's home: you simply have to notice), there was no direct link between the president and the funds.

The second critical factor in the president's survival was his popularity, which remained relatively high throughout the scandal. This provided legislators with little incentive to vote to oust a popular president. A third factor was the control the Liberal Party maintained of both the upper and lower chambers of Congress. Yet this was not enough to ensure the president's survival, because the Liberal Party was divided between those loyal to Samper and those loyal to former President Gaviria. A united opposition could have placed Samper in a precarious position (within three votes of removal). As our data and analysis suggest, Samper was able to overcome this potential threat by allocating the Co-Financing Funds in such a way as to reward opposition legislators who would vote for him. These funds had little impact on disaffected Liberals, but a significant impact on opposition legislators. Indeed, we suspect that these funds helped "the president who was going to fall" overcome a dramatic impeachment crisis.[31]

CHAPTER 5

Madagascar: Impeachment as Parliamentary Coup d'Etat

Philip M. Allen

INTRODUCTION

During the past century, the Indian Ocean's "Great Island" practiced virtually all forms of regime change except the electoral defeat of an incumbent; that experience occurred in 2001 and proved more difficult to implement than any of the others. Five years earlier, Madagascar became the first African state ever to dismiss a sitting president through constitutional impeachment. This chapter tells a tale of presidential exit.

The fifth chief of state to govern Madagascar since its independence from France in 1960, Dr. Albert Zafy was elected president in February 1993 and removed from office by impeachment in September 1996. Zafy's presidency was beset from the start by constitutional anomalies and by the failure of the opposition to cohere into a stable governmental coalition. A National Assembly, elected in June 1993, only reflected the fissiparous tendencies of Malagasy politics. Zafy and his succession of prime ministers never controlled an effective legislative majority, and the president's efforts to defeat parliamentary recalcitrance proved maladroit. Eventually, he blamed all failures of governance on the legislators and/or his own ministers. Seeking to mobilize popular enthusiasm, he espoused radically nationalist economic policies regarded as ruinous by the international agencies on which the Great Island depended for viability in an unsympathetic global system.

Ultimately, the alienation of both domestic and foreign stakeholders cost Dr. Zafy his presidency. He was both an obstacle to the fundamental adjustments that would invigorate a desperately stagnant economy, and an unstable factor in a fragile new experiment in parliamentary democracy. On July 26, 1996, by which time the majority of his erstwhile coalition partners had deserted him, he was impeached by a more than two-thirds majority of the unicameral legislature. He was formally removed from office on September 4 by decision of the High Constitutional Court, Madagascar's supreme tribunal. To this day, two presidencies later, Zafy persists in denouncing his impeachment as irregular and unjust and his successors as usurpers. But the 1996 process has proved definitive. Although still active in politics, the disgraced ex-president has steadily lost his audience, and his polemics have become increasingly shrill, the ignorable rantings of a marginalized failed statesman.

THE IMPEACHMENT PROCESS IN MADAGASCAR

The term *empêchement* used in both the Malagasy and the French constitutions does not carry connotations of retribution against crime or misdemeanor. There is no provision for criminal proceedings to warrant removal of an official from office. Rather, once indicted by the National Assembly (in France, the government brings charges), a president is formally declared incapacitated, precluding him/her from carrying out prescribed duties. Whereas the French precedent does not itself provide definitions for the causes or motives of such incapacitation, Madagascar's constitution is somewhat more explicit, albeit still ambiguous. In Article 44 it identifies a president as *Ray aman-dreny*—literally "father and mother"—prime custodian of the public well-being. In Article 50, it defines grounds for the court's finding that a president is incapable of continuing in office if either (1) s/he has violated the constitution, the integrity of which is to be safeguarded under presidential oath, or (2) s/he is incapable of functioning for some other valid reason—presumably, a medical or comparable disabling condition. Thus, *empêchement définitif* (or categoric incapacity) can be moved either by acts of commission or omission that in United States law might not be subject to impeachment, or under circumstances that might be beyond the incumbent's control, leaving the constitutional court to decide the remedy.

As articulated in Article 50 of the 1992 constitution, "Irrevocable incapacitation (*empêchement définitif*) of the President of the Republic may be declared by the Constitutional Court upon receipt of a resolution adopted by a majority of no less than two-thirds of the deputies comprising the National Assembly, for violation of the Constitution, or for any other duly affirmed and proven reason entailing his permanent inability to carry out his responsibilities."[1]

ZAFY'S RISE TO THE PRESIDENCY

From independence on June 26, 1960, until May 1972, Madagascar was governed by President Philibert Tsiranana and his Social Democratic Party (PSD). For 12 years while the PSD expanded its electoral and parliamentary dominance, the Tsiranana regime, or the First Republic, sought national security and prosperity through orthodox Western prescriptions for development, ideology, and cold-war alignment. The Republic fell amidst a protest movement that joined nationalist aspirations, particularly among students, to dissatisfaction in labor and small business classes over the pace of progress. Tsiranana conferred extraordinary powers on Army Chief of Staff General Gabriel Ramanantsoa, but the Ramanantsoa interregnum itself collapsed in the aftermath of a counter-coup staged by disaffected pro-Tsiranana military in December 1974. Unable to pacify his own army, Ramanantsoa resigned in favor of interior minister Richard Ratsimandrava. However, Ratsimandrava was assassinated on February 11, 1975, less than one week after taking office. Following four months of deliberation, an 18-member military directorate declared Ratsimandrava's rival, Navy Captain Didier Ratsiraka, president.

Unable to force Madagascar's unruly politics into an obedient monolith, Ratsiraka allowed his Second Republic to resemble a multi-party state, although all participating factions had to subscribe to his socialist charter and join a National Front for the Defense of the Revolution. He controlled this anomaly for 17 years through manipulation of conflicting interests and in spite of mounting dismay over a dramatically deteriorating economy. Managing to prevent critical linkages among contending groups or between those groups and the island's traditionally loyalist military, the self-appointed admiral sustained control until 1991 through a combination of local party leverage and deft police intimidation.

A cardiovascular surgeon trained in France, Dr. Albert Zafy was elected president in February 1993, to become the fifth chief of state to govern Madagascar since independence in 1960. A man of moral and physical courage, but lacking in political experience or consistently sound judgment, Zafy emerged from virtual obscurity as a surgeon in 1990 to join and eventually (by default) lead the Vital Forces, the burgeoning opposition to Didier Ratsiraka's foundering dictatorship. For two years, while other, more practiced politicians explored alternative forms of accommodation with the regime and its international supporters, Zafy invariably chose the line of least compromise with the beleaguered tyrant and the foreign institutions that, in spite of themselves, had become reconciled to him. The disintegration of the USSR and exit of other socialist props for Ratsiraka's 17-year Second Republic sharpened Zafy's profile as a nationalist alternative.

Once Ratsiraka had been ousted by constitutional convention and plebiscite in August 1992, Zafy stood for the presidency, winning a plurality of votes on November 25 and defeating his predecessor in a two-man run-off on February 10, 1993. Democracy appeared to have triumphed. But the Vital Forces owed their brief coherence primarily to antagonism against Ratsiraka, not to consensus on political directions, let alone fidelity to the new president. The new presidency was beset from the start by constitutional anomalies and by the conflict between the president and the parliament.

EXECUTIVE-LEGISLATIVE CONFLICTS

The Third Republic's constitution, adopted by the canonical referendum in 1992, departed significantly from its predecessors by modestly empowering parliamentary authority over the executive. This shift in balance represented an expected response to the predominance of an excessive presidency, exploited in both Tsiranana's First Republic and especially during Ratsiraka's mercurial dictatorship.

True to the juridical philosophy of its framers, the 1992 constitution was strongly influenced by French precedents. Under its provisions the National Assembly appointed and dismissed a prime minister who shared with the Assembly the right to propose a budget and initiate legislation—prerogatives denied the president.[2] The success of the new system would depend of course on the ability of a multitude of political factions to form stable alliances for or against the executive. It also required a chief of state who could respect legislative legitimacy, allow administrative authority to be exercised by a prime minister and cabinet, and encourage these alliances toward the national interest. Blunt, inexperienced in administration, demagogic in demeanor, Albert Zafy could not function under such constraints.

Signals of instability in the political structure appeared early. The Vital Forces coalition began to show serious fissures as it entered the crucial legislative elections of 1993. The geographic distribution of seats in the National Assembly became subject to a welter of differing interests, and the resulting electoral process represented a clumsy compromise among them. These controversies captured so much attention that elections were delayed for several months, and a corresponding attempt to create a Senate, as called for by the constitution, had to be postponed indefinitely.[3]

Fully 121 self-styled parties competed in the June 16, 1993, race, sending over 4,000 candidates after 138 seats in 59 constituencies of radically unequal size, with seats apportioned through a complicated variation on proportional representation. Confusion over balloting procedures and awkward administration caused defections in a weary and often befuddled Malagasy electorate, called to the polls for a fourth time in ten months; only 55.8 percent turned out to vote. The Vital Forces, victors in 1992, claimed only 52 of the 138 seats, with 20 to 24 additional deputies more or less pledged to support Zafy's preference for prime minister. This gave the eventual government a bare, unstable majority. The legislative sequel consisted of shifting affinities and changing loyalties among many competing factions.

The first challenge came in the selection of prime minister. This contest pitted against one another several aspirants claiming to have played critical roles in the Vital Force success, a harbinger of what was to come. Zafy's compromise choice for prime minister fell upon Francisque Ravony, another major player in the Vital Forces movement who won an unimpressive plurality of 54 votes for the premiership, a handicap that troubled him and his impatient, suspicious president throughout the premier's embattled tenure.

Never able to command a consistent majority, Ravony also contested presidential options on virtually every major issue. Seeing hope for the dismal Malagasy economy only in a reinvigorated program of foreign investment and assistance, the prime minister proved far too ardent an internationalist for a president convinced that Madagascar could go it alone in the global system. Calling World Bank/IMF conditionality requirements a "sell-out to foreigners," Zafy pressed for inflationary subsidies to rice farmers, a costly three-tiered local administrative structure, and recourse to what the Washington advisors denounced as "parallel financing" for expensive imports.[4] Ravony and the Assembly were locked in stalemate against a president unreconciled to cooperation with either of them. Dubbing himself "the straw-hat man" (*l'homme au chapeau de paille*) in homage to the First Republic's popular president Tsiranana, Zafy toured the country denouncing the politicians of the capital city of Antananarivo, including his own prime minister, and making matters all the worse for a hapless economy.

In September 1995, Zafy struck directly against his antagonists to correct what he regarded as a prejudicial subordination of president to legislature. He initiated still another referendum, asking for presidential authority to name and dismiss the prime minister and cabinet, to dissolve parliament, and to ignore certain of its resolutions. With only 65.39 percent of a sadly confused electorate voting (far less in the cities), Zafy obtained a majority of 63.56 percent in this referendum, effectively employing one-half the electorate to change the balance of political forces devised by the 1992 constitution. "I am now in a position to guide the government," claimed President Zafy after the referendum.[5] Antagonized by the president's defiance, the IMF responded by postponing negotiations for yet another year, allowing Madagascar to founder in debt, deficit, and indecision. In this accomplishment, Zafy also inadvertently betrayed once more how little "the governed [in Madagascar] recognize themselves . . . in their governors."[6]

Zafy's third prime minister was a respected Antananarivo jurist, Norbert Ratsirahonana, who left his position as president of the High Constitutional Court to enter the chaotic political arena, staking his ministry on a successful return to the favor of the international institutions that hold Madagascar's livelihood in their dossiers. With a modicum of parliamentary support, Ratsirahonana was able to sign a new IMF Enhanced Structural Adjustment Facility in Washington on November 27, 1996. But Zafy's by now notorious incompetence in critical economic matters, combined with perceptions of vindictiveness and obvious dissension within his administration, finally induced Vital Forces defectors to form a loose front called the Rally for the Third Republic. Thereupon they joined the Ratsirakist movement toward impeachment of the president. Ominously for Zafy, this revolt was also supported by the leadership of the influential National Council of Churches.

ALBERT ZAFY'S PARLIAMENTARY DISGRACE

Once the original Vital Forces had dissolved, Zafy's legitimacy rested on his election by universal suffrage and his rather tainted triumph in the September 1995 referendum. That victory turned into disaster for Zafy within a year's time. While managing to obtain popular approval, his campaign tactics appeared deceitful and his motives—aggrandizement of personal/presidential power—offensive to the contemporary political mood. Under these circumstances, a vehemently alienated parliament had only one effective weapon against him—impeachment.

In spite of the presidential power-grab, the National Assembly remained a vital political body in Madagascar. According to one analyst, the "constitutional amendment did not disarm the National Assembly"; another analyst concluded, "on the contrary. In a climate of instability, the parliament remains a key component of the political structure of the Third Republic and also probably a factor in the preservation of democracy. It confirmed its role as balancing power against the expansion of presidential prerogatives."[7]

The impeachment complaint transmitted to the High Constitutional Court (HCC) by parliament on July 26, 1996, charged President Zafy with several violations of the constitution and other abuses of his authority. Specifically, the president was accused first of violating the principle of continuity of public services in his interference in the formation of the second government of Francisque Ravony in 1995 (prior to the September referendum), illegitimately opposing the nomination of several of Ravony's choices for ministerial posts, and again in his subsequent imposition of certain ministers on the newly confirmed prime minister Norbert Ratsirahonana against the latter's wishes in May 1996.

Secondly, the complaint charged Zafy with violating the principle of separation of powers by incorporating the office of the state controller into the presidency, rather than respecting the authority of the prime minister to supervise the audit process; by organizing a national forum on the judiciary during the time the National Assembly was debating governmental motions on this subject; and by refusing to allow the National

Assembly to vote on promulgation of the results of the referendum of September 17, 1995.

Finally, the president was charged with frequently violating his oath of office through failure to implement various policies as authorized by legislation, failure to make obligatory appointments to ranking civil service vacancies, and abusing the constitution in his actions, declarations, and messages to the nation; with violating his oath of office in failing to promulgate and to implement a number of laws within the 15-day period required by Article 57 of the constitution; and with obstructing the normal process of negotiations with external donors of assistance.

The National Assembly voted its resolution against Zafy by a majority of 99 to 32, with three abstentions (blank votes, actually) and four deputies recorded as absent or not voting. Hence, the articles of impeachment were approved by seven more votes than the required two-thirds (92). The National Assembly thereupon requested the court to declare Albert Zafy "irrevocably incapacitated." The resolution asked the court to designate an acting president for the period of time necessary to organize new elections to the office. Beyond the solemn rebuke implicit in this action against a particular president whose performance it found defective, the Assembly was seeking through judicial process to reassert the parliamentary character of the Third Republic as originally determined in the 1992 constitution, notwithstanding the assault on that principle embodied in Zafy's referendum of September 1995.

On receipt of this parliamentary resolution, the HCC invited Mr. Zafy to submit a formal rebuttal to the charges made against him by parliament. He did so in a memorandum on August 29. In particular, the president challenged the competence of the High Constitutional Court to consider the Assembly's resolution in view of the constitutional designation of another tribunal, the (hitherto nonexistent) "Constitutional Court" as empowered to entertain such charges. He also sought dismissal of the resolution based on the casuistical nature of most of the arguments deployed against him during the Assembly's debates, reflecting purely subjective and personal complaints for legitimate actions that merely failed to please certain deputies.

In the event that the HCC should declare itself competent to decide the case and that it accept the Assembly's "truncated and amputated" resolution, the president defended himself against all charges, contending that the president had the right, even prior to the enactment of the September 1995 constitutional amendments, to oppose nomination of ministers (in this instance, those designated by Prime Minister Ravony) in order to ensure that all ministers enjoyed their civic and political rights and that none was subject to doubts over her/his "reputation and civic virtue," according to reliable information at the president's disposal. Zafy also claimed that subsequent to the 1995 referendum, and hence in the case of

Prime Minister Ratsirahonana in 1996, the president no longer had to respect the prime minister's wishes in the designation of members of that government. In any case, he continued, the nomination of ministers constituted an administrative act only susceptible to explicit challenge before the courts within 90 days of such act, and since that challenge had not taken place, the president's behavior in both instances became acceptable by default.

Zafy went further, claiming that the organization of the national forum on the powers of the judiciary took place at the request of certain deputies representing constituents who contested judicial behavior in their respective districts; moreover, the forum had a purely consultative character, not binding on any members of either the legislative or the judicial branch; hence in no way had the president infringed on the authority of the legislature.

Zafy also contended that:

- the charges of violation of oath of office lacked specificity, and no discretionary presidential actions were subject to jurisdiction of the HCC, the president deriving his powers directly from the nation through universal suffrage;
- the absence of appointments to certain high offices was again a matter of presidential discretion not subject to sanction, and the right to appeal against such actions before the administrative courts had not been exercised at the time;
- the National Assembly had no constitutional role to play in promulgation of the results of the referendum of September 17, 1995;
- since the president enjoyed absolute immunity against challenge to his "acts of government," an absence or delay in promulgating laws could be appealed only to the president himself and only by the president of the Senate (which, it is understood, did not exist at the time); in addition, certain clauses in some unpromulgated laws had been declared unconstitutional by the HCC;
- the impeachment resolution constituted a political attack against the legitimate authority of the president and was thus void of juridical validity.

In conclusion, Dr. Zafy requested the that High Constitutional Court concede its incompetence to decide on the impeachment of a president and, if the court should affirm its competence, to reject the impeachment resolution as without legal foundation, hence not receivable.[8]

The HCC responded promptly and without hesitation over the appropriateness of its jurisdiction in the matter of presidential impeachment. It dismissed this challenge on the grounds that, since the so-called Constitutional Court had never been established, only the HCC itself had jurisdiction over charges of constitutional violation. The court considered Zafy's August 29 rebuttals in detail and called several witnesses to testify on the issue of impeachability. On September 4, its decision upheld the validity of two charges filed by the Assembly, rejecting all others. Specifically, the court found against President Zafy that he was constitutionally bound to promulgate promptly and execute laws duly voted by the National Assembly, and the president had failed to do so in 15 instances, two of them (establishing decentralized administrative units) having been left without promulgation for more than one year. Moreover, while the president was authorized to incorporate a unit of control in his own office, the function of State Inspector General belonged appropriately to the office of chief of government, namely the prime minister, and had thus been absorbed by the presidency in violation of the constitution.

With considerable analysis and certain marginal reservations, the court exonerated Zafy on the following charges:

- the formation of the August 1995 Ravony government, which had occurred in conformity with constitutional provisions, albeit simultaneously with a decision of the HCC confirming the duty of the president to endorse a prime minister's nominations;[9]

- nomination of cabinet ministers in the Ratsirahonana government of May 1996, since no challenge to that presidential action had been filed with the court;

- holding the forum on judicial power during parliamentary debates on the subject, since the proceedings of the forum did not necessarily bind legislators to act one way or another;

- absence of appointments to certain high offices, where governing legislation remained incomplete and inconclusive;

- promulgation of the results of the September 1995 referendum, since those results automatically became law once the HCC confirmed the constitutionality of the proposed text and the electorate voted affirmatively for that text;

- the complaints of violation of oath and propriety of office, which remained insufficiently articulated in the resolution.

Confirming infringements of the constitution in two instances, the HCC proclaimed the office of president to be vacant as of the date of the decision, September 4, 1996, which aborted Albert Zafy's term by almost 19 months. In the absence of a senate president who would normally exercise the functions of acting president, the HCC charged Prime Minister Ratsirahonana and his government to carry out those functions—except for the prerogative of dissolving the National Assembly; in return, Ratsirahonana was held immune from a parliamentary motion of censure during his acting presidency. That interim government was enjoined to organize elections for the vacant presidency within a period of 30 to 60 days following the declaration of impeachment.[10] Specifying this electoral period made the best of a poor bargain, since Article 47 of the constitution required presidential elections to be held within 30 to 60 days *prior to* the expiration of a presidential mandate, not subsequent thereto. There was no legal authority governing the establishment of a date for elections once a term had expired, so the court was in effect making law (a similar consideration might of course have to be invoked in the event of the sudden death or medical incapacity of a sitting president).

THE CONSEQUENCES, ACCORDING TO ZAFY

In an ambiguous reaction, the deposed president accepted the court's decision as law, but sought to avoid its implications. On September 5, the day after he ceased being president, Zafy sought to announce his resignation, effective October 10, as though he still retained so much discretion. Parliament, he alleged, had committed a "constitutional coup d'état" in retaliation against him for having criticized its "naughty behavior." Moreover, in defiance against Prime Minister Ratsirahonana, the court-appointed acting president, he told the press that he would surrender the regalia of office (presidential seal, coat of arms, vehicle insignia) only to a duly elected chief of state. That election must ensue quickly, he insisted, fearing a power vacuum that might lead to civic disturbance if the interim were prolonged (as certain rival politicians might have wished).[11]

Such bravado was designed, it seems, toward one end—to anchor Zafy's candidacy for reelection at the earliest opportunity, catching his eventual opponents unprepared. Zafy nearly made it. Curiously, his right to candidacy went unchallenged, implying that in this highly permissive culture, irrevocable incapacitation concerned an institution, not the individual holding it. At least, such indulgence confirmed that constitutional violations in Madagascar's Third Republic entailed no disabling taint of turpitude (no high crimes or misdemeanors). In this regard, Zafy reminded the public that he had posed no objection in 1992 to the candidacy of the "assassin Ratsiraka" under comparable circumstances.[12]

Although abandoned by all national parties except his own National Union for Democracy and Development, Zafy found encouragement in the provinces (particularly in his native North) where substantial audiences accepted his arguments blaming chronic domestic insecurity and government paralysis on his political opponents and on interference by the IMF. He assured the nation that he had used his powers to frustrate the corruption of politicians in the capital and that the impeachment decision found only trivial flaws in his presidency; for instance, he rhetorically reduced the number of unpublished laws from 15 to four or five, which had only to await his return from an important labor mediation mission in the North, and he talked as though the permissible lapse of time for promulgation was 30 days, not the actual, constitutional, 15. Furthermore, if taking over the inspector general's office was illegal, he claimed, it should have been blocked by the administrative courts.[13] The interim remained relatively calm, as a new Ratsirahonana cabinet went about its business devoid of Zafyites, and the Malagasy army retained its habitual indifference to political controversy.

THE SEQUEL: RETURN OF THE DESPOT

The democratic opposition on which Albert Zafy had depended for his vindication was not prepared to return to his side; nor was it able to maintain the solidarity of the parliamentary majority that had voted his ouster. As Zafy predicted, his arch-rival and predecessor in disgrace, Didier Ratsiraka, duly announced his own candidacy for leadership of the republic that had repudiated him in 1993. Rather than leave the field to an immediate rematch between two discredited ex-chiefs of state, Madagascar's contentious parties fielded 15 candidates for the presidential vacancy. These included acting president Ratsirahonana who, partly to prepare his own ill-fated candidacy, waited the entire legal limit of 60 days following the act of impeachment before calling the voters once more to the polls. Far from being the sole contestant prepared to run effectively in a brief 60-day campaign, Zafy managed to tally only 23.4 percent of the vote on November 3, 1996. Ratsiraka, fresh from a busy exile in France, had kept his core of party support intact, bringing in 36.6 percent, setting the stage for a run-off between the two former presidents. Between these veteran foes stood a dozen dignitaries, all claiming key roles in the impeachment of Zafy and in the eviction of Ratsiraka before that, all eager to inherit an unsullied democratic mandate. They were disappointed—and Ratsiraka favored—by a light turnout of 58.4 percent.

In round two on December 29, although Ratsirahonana and other moderates urged support for Zafy as a lesser evil, Ratsiraka pulled through with the narrowest of margins—1,608,321 votes against Zafy's 1,563,137. Once more, the outcome turned on apathy, as only 49.66 percent of the electorate came to the polls, a record low turnout. Half the electorate seemed truly disgusted with politics in Madagascar,[14] the rest with Zafy; impeachment was fresh in their minds, and the most recent president was held responsible for ubiquitous corruption and stagnation in economic life. Later, the intrepid Zafy would characteristically accuse the HCC of deliberately reversing his and Ratsiraka's second-round percentages; he kept silent, he claimed, only to preserve the peace.[15]

Whatever the reasons for Ratsiraka's razor-thin victory, the most serious loser in this sorry episode was the very parliamentary democracy that had ousted Zafy in the first place. Never an admirer of the Third Republic, Didier Ratsiraka set about deliberately changing its constitution to resume the executive prerogatives he had enjoyed during the 17 years of the Second Republic.

Ratsiraka's referendum, presented to the public on March 15, 1998, did not seek to demolish the Third Republic entirely, as he had originally threatened. Rather, it proposed amendments to that constitution that, among other achievements, weakened parliament and strengthened presidential authority over elected provincial governors. Ratsiraka could now dissolve the National Assembly at will and appoint a prime minister and cabinet without parliamentary approval. He assumed presidential control over judiciary appointments and rendered himself less vulnerable to impeachment.[16] This effort was opposed by a still disorganized parliamentary opposition and by the National Council of Church leaders who interpreted Ratsiraka's intentions as a return to the socialist paradise of his pre-1992 dictatorship. Miscalculating, the National Council of Churches called for a boycott of the referendum instead of outright opposition, and when the referendum drew 70.37 percent of the voters to the polls, the missing nay votes gave Ratsiraka another slender majority—50.96 percent, with a margin of 57,184 votes.

In February 1998, taking advantage of resistance against the amendments proposed for the ensuing month's referendum, Albert Zafy had sought to dose his successor with the medicine that he'd swallowed himself. Together with 48 deputies, Zafy filed a motion to impeach Ratsiraka on grounds of perjury, violation of the constitution in his use of federal devolution as a disguise for presidential dictatorship, refusal to assume the role of supreme arbiter in disputes, nepotism, and even poor health. Although of dubious constitutionality, the motion would have reached the HCC had it obtained the requisite two-thirds majority of 92. As it turned out, only 60 deputies voted in favor of impeachment on February 4; they included former prime ministers Francisque Ravony and Norbert Ratsirahonana, both comparative moderates willing at considerable personal risk to transcend their previous disagreements with Zafy. Ratsiraka's 49 adherents abstained, and 25 deputies filed blank ballots. Dubious as it seems, this legislative victory seems to have strengthened Ratsiraka's hand in the next month's delicate referendum vote. Once again, the partisans of parliamentary democracy miscalculated.

Never reconciled to repeated defeats at the polls, Zafy sought to bring his home province of Antsiranana into outright secession from Ratsiraka's putative federation. When that effort failed to mobilize the northerners, he seized the rostrum at the opening of the new National Assembly (to which he had been elected) session after the parliamentary elections of May 1998, where as self-appointed opposition leader, he commanded a basic faction of only six votes, with some sympathy among another two dozen deputies implacably opposed to Ratsiraka.[17] On July 7, 1998, as a senior member of parliament (*doyen d'âge*), he issued his characteristic diatribe against Ratsiraka's alleged cronyism, opacity, financial irregularities, and tyrannical ambitions. Having nothing to lose, he could even endorse a three-fold pay raise for civil servants, something no government would have been able to afford.

On March 18, 2001, Ratsiraka's Alliance for the Rebirth of Madagascar (AREMA) captured 49 of 60 seats chosen by an electoral college of grateful notables in the first formation of a Third Republic Senate. The president then added another 30 loyal senators by virtue of his right of appointment. Provincial elections in December 2000 had prepared for this

Ratsirakist groundswell through the endorsement of large AREMA majorities everywhere outside some of the major cities. But as the nation searched for remedies to its disillusion with politics, the appalling state of its infrastructure, its economy in international receivership, and its culture of mutually defiant localities, new leadership was emerging—in Antananarivo itself.

In December 1999, the capital elected a new kind of mayor unblemished by the political wars of the successive republics. Marc Ravalomanana was a Merina (a highlander) but not of the aristocracy whose conspicuous privileges allowed demagogues to confuse class resentment with ethnic hostility. The young mayor was rural in origin, piously Christian, industrious and enterprising in character, a self-made millionaire (in agro-dairy businesses), and a skillful promoter of himself along with his brands. Sprinkling his discourse with English rather than the conventional French, and advocating MBA-certified solutions for national problems, Ravalomanana appealed to younger Malagasy throughout the country and to exasperated foreigners, albeit not the French establishment or the international donors that had become used to dealing with Ratsiraka's diligent ministers. From his reasonably successful mayoralty of two years duration, Ravalomanana confronted Didier Ratsiraka and four other candidates in the presidential election of December 16, 2001.

After a lengthy, economically injurious stalemate, during which Ravalomanana contested the HCC's original vote-count giving him a plurality but not a majority of the first-round votes, he succeeded in forcing a recount. With endorsement from churches, election observer groups, and eventually the U.S. and other outside powers (albeit not yet from Paris), a new High Constitutional Court recounted ballots and on April 29, 2002, confirmed a 51.46 percent victory for Ravalomanana. Ratsiraka's second-place finish dropped to 35.9 percent, thus nullifying his claim to the right of a second-round run-off. The canonically neutral armed forces thereupon regrouped behind the victor and, province by province, subdued resistance by Ratsirakist militias throughout the vast landscape. Ratsiraka's threats of coastal secessions from the nation thereupon evanesced.

This outcome proved remarkably popular in a country beset by political conflict, disillusion with institutions, and deep-seated cultural suspicions of all government pretensions. It was particularly noteworthy for the absence of hitherto overriding coastal majority objections to a chief of state from the highland Merina. In France, scene of frequent, unmistakably pro-Ravalomanana demonstrations among a large expatriate Malagasy population, the new French government led by Jean-Pierre Raffarin promptly reversed Parisian predilection for Ratsiraka. This was a clear signal for surrender by Ratsiraka, who left the island furtively, with family and a number of aides, on July 7.[18] Although the newly titled African Union (AU) raised objections over the way Ravalomanana had taken

power, its reservations seemed to emerge more from traditional preference for the status quo (namely, Ratsiraka) than from a concern for popular sovereignty. In any event, Senegal (appointed by the Organization of
African Unity early in the year to mediate between the deadlocked con-
testants) and nearby Mauritius both intervened to reconcile the AU to
Ravalomanana's legitimacy.

The HCC's self-contradictory role between December 2001 and April
2002 has inevitably raised a matter of concern for that legitimacy. In what
seems a flimsy juridical accommodation, a reconstituted court proceeded
on its own authority to recount the December 16 ballots, as demanded by
one candidate against opposition by the other (incumbent). Confirmed by
the electoral observation coordinators and subsequently by the U.S.
Embassy, the belated recount significantly revised the predecessor court's
initial tally, leaving little objective doubt of Ravalomanana's slender
majority. The doubt that lingers refers more to the way the court functions
in relation to prevailing political power than to the specific outcome of the
December–April crisis.

Madagascar's institutions and, gradually, the island's international col-
laborators, conceded an evident desire on the part of the Malagasy for a
new political culture. Once again, the court that confirmed the eviction of
Albert Zafy in 1996 acted to recover honor lost in the interim. The new
president still had to come to grips with a National Assembly bent on
restoring lost prerogatives of parliamentary democracy, a confrontation
that would not be settled until legislative elections in December 2002
replaced the lame-duck legislature inherited from Ratsiraka's victories of
May 1998. While the blatant inefficacy of the Zafy era and the smiling
authoritarianism of the Ratsiraka era seem to have been put behind them,
the new leaders confront fundamental problems of governance. They
must repair a dramatically crippled economy, earn national and international confidence for weakened institutions, solve the abuses of a thor-
oughly corrupt administrative apparatus, and mobilize a population that
has never truly accepted the legitimacy of any regime, no matter how
established.

CHAPTER 6

Impeachment, Russian Style (1998–99)

Jody C. Baumgartner

INTRODUCTION

Boris Yeltsin's nine-year tenure as president of Russia was a strange mix of highs and lows, the latter including numerous efforts by an opposition legislature to impeach him. This chapter focuses on the 1998–99 impeachment effort in which the Russian Duma came very close to successfully impeaching Yeltsin on one of the five charges he faced. The story is one of partisan politics, in particular of an almost continual effort on the part of the Communist opposition and their allies to remove the president or force him to resign. The effort reached the stage of deliberation and voting on impeachment, and ended in presidential survival.

Part of the reason for the failure can be found in the Russian constitution, which sets the bar exceedingly high for impeaching and removing a president. Understanding this, however, suggests other questions. Why was the attempt made at all, especially considering that initially few—indeed, almost no one—believed that it would succeed? Why did it take the course that it did? How did the Chechen War charge gather the momentum that it did? Finally, why did the attempt to impeach Yeltsin on that charge, which in the end looked as if it might succeed, ultimately fail? This chapter illuminates the setting in which the impeachment attempt took place and addresses these questions, suggesting that partisan and strategic considerations drove the process from beginning to end, an explanation that is consistent with the theme of this volume, namely that presidential impeachment is a political process and can only be understood in those terms.

THE SETTING

Presidential History and the Institutional Balance of Power

Boris Yeltsin easily won Russia's first presidential election in June 1991, when Russia was still part of the Soviet Union. Two years of turbulence, including a protracted stalemate with the legislature over the shape of a new constitution, ended in early October 1993, when Yeltsin, reluctantly aided by the military, forcibly disbanded the legislature. In December, voters were presented with, and a small majority ratified, a draft constitution that was produced mainly by individuals loyal to the president.[1] Fairly labeled "Yeltsin's" constitution, the regime it created is, according to many observers, "super-presidential" with respect to its institutional balance of power.[2]

The Russian Federal Assembly, a bicameral legislature, is comprised of a 450-member lower house (the State Duma) elected by the people and a 178-member upper-house Federation Council, made up of two members from each of Russia's 89 regions. The president formally shares executive power with a prime minister appointed by the president and is subject to approval by the Duma; if the Duma rejects the president's choice three times, the president may dissolve the Duma and appoint an interim prime minister. Other government ministers are appointed jointly by the president and the prime minister; the Duma has no say in the matter. The Duma can vote no confidence in government, but only if another vote is passed within three months is the president required to respond, at which point he may dismiss either the government or the Duma. In short, the government is accountable to the Duma in only the loosest sense. Russia also has both a Supreme Court and a Constitutional Court; members of both are appointed by the president subject to approval by the Federation Council.

Throughout his tenure, Yeltsin's relationship with the lower house Duma was difficult at best; this is hardly a surprise, since that body was controlled by opposition parties during that time. On the other hand, the Federation Council was for the most part sympathetic to the president. This is at least partly because its members are not elected, and the president had some, albeit informal and imperfect, influence in the appointment of its members. The high courts were also fairly reluctant to challenge Yeltsin, primarily because they were packed with judges who were very conscious of the fact that Yeltsin had disbanded the previous Constitutional Court during the fall 1993 crisis.

The Impeachment Process

The constitutional provisions for the impeachment of a Russian president are found in Articles 93, 99, 107–110 ("On the Constitutional Court of the Russian Federation"), and 176–180 ("The Rules of Order of the State Duma") of the Russian Constitution.[3] Article 93 states, in part, that a decision to impeach and remove a president from office is based on the commission of "high treason or another grave crime" by the president and "must be adopted by a vote of two-thirds of the total number [of members] of each chamber [of the legislature]."

The first phase of a presidential impeachment begins if and when one-third of the Duma deputies support a motion to indict the president. In this event, the Duma forms a special commission to evaluate the charges against the president and the rules that will be adopted to examine them. The commission is constituted similar to the way all Duma committees are constituted, namely with an eye toward ensuring that all parties and factions are fairly equally represented.[4] The commission evaluates the charges against the president, examines evidence, hears testimony, and so on, and if a majority supports the motion to indict, the resolution is sent to the Duma; the commission then acts as prosecutor for the case.[5] If, by a two-thirds majority of all deputies, the Duma votes to accept charges and indict the president, the case is sent to the Supreme Court within five days (if there is more than one charge, an affirmative vote is needed on only one charge).

The next phase of impeachment occurs in the high courts. First, the Supreme Court must render a decision as to whether the charges leveled against the president constitute an impeachable offense. Next, the Constitutional Court, on the request of the Federation Council, renders a decision regarding the constitutionality of how the procedure has been carried out; this must be done within one month after the Duma has voted to indict. Should the Constitutional Court approve, the case moves to the final phase, where, within three months of the passage of the original Duma resolution to impeach, the Federation Council must vote on whether to remove the president. If no action is taken within three months, the effort dies and the president remains in office. If two-thirds of the members of the Federation Council vote for removal, the president must resign.[6]

In conclusion, the odds of successfully impeaching and removing a Russian president are, at best, slim. There are at least four possible veto points where the process can be stopped (not including the Duma special commission), and the threshold in both legislatures is fairly high (supermajorities). At several points the process is time-bound, meaning that inaction can kill the process as well. One final aspect of the process that should be noted is the constitutional provision that if and when a president has been successfully indicted (impeached), he cannot dissolve the Duma. This provision seemed to have played a strategic role for many deputies in the 1999 impeachment effort.

Political Parties and the Party System

Russian parties can be grouped according to whether they are reformist, centrist, national-patriotic, or leftist in their orientation.[7] Generally speaking, they are elite-based organizations, still somewhat disconnected from a shifting electoral base and relatively underdeveloped. Partial exceptions do exist, in particular the Communist Party of the Russian Federation and Vladimir Zhirinovsky's Liberal Democratic Party of Russia.

This said, parliamentary parties in Russia are fairly well developed. After election to the Duma,[8] deputies form parliamentary groups known as factions.[9] Factions, which must be comprised of at least 35 members, are generally made up of members of the same political party (e.g, Communists, Yabloko), but this is not a requirement. Faction membership for deputies is not mandatory, but without it individuals are hard-pressed to influence the legislative agenda, gain access to the floor, or even procure office space.[10] Interestingly, considering the relatively underdeveloped state of political parties in Russia, a surprising degree of cohesion exists within Duma factions;[11] this is significant as it relates to how one would expect an impeachment vote to play out in the Duma. Table 6-1 outlines the major parties, their ideological orientation, and associated Duma factions in Russia, as of 1999.

Table 6-1.
Major Russian Political Parties, Their Orientation, and Associated Duma Factions (1999)

	Leftist	Centrist	Reform	National-patriotic
Orientation	Anti-reform, although their rhetoric has softened somewhat since 1996 presidential election	Not unfriendly to reform, but slightly more to the left; also parties formed to support the government	Associated with western notions of democratic and market reforms	Extreme right wing, though some are less extreme than others
Parties	Communist Party, Agrarian Party	Our Home is Russia, Russia's Regions, Women of Russia	Russia's Democratic Choice, Yabloko	Liberal Democratic Party of Russia, Congress of Russian Communities
Duma Faction(s)	Communist Party, Agrarian Party, People's Rule	Our Home is Russia, Russia's Regions	Yabloko	Liberal Democratic Party of Russia

Throughout Yeltsin's tenure, there was no formal presidential party in the legislature. While he informally (not publicly) backed so-called parties of power like Our Home is Russia and (earlier) Russia's Choice, Yeltsin eschewed formal association with any political party after his resignation from the Communist Party of the Soviet Union in 1990. Generally speaking, the president was forced to rely on temporary coalitions in policymaking.[12] By extension, when it came to impeachment, Duma members had no formal partisan incentives to support Yeltsin, and the task of building a legislative shield was a bit more difficult. On the other hand, the Communists were able to rely on consistent support from the Agrarian Party and People's Rule factions. Together, they commanded roughly 211 votes in the Duma (just short of a 226 majority), and, like other far-left parties around the world, generally displayed a high degree of party discipline.

Other Factors

Russia faced a variety of political, social, and economic crises during Yeltsin's tenure: an abortive coup attempt in August 1991, the breakup of the Soviet Union later that year, executive-legislative deadlock throughout 1993 and the forceful dissolution of parliament in October, a constitutional referendum in December that ushered in a new regime, and a disastrous and wildly unpopular war in Chechnya starting in December 1994. Throughout, the economy was in free-fall, suffering severe contraction, runaway inflation, and double-digit unemployment.

The 1990s were, in short, a period of radical social, political, and economic change for Russia, and precious little consensus about the nature of the problems or solutions existed. Therefore, it is hardly surprising that by the time impeachment proceedings began in May of 1999, popular support for Yeltsin had steadily declined. One study shows that after his election in 1991 he enjoyed the support of over half of the population. However, with the exception of a few brief upturns, including the months immediately prior to and after the 1996 election, this support declined steadily over the next few years to roughly 30 percent. It remained fairly constant at this level until the spring of 1998, when it took a sharp downturn, leveling off at just under 20 percent; it remained at or near this level throughout the remainder of his second term.[13]

Given this, and the fact that he faced a hostile legislature throughout this entire period, it is not surprising that seven attempts to impeach Yeltsin were initiated from 1992–1998.[14] These impeachment attempts, none of which made it to the point at which a commission was formed to formally investigate charges, are summarized in Table 6-2.

Several points stand out with respect to these impeachment efforts. First, three attempts were centered around relations with Chechnya (the

Table 6-2.
Impeachment Attempts in Russia, 1992–1997

Date	Circumstances and/or Charges	Stage Reached & Outcome
Dec. 1992	Failed economic reform policies	Impeachment vote defeated*
March 1993	Yeltsin claim of emergency rule powers	Impeachment vote defeated*
Jan. 1994	Initiation of the Chechen War	Duma debate on resolution to start proceedings defeated
June 1994	Handling of the Chechen War and the Budennovsk crisis	Duma debate only; vote to start proceedings defeated
Sept. 1995	Yeltsin ignoring of Duma resolution to call for end to NATO bombing of Serbia	Duma debate only
Nov. 1996	Presidential decree withdrawing troops from Chechnya and postponing resolution of region's status	Duma debate only; resolved
Jan. 1997	Medical; presidential incapacity and succession issues	Legality of charge examined; vote on resolution defeated

* Simpler impeachment rules governed the 1992 and 1993 attempts. For 1992, see Robert G. Moser, "Executive-Legislative Relations in Russia, 1991–1999," in Zoltan Barany and Robert G. Moser, eds., *Russian Politics: Challenges of Democratization* (Cambridge, UK: Cambridge University, 2001, p. 86), and David Lane and Cameron Ross, "The Changing Composition and Structure of the Political Elites," in David Lane, ed., *Russia in Transition: Politics, Privatization, and Inequality* (London: Longman, 1995, pp. 59–65); For the 1993 attempt, see Lilia Shevstova, *Yeltsin's Russia: Myths and Reality* (Washington, D.C.: Carnegie Endowment for International Peace, 1999, pp. 71–73). For subsequent impeachment attempts, see *Radio Free Europe/Radio Liberty (RFE/RL) Daily Digest*, 1994–1997 (various); available online at *http://rferl.org*.

war and its resolution), a contentious issue that eventually formed the base of the 1998–99 impeachment attempt. It is probably not accidental that most of 1995 and the first half of 1996 were quiet on the impeachment front, since Russia's political elite were preoccupied with the Duma elections of December 1995 and the presidential election of 1996. In 1996 the impeachment attempt clearly revolved around a constitutional question, namely Yeltsin's unilateral alteration of Chechnya's federal status.[15] This situation was defused when Yeltsin and Prime Minister Chernomyrdin allowed the Duma to scrutinize the decision. The 1997 impeachment attempt was centered around Yeltsin's health, which made it politically expedient to attack him, but also pointed to the need for constitutional or statutory clarification of succession procedures in the case of presidential incapacity.[16]

In addition to these impeachment attempts, political discourse in Russia throughout the 1990s was rife with calls for early presidential elections, questions and criticism about Yeltsin's health (in particular, from 1995 onward), calls for the Supreme Court to clarify whether the period of 1991–93 constituted a presidential term or not, and calls for Yeltsin's resignation. Taken together with the impeachment efforts, they represent an almost continual attempt to remove President Yeltsin from power. The Duma, and in particular, the Communist Party and its allies, did not always lead these efforts, nor were they alone when they did; they were, however, never too far behind. It was in this setting that the 1998–99 impeachment attempt emerged.

IMPEACHMENT, 1998–99

The 1998–99 impeachment attempt of Boris Yeltsin began in March 1998, when Duma Defense Committee Chairman Lev Rohkin (previously a member of the pro-government Our Home is Russia) and Security Committee Chairman Viktor Ilyukhin (part of the radical wing of the Communist Party) formed a committee to investigate the possibility of impeachment. Headed by Aleksandr Morozov, one of their rather far-fetched goals was to bring Yeltsin and other Russian leaders before the International Court of Justice in the Hague for genocide against the Russian people. This was one of the five charges Yeltsin faced in the eventual impeachment attempt, and was based on a theoretical decline in the population of close to eight million people due to the spread of AIDS (and other sexually transmitted diseases), an increase in the number of abortions, and a decrease in the number of live births, all blamed on Yeltsin's (and his government's) failed economic policies.[17] By itself, it is likely that, as in previous attempts, nothing would have come of this charge.

However, on March 23, Yeltsin dismissed long-time Prime Minister Viktor Chernomyrdin, proposing the virtually unknown 35-year-old Sergei Kirienko as his successor. This appointment led to a month-long struggle, with Yeltsin sending Kirienko's name to the Duma three times (the limit) before he was eventually confirmed; the Communists and their allies (the Agrarians and People's Rule) were opposed to the appointment. By early April, Rohkin and Ilyukhin were actively collecting the 150 signatures needed to put the question of forming a commission to investigate impeachment of the president on the Duma agenda.[18]

On May 20, with coal miners striking around the country and widespread discontent in other sectors over unpaid wages, Communist Party leader Gennadi Zyuganov issued a 12-page statement outlining Yeltsin's "crimes"and announced that the party had collected enough signatures (177) to start impeachment proceedings. Although the process picked up momentum as a result of the strike, the Communists delayed action at this point, perhaps betraying the symbolic rather than the substantive nature of the effort. However, on May 25, Duma Speaker Gennadi Seleznev announced that the Duma would consider the motion in early June, and on June 9 a formal request to begin the process of impeachment, signed by 215 deputies, was submitted to the Duma.[19] Moving forward again may have reflected what some believe to have been a deliberate decision within the Communist Party at an Extraordinary Congress on May 23 to adopt more confrontational tactics in dealing with Yeltsin;[20] the miners' strikes and the struggle over Kirienko's confirmation had galvanized many in this respect.

As shown earlier, the effort to impeach Yeltsin began shortly after he assumed the presidency; in terms of the framework of this book, the process actually began formally on June 19, 1998, when the Duma voted to form an impeachment commission to investigate charges against him; the commission convened for the first time on June 29. The commission was composed of 15 members, which required approval by a simple majority of the Duma. Of these, the Communist Party had four seats, including the chair (Vadim Filimonov, a former law professor, elected by secret ballot); Our Home is Russia, three seats; Yabloko and the Liberal Democratic Party, two seats each; the Agrarians, People's Rule, and Russia's Regions, one seat each. Thus, the Communists and their allies controlled seven of the 15 seats (five for the Communists, one each for the Agrarians and People's Rule), including the chair. The term of the commission was indefinite, or through the end of the Duma's term (December 1999). The commission convened on June 29, announcing that it would work through the Duma's summer recess; this was hardly a surprise, since one of its primary tasks was to have a list of charges ready to present to the Duma should Yeltsin have made a move to dissolve parliament.[21]

In late July the commission considered the first of the five charges it was tasked to investigate, that of high treason for signing the Belovezha agreements with the Ukrainian and Belorussian Republics in November 1991, which effectively dissolved the Soviet Union. He was also charged with inciting civil unrest by improperly using force in dismissing parliament in the autumn of 1993; abuse of office, for initiating and conducting the war in Chechnya; for overseeing the disintegration of the country's military forces; and, as mentioned earlier, genocide.[22] The work of the commission was, according to Communist Party leader Gennadi Zyuganov, originally scheduled to wrap up in September; correctly, few believed this forecast.[23]

Russia's financial meltdown in August 1998, which culminated in the devaluation of the ruble, added fuel to the impeachment fire.[24] As a result, the Duma called on Yeltsin to resign and to replace Kirienko; the president, predictably, did not resign, but in late August he dismissed Kirienko, proposing former Prime Minister Viktor Chernomyrdin as his replacement. In large part led by the Communist Party, the Duma rejected Chernomyrdin twice, and in accordance with earlier strategy, protecting the Duma from dissolution, threatened to move the impeachment process to the next stage if Yeltsin put his name forward a third time.[25] By this time (mid-September) the commission had completed work on the first of the five charges it was examining and could have accelerated the impeachment proceedings; in any event, Yeltsin acquiesced and compromised by nominating Yevgeny Primakov (loosely associated with the Communist Party) as prime minister.

Primakov's confirmation led some to hope that the crisis was over, but impeachment was not dead. In the glow of victory, Communists continued pressing the issue, this time focusing also on the issue of the president's health, and proposed a nationwide protest calling for Yeltsin's removal in mid-October.[26] By late November the commission had voted in the affirmative on two more of the impeachment charges (the forceful dissolution of the Duma in 1993 and the initiation of the Chechen War), and by late December Duma Speaker Seleznev was signaling that the Duma would launch impeachment proceedings in January. By this time the focal point of the effort was the Chechen War charge, inasmuch as it had the support of other, non-leftist deputies, most prominently, members of the Yabloko faction. It seemed at this stage as if charges of genocide and ruining the country's defense capabilities would be forgotten.[27]

From January through April there was protracted debate over the timing of the impeachment hearings in the full Duma, each side attempting to maximize its own political advantage. This included discussion in January and February, spearheaded by Primakov, of a proposed political truce between the legislature and the executive involving an agreement in which both the president and the Duma agreed that each was to stay in office until 2000.[28] The plan ultimately collapsed and proved ineffective in sidetracking the impeachment effort. The commission's work on the charges of genocide and ruining defense capabilities resumed, and by late February had been completed; in total, Yeltsin now faced five charges.[29] It was announced in mid-March that impeachment hearings in the full Duma would start on April 15, but debate over the issue of whether voting would be conducted by open or secret ballot delayed them further (proponents of impeachment favored the former). This issue was eventually resolved in late April when the Duma passed an amendment (329–42) that made it easier for factions to enforce voting discipline, and hearings were finally scheduled for May 13.[30]

However, the day before hearings were to commence, Yeltsin made a move which cast the proceedings in a completely different light. Citing poor economic conditions, he fired the extremely popular Primakov, a move decried by virtually all. Hours afterwards, before impeachment hearings began, the Duma passed (by a vote of 243–20) a nonbinding resolution calling on the president to resign.[31] Importantly, the move created the potential for a constitutional stand-off between the President and the Duma, since the president cannot dissolve the Duma if they vote to impeach, and if the Duma rejects the president's choice of prime minister three times, the president may dissolve the Duma. It was under this cloud of uncertainty that impeachment hearings began.

Voting on all five charges took place two days later, on May 15. Of 442 Duma members, 408 registered on the morning voting took place; however, only 348 valid ballots were cast.[32] In the end, as predicted, the Chechen War charge garnered the most support, but even this fell 17 votes short of the 300 necessary to move the process to the next stage. The 1998–99 impeachment attempt of Boris Yeltsin reached the stage of deliberation and voting on impeachment, resulting in a case of presidential survival. Table 6-3 summarizes the voting.

UNDERSTANDING IMPEACHMENT 1998–99

Two questions arise from the 1998–99 impeachment attempt of Boris Yeltsin. First, why did the attempt emerge at all, when, given the exceptionally high constitutional bar that is set for presidential impeachment in Russia, it was all but certain that it would fail? Second, why, after the process gained momentum against such high odds, did the attempt ultimately fail?

Table 6-3.
Summary of Voting on Impeachment Charges Against President Yeltsin, May 15, 1999

	In Favor	Opposed
Dismantling the Soviet Union	239	78
Illegally dismissing parliament in 1993	263	60
Illegally unleashing the Chechen War	283	43
Destroying the army	244	77
Genocide	238	88

From Michael Wines, "Drive to Impeach Russian President Dies in Parliament" (*The New York Times*, May 16, 1999, Section 1, p. 1).

Why Did the 1998–99 Impeachment Attempt Emerge?

In trying to understand why the impeachment attempt of 1998–99 emerged, we can look first to the setting in which it took place. In particular, the constitutional structure of government, the party system in the 1990s, public opinion, and past impeachment attempts converged to make conditions ripe for the 1998–99 attempt. First, the Russian super-presidential system provides an incentive for the less powerful legislature to seek other ways in which to exert its influence; impeachment constitutes such an attempt. Second, party politics in the 1990s in Russia were, in the words of one analyst, sharply polarized between reform and anti-reform camps (Yeltsin occupying the former); this created a scenario similar to cases of divided government in the United States (see Chapter 2).[33] Public opinion, while not overwhelmingly in favor of impeachment, was at least amenable to it at the beginning of the process. As mentioned, Yeltsin was a fairly unpopular president. Moreover, surveys suggested that at various times during the fall of 1998, for example, as many as 75 percent of Russians were in favor of impeachment, and those who thought Yeltsin was guilty of the crimes with which he was charged ranged from a low of 67 percent (genocide of the Russian people) to a high of 87 percent (the war in Chechnya).[34] Finally, it is useful to remember that the 1998–99 attempt was the latest in what was a continual effort to remove Yeltsin from office. Yeltsin himself suggested (quite naturally, and correctly) that the opposition Communist party was looking "for any means to destroy the president, any way to remove him from his post."[35]

It is hard to believe that impeaching Yeltsin was solely about policy or principles, as year after year the Communists passed government budgets largely intact. Even more to the point, it was understood that unlike Yabloko, the Communists were not opposed to the war in Chechnya but to the idea that it had not been successfully prosecuted.[36]

This last point leads to a discussion of strategic behavior. It seems quite clear in examining the emergence of the 1998–99 attempt that there was some amount of political strategy being contemplated on the part of Duma deputies; this can be seen in earlier impeachment attempts as well. For example, the impeachment attempt in 1995 was likely an electoral ploy designed to criticize the president and boost the Communist Party's popularity; fearing electoral backlash, all impeachment activity ceased six months prior to elections.[37]

In strategic terms, impeachment served as political leverage against the president, and more specifically, a form of immunity against parliamentary dismissal. For example, the impeachment commission was formed right after the Communists lost the battle over the Kirienko appointment when coal miners went on strike; little progress was made in the investigation throughout the summer, but efforts were stepped up when Yeltsin proposed Chernomyrdin as prime minister in the fall; activity again abated somewhat when Primakov was proposed. The point is that the impeachment commission could quickly draft a motion and get it on the Duma agenda if dissolution seemed imminent, thus protecting them, since the president cannot dissolve the Duma once he has been impeached.[38] It very likely also served to quell a certain amount of intra-party dissent between the more moderate and hard-line wings of the Communist Party; propagating an impeachment attempt that had little chance of removing the president was a low-cost strategy to appease hardliners. In this respect, the role of Viktor Ilyukhin, who throughout the years seemed to have made Yeltsin's removal a personal crusade, was likely pivotal (this recalls Bill Perkin's point in Chapter 2 about the impact of personal hatred of presidents on impeachment).

Why Did the 1998–99 Impeachment Attempt Fail?

Few people in Russia, including public officials, party leaders, and even the public, believed that the 1998–99 impeachment attempt by the Duma would lead to Yeltsin's removal. For example, only about 33 percent of polled respondents believed that the proposal to initiate impeachment proceedings would gather the necessary votes.[39] But by the spring of 1999, with Yabloko support, it was widely believed that the Chechen War charge would be able to garner the votes necessary to move the process to the next phase.[40] On the eve of the vote, Gennadi Zyuganov claimed that he and the Communist Party had the support of as many as 312 deputies.[41] Yeltsin himself admits to having been "rather worried".[42] So why did the attempt fail?

While super-presidentialism may have encouraged the emergence of several of the impeachment attempts, it remains the case that the institutional balance of power in Russia is heavily weighted in favor of the president. In the end, the constitutional provisions for presidential impeachment in Russia make it extremely unlikely that any president can be removed from office. Recall that there are several veto points where the process can be stopped, and the threshold for success in the lower and upper houses is fairly high; also, the process is time-bound.

In addition to a high constitutional hurdle, the charges against Yeltsin, with one exception, were not the sort that were likely to gain much momentum. Most of the charges centered around his policies; three of the five (at minimum) referred to policies or actions that took place prior to the 1996 presidential election. Thus, the scandals around which the attempt was centered were for the most part relatively diffuse and had difficulty gaining traction. The exception to this was the charge that gathered the most support in the Duma, namely, Yeltsin's prosecution of the war in Chechnya. Here there was arguably a constitutional issue at stake—an abuse of presidential power in unilaterally starting the war; moreover, the war proved extremely unpopular and was the subject of intense media scrutiny. However, in July 1995, the Russian Constitutional Court ruled that this action on Yeltsin's part did not constitute an abuse of his power; in addition, at least one member of the Supreme Court publicly suggested that the legal quality of the arguments for impeachment were such that the Court would quickly dismiss them.[43]

That the charges against the president did not translate into politically effective scandals for the opposition can be seen in the public's reaction to them. Low levels of overall support for the president throughout the 1990s and his perceived guilt did not necessarily translate into an over-whelming amount of concrete support for impeachment. While impeach-ment had been favored by many survey respondents in the late fall of 1998, that support waned as the date for voting approached. By April 1999, only 47 percent of those surveyed were in favor of the Duma initi-ating the proceedings, while a full 40 percent were opposed.[44] In a poll surveying what Russians felt was the most important event of 1999, only ten percent cited the Yeltsin impeachment (fewer than the 13 percent that cited the Clinton-Lewinsky scandal).[45]

Elite opinion on Yeltsin's impeachment seemed to be divided, but gen-erally negative. For example, many regional governors appealed to the Duma on more than one occasion to halt the procedure.[46] The Russian press, generally not noted for being Yeltsin sympathizers, was filled throughout the period with statements by various leaders chastising the Duma for proceeding with impeachment; few seemed to take the impeachment hearings seriously. In fact, most of the witnesses (including notables like Mikhail Gorbachev, former Vice President Aleksandr Rut-skoi, former defense minister Pavel Grachev, Ruslan Khasbulatov, and Sergei Shakhrai) did not attend; in the end, only six of 40 actually appeared.[47] The hearings were not televised, partly because of a lack of adequate facilities; the one television crew that came to cover the pro-ceedings left after being unable to find an electrical socket.[48] Many print journalists were similarly disinterested, and it was reported that some leg-islators could be seen sleeping during the hearings as well.[49] In sum, while public and elite opinion may have been somewhat divided, opinion was generally unfavorable regarding the attempt to impeach and remove the president.

In the end the impeachment effort against Yeltsin failed because fewer than 300 Duma deputies supported it. It is instructive to examine the vot-ing on impeachment with respect to partisanship, principles, and other incentives deputies may have had. It is here that the effects of the party system on the impeachment effort are seen in vivid detail. Table 6-4 details the voting by Duma faction and charge.

Table 6-4.
Russian Duma Voting on Presidential Impeachment, 1999, by Charge and Faction

Faction Name (Number of Members)	Dismantling the Soviet Union	Illegally Dismissing Parliament, 1993	Chechen War	Destroying Army	Genocide
Communist Party (129)					
In Favor	127	128	128	127	127
Opposed	0	0	0	0	0
Abstained	1	1	1	1	1
Spoiled Ballot	1	0	0	1	1
Our Home is Russia (60)					
In Favor	1	0	1	2	2
Opposed	38	38	34	36	36
Abstained	21	22	24	22	22
Spoiled Ballot	0	0	1	0	0
Lib. Dem. Party (49)					
In Favor	1	2	1	2	2
Opposed	0	0	0	0	0
Abstained	47	47	48	47	47
Spoiled Ballot	1	0	0	0	0
People's Rule (47)					
In Favor	43	43	42	43	43
Opposed	0	0	1	0	0
Abstained	4	4	4	4	4
Spoiled Ballot	0	0	0	0	0

Yabloko (46)					
In Favor	6	24	37	3	0
Opposed	21	8	1	24	34
Abstained	11	10	7	11	9
Spoiled Ballot	8	4	1	8	3
Russia's Regions (44)					
In Favor	20	22	28	19	19
Opposed	8	6	3	8	9
Abstained	12	12	11	13	12
Spoiled Ballot	4	4	2	4	4
Agrarian Party (35)					
In Favor	35	35	35	35	35
Opposed	0	0	0	0	0
Abstained	0	0	0	0	0
Spoiled Ballot	0	0	0	0	0
Independent (30)					
In Favor	9	9	13	9	9
Opposed	9	9	5	9	9
Abstained	12	12	12	12	12
Spoiled Ballot	0	0	0	0	0

From "Game's Over" (Current Digest of the Post-Soviet Press. 51(20). June 16, 1999, p.1). This account differs somewhat from many summary accounts of the voting published elsewhere. This is explained by the fact that one or two deputies inevitably forget their electronic voting card and their votes had to be recorded manually later; this table reflects those later, complete, totals (personal conversation with Thomas Remington, April 7, 2002).

Unsurprisingly, all but six of the 211 deputies from the Communist Party and their two smaller allies (People's Rule and the Agrarian Party) voted in favor of the Chechen War charge; voting on the other charges was also overwhelmingly in favor of impeachment. This is not surprising, since, like other parties of the far left, the Communists tend to exhibit greater party discipline. For example, in the 1997 impeachment effort, their combined vote total was 114 to 6.[50] In fact, in 1999 the Agrarians were the most disciplined of all parties, with all 35 deputies voting in favor of all five impeachment charges. In other words, partisanship would seem to have driven the behavior of the Communists and their allies, from the inception of the impeachment effort through voting.

The pro-government and centrist Our Home is Russia fairly solidly backed the president; 34–38 of 60 members voted against the various charges. Only one member voted in favor of the Chechen War charge; more than a third of party members abstained; one member spoiled his ballot. This was hardly a surprise, since this was the party of former Prime Minister Viktor Chernomyrdin, a close Yeltsin ally. Moreover, being a pro-government party, members of Our Home could expect to be rewarded (either materially or with government posts) by adopting a pro-Yeltsin position. Russia's Regions, another centrist party, was fairly evenly split between those who voted in favor and those who were either opposed or abstained; the exception to this was the Chechnya charge, which drew 28 of 44 votes in favor. The behavior of the 30 independent deputies was more heavily weighted toward acquittal (again, either by a no vote or by abstention); here too, the Chechnya charge drew slightly more votes (13).

The behavior of Vladimir Zhirinovsky's Liberal Democrats (LDPR) was, like the Communist Party, consistent, although historically their support of the president was contingent, shifting from one impeachment attempt to the next.[51] The party generally backed impeachment attempts against the president and initially supported the 1998–99 effort. In the end, however, they came out strongly against it. Informed speculation suggests that the behavior of Zhirinovsky (and by extension, his party) was motivated by material incentives; reports suggest that the leader routinely offers his party's votes for sale.[52] In the end, all but two of the party's 49-strong delegation walked out of the hearings after a bombastic speech by Zhirinovsky just before the vote; this constituted almost half of the 107 to 110 abstentions in the final vote count (one LDPR deputy did vote in favor of the Chechen War charge).[53]

Yabloko voting was also consistent, at least in terms of their stated intentions. Although generally opposed to impeachment, party leader Grigori Yavlinski supported the Chechen War charge throughout, based on a repeatedly stated desire to help ensure that future chief executives understand that they are accountable.[54] He also made it clear that charges other than the Chechen War charge were political in nature and thus inappropriate to consider.[55] Although party members could vote as they saw fit, as a whole they supported the charge and delivered 37 of their 46 promised votes. What is significant about this is that prior to the vote there were widespread reports that the administration was trying to buy votes, including those of some Yabloko members, who were seen as having crucial swing votes. Yavlinski himself implied at the start of the hearings that members of his faction might be offered positions in government in exchange for a no vote.[56] This said, most of the party followed the party line. The charge of illegally dissolving parliament in 1993 drew the support of 24 Yabloko deputies, but none of the other charges garnered more than six votes.

Looking at the vote from a broader (non-party) perspective, Yeltsin clearly succeeded in building a sympathetic legislative coalition. The strategy seemed to be three-pronged, as the administration either persuaded, bribed, or threatened various members (1) to abstain or to spoil their ballots; (2) to vote strategically, against the Chechen War charge and for other charges that were less likely to pass; or (3) to vote against impeachment altogether.[57]

With respect to abstentions, Zyuganov had feared just such a strategy, and had attempted to hold the vote on impeachment the previous day. Communists claimed that the Kremlin had offered up to $30,000 to deputies to boycott the session. As it turned out, only 408 of 442 deputies attended (many claimed they were sick), LDPR deputies walked out as a block, and as many as 18 spoiled ballots (either unsigned or defaced) were submitted and had to be discarded.[58] Another tactic that deputies appeared to take, whether at the behest of the Kremlin or otherwise, was that of strategic voting. There is some reason to believe that the scattering of yes votes across different charges was a deliberate effort on the part of at least some deputies to be seen as being on the right side of impeachment (in favor) while ensuring that it did not succeed. A total of 294 deputies voted yes on one or more of the charges (still short of the 300 necessary for impeachment), but as we saw above, the charge that garnered the most support (Chechen War) received only 283 votes.[59]

As Victor Hinojosa and Aníbal Pérez-Liñán describe in Chapter 4, a president succeeds in building a "legislative shield" when he persuades enough legislators to vote against impeachment and/or removal. A president's strategy and success in building this shield revolves to some extent around the nature of party politics in the country. In this respect, the story in Russia is mixed. In one sense the Communists and their allies behaved as expected, strictly adhering to the party line. With some exceptions, Yabloko and Our Home did so as well. This is the behavior one might expect in a stronger party system. On the other hand, while it is true that the no vote of some deputies was a vote of their conscience, others appear to have been influenced in their decision by material incentives by the Kremlin. This is a reflection of Russia's weaker party system, and is consistent with discussions of the role of patronage in other cases in this book, especially the chapters on Colombia and the Philippines.

SUMMARY

Russian politics have, throughout the 1990s, been polarized over basic questions surrounding her multiple transitions. The 1998–99 impeachment effort, like those before it, can be seen as part of an ongoing referendum of sorts on the reform course of the Yeltsin administration. Driven mainly by the Communist Party, this ongoing attempt to remove Yeltsin from office makes sense when one recalls that the party was (and elements remain) both anti-reform and anti-system. In addition, impeachment efforts throughout the 1990s seemed to be a cover for a strategic struggle for political advantage. One deputy noted simply that "ninety percent of all deputies have no real opinion about impeachment but are concerned with only one cause—making sure their Duma stay is not cut short by a single day."[60] In this respect, the Russian case resembles the American one in that in a general sense, impeachment can be understood in terms of the divided government phenomenon.

It might be the case more generally that the attempts to remove President Yeltsin can be attributed to the growing pains of a still nascent regime, which should come as little surprise. Regime transitions are situations of fluid power. Various actors jockeying for position in a young regime is most definitely not unexpected behavior; one need only look at the behavior of George Washington during his eight years as president to support this (e.g., his refusal to go back to the Senate for consultation after being snubbed). In this sense, the lesson for newer presidential democracies, especially those with anti-system parties in the legislature, might be to expect impeachment attempts and other extra-constitutional moves.

CHAPTER 7

Impeachment as a Punishment for Corruption? The Cases of Brazil and Venezuela

Naoko Kada

INTRODUCTION

In 1992, Brazilian president Fernando Collor de Mello became the first popularly elected president to be impeached and removed from office in Latin America. Within a year, Venezuelan president Carlos Andrés Pérez followed suit. Both are cases of presidential exit. Both presidents were accused of corruption, and public opinion in each country supported—if not demanded and welcomed—each president's departure.

On the surface, these two cases of impeachment seem to be success stories of checking executive power. In both countries, it was the democratically elected legislature, not the military barracks, that made the final decision to remove the president from office. At the time of removal, both presidents were widely believed to be corrupt. Their removal by the legislature, therefore, was viewed by both national and international media as proof that democratic institutions could effectively check abuse of power by executives in Latin America, a region that has witnessed many presidents leaving office, as a result of a *coup d'etat*.

While it is indeed remarkable that no extra-constitutional means were used to remove these two presidents, a closer examination of the cases leads one to wonder whether they should be considered equally as regards the checking of executive power. Such an examination also casts doubt on the effectiveness of the impeachment and removal process as a check on the particular type of executive abuse of power in question, i.e., executive corruption.

In this chapter, I first contrast the two countries' institutional settings and their impeachment and removal processes, which differ greatly from one another. Next I discuss how the two presidents were accused, impeached, and removed from office. Finally, I analyze why these two presidents became the first to be removed for charges of corruption, among a large number of presidents accused of corruption in the region, and whether their removal constitutes an effective check against executive corruption.

INSTITUTIONAL SETTING

The procedural rules on impeachment and removal of the president determine who participates in the impeachment and removal process. These rules differ greatly between Brazil and Venezuela. Once we identify the players, we will examine the relationship between and among them, relationships that may influence their decisions regarding impeachment and removal of the president.

Impeachment and Removal Process in Brazil and Venezuela

The process by which a president is impeached and removed in Brazil is quite different from the process used in Venezuela in 1993 (Venezuela adopted a new constitution in 1999). While the Brazilian process is handled almost exclusively by the legislature, the Venezuelan process is characterized by the broadest amount of participation of the judiciary among those presidential systems that have rules on impeachment proceedings (see Figure 7-1).[1]

Brazil's impeachment process is legislature-dominant in that the legislature handles the investigation, impeachment, and trial of the president.[2] The legislature conducts the investigation through an ad hoc committee, created whenever at least one-third of the members of one or both of the chambers request its creation. It can be a committee created in only one of the chambers, or it can be a joint committee of both houses. The investigative committee is not a formal part of the impeachment process, for the vote on impeachment can take place without any investigation by Congress. However, a congressional investigation often forms the basis for a request for impeachment. The lower chamber, the House of Deputies, has the sole power of impeachment, requiring two-thirds of the members' vote in favor. If the House impeaches the president, the president is suspended. The Senate handles the impeachment trial, which is called a trial for the crime of responsibility. The decision to convict the president requires a vote of two-thirds of its members. If the president is also accused of common crimes, the criminal trial is conducted by the Supreme Court.

In contrast, in Venezuela, according to procedural rules in effect until 1999, the Supreme Court handles the pre-impeachment investigation. The Court does not initiate its investigation unless it receives a request to do so.[3] Any citizen can present such a request, but the likelihood that it would lead to an investigation was, until 1993, quite small, due to political ties between the Supreme Court and the other two branches. The one

Figure 7-1.
Impeachment and Removal Process in Brazil and Venezuela

Brazil	Venezuela
Accusation	Accusation
Request to form an investigative committee ($1/_3$ members of House or Senate or both)	Request to open a trial presented to the Supreme Court
Investigation by the Committee (not required for impeachment)	Investigation by the Supreme Court
Request for Impeachment presented to the House	Supreme Court recommendation of a trial ($1/_2$ votes)
House vote on Impeachment ($2/_3$ members)	Senate vote on Impeachment ($1/_2$ members)
*Impeachment**	*Impeachment*
Senate special committee composes the charges against the president	Supreme Court trial ($1/_2$ votes)
Impeachment Trial: Senate vote on conviction ($2/_3$ members)	*Conviction* (punishment determined by Supreme Court)
Conviction (president is permanently removed)	

* Common crime charges are handled by the Supreme Court after impeachment.

individual that held more sway than others in this regard was the Prosecutor General, whose institutional prerogatives included overseeing public officials' conduct, including the judicial branch.

The legislature can conduct investigations into matters of its choosing, but the 1961 constitution, in effect until 1999, specifically stated that congressional investigation should not interfere with judicial investigation. The legislature was limited not only in its investigative authority, but also in its power to impeach the president; without the Supreme Court's recommendation to hold a trial, the legislature could not impeach the president. If the Court did recommend a trial, the Senate decided, by the majority vote of its members (i.e., absolute majority), to impeach the president and the president was suspended. Following impeachment, the Supreme Court conducted the trial. The legislature had no role in the impeachment and removal process once the Senate authorized the trial. The Venezuelan impeachment process prior to 1999 can thus be called judiciary-dominant.

Aside from the active role the Supreme Court played, Venezuela's impeachment and removal process was characterized by a low voting threshold: all of the Supreme Court's decisions were made by a simple majority (i.e., the majority of those present at the time of voting), and the Senate's decision on impeachment was made by an absolute majority. Unlike in Brazil, none of the decisions throughout the process require a super-majority in Venezuela.

Given the differences in the impeachment and removal process of the two countries, the actors in the process naturally differ. In legislature-dominant Brazil, the principal actors are legislators and the president. In judiciary-dominant Venezuela, the principal actors are Supreme Court justices and the president; senators also play a role, since they do impeach the president, and without impeachment the president cannot be tried. Having identified the key actors in the impeachment and removal process, our next task is to understand the positive and negative incentives to proceed with or stop the impeachment and removal process. These incentives are shaped, at least in part, by the existing party system and the president's ability to influence others in the process.

Party System and Presidential Power in Brazil

The commonly held view about Brazilian legislators is that their loyalty to regional bosses is stronger than to political parties and that patronage plays an important part in advancing their political careers. The president is equipped with a wide range of distributional powers, and, given the patronage-seeking behavior of legislators, would be in a strong position to bargain with legislators if faced with the danger of impeachment. Brazil's fragmented party system is both a blessing and a curse for the president: while the fragmentation opens up many opportunities to bargain with legislators, the president can rarely count on a single-party support base large enough to weather impeachment crises.

In Brazil, not only senators but also representatives to the lower chamber are elected in statewide districts. The average number of representatives elected from each electoral district (the district magnitude) is about 19, one of the highest in the world. Since a party can win a seat with a small number of votes, small parties have a good chance of winning seats, which is one reason there are so many parties in Brazil. The effective number of parties in the Brazilian Congress since 1990 has consistently been five or more. Brazil's multi-party system has resulted in power-sharing arrangements, both formal and informal, where delegates from more than one party hold important positions on congressional committees, and nominations are discussed among leaders from all the major parties.

The Brazilian party system is also characterized by a lack of cohesion within parties.[4] Leftist parties such as the Workers' Party and the Communist Party are exceptions, demonstrating a high level of cohesion; larger, "catchall" parties are characterized by a lack of cohesion,[5] due in large part to the open-list electoral system. In a closed-list system, party leaders can discipline party members by placing party-loyalists at the top of the list and dissidents at the bottom. However, in Brazil party lists are open, which means that party leaders have no influence on which candidates are elected (much like in the U.S.). The lack of disciplinary measures available to party leaders in most parties makes it less costly for individual legislators to defy party leadership.

Additionally, open-list proportional representation encourages intra-party competition where legislators seek personal, instead of party, support bases. Many politicians use patronage, or delivery of state resources, to cultivate and maintain the support base, and some switch parties to gain better access to those resources[6]. Furthermore, because of a strong tradition and practice of federalism in Brazil, regional leaders are often said to have more influence on legislators than party leaders do.[7] As many legislators rely on patronage to maintain their constituent support base, and given the absence of strong party discipline, legislators are likely to be interested in negotiating their vote with the president, who enjoys vast distributive powers.

Brazilian presidents are equipped with a wide range of powers to distribute positions and resources and thus are well positioned to make attractive bargains with legislators. In one well-known measure of presidential power, the Brazilian president ranks among the strongest in terms of budgetary and cabinet nominating powers.[8] The executive prepares the multi-year economic plan and annual budget, and Congress cannot pass amendments to the budget if the change is incompatible with the multi-year plan presented by the executive. The president in Brazil is indeed in a strong bargaining position *vis-à-vis* legislators who rely on delivery of state resources and positions in federal government for electoral survival.

Party System, Presidential Power, and the Supreme Court in Venezuela

The Venezuelan Supreme Court is tightly knit into the impeachment and removal process, and therefore it is imperative that we understand the justices' incentives as well as those of the legislators. Under the 1961 constitution, Supreme Court justices were selected by Congress in joint session for nine-year terms (with the possibility of reappointment). This selection rule resulted in a Supreme Court whose overwhelming majority was strongly aligned with one of the two major political parties. The president had no formal role in the selection of the Supreme Court justices, although he might exercise informal influence through his party. The Supreme Court's budgetary independence was limited, in that while it proposed its own budget (instead of the executive branch making the proposal), that budget had to be approved by Congress. Thus, Congress had considerable influence over the Supreme Court; presidents had virtually no leverage whatever. However, because presidents from 1958 until 1993 were prominent leaders of the two largest parties, they could influence Supreme Court magistrates indirectly.

Until the early 1990s, Venezuelan party politics could be characterized as a quasi two party system that developed after the dictator Marcos Pérez Jiménez was ousted in 1958. Between 1958 and 1968, three parties, Democratic Action (AD), the Republican Democratic Union (URD), and the Christian Democrats (COPEI) shared power. This power-sharing was institutionalized in a formal agreement known as Pact of Punto Fijo. The Republican Democratic Union rapidly lost its initial electoral strength, and between 1968 and 1993 Venezuelan politics centered around two major parties, Democratic Action and the Christian Democrats.[9] As the Pact of Punto Fijo expired in 1968, the two parties formed a series of agreements known as the *Pacto Institucional* to maintain the practice of power-sharing. A good example of power-sharing were the informal agreements by which the 15 Supreme Court magistrates were selected from those who identified closely with Democratic Action or the Christian Democrats. Because of this, the Supreme Court was widely viewed as ineffective, lacking both independence from political parties and in professionalism.

The ideological distance between Democratic Action and the Christian Democrats shrunk increasingly as both headed toward the center, which made room for a third party to capture votes, especially from the left. Indeed, a leftist party, the Movement Toward Socialism, became the third largest party between 1974 and 1993. Another leftist party, Radical Cause, has captured urban voters since the 1980s, and in the 1993 election passed the Movement Toward Socialism to become the third largest party.[10] The party gained increased visibility in the early 1990s for its attacks on corrupt government.

Under the 1961 constitution, Venezuelan party leaders exerted strong power over party members, for they were in absolute control of candidate selection due to the closed-list system. Party members who publicly opposed the party line were punished with disciplinary measures such as expulsion from the party and removal from important party posts. In fact, the party discipline in Venezuela was so strong that roll-call was never taken in Congress: a party leader's statement was assumed to represent all the party members' votes. Dissent was expressed only by issuing individual statements apart from the party leader's, and this at the risk of harsh punishment.

Nevertheless, parties were not free of internal divisions. As one analyst aptly shows, Democratic Action's history as a party has been filled with internal conflicts, mostly when it held the presidency.[11] The existence of a rival faction makes it difficult for a president to enjoy solid support from his party, especially when the rival faction controls crucial posts within the party. President Pérez found himself in precisely such a situation in 1993.

The Venezuelan presidency, under the 1961 Constitution, was one of the weakest among presidential democracies in terms of its power to legislate and to define the national budget.[12] Strong party discipline also limits the president's ability to influence individual legislators' actions and decisions. As the president had no institutional influence on the Supreme Court magistrates under the 1961 constitution, the president's influence depended on his command of the party to which he belonged. In other words, once a president's command of the party weakened, his power to influence the impeachment process was quite small.

Another player that could influence the decisions of the Supreme Court under the 1961 constitution was the Prosecutor General, who was selected by the Congress just as Supreme Court magistrates were. The Prosecutor General's office was responsible for seeing that the judicial system worked in accordance with the constitution, as well as helping ensure that public officials behaved within the limits of law. The position of the Prosecutor General was viewed as a more prestigious position than that of a Supreme Court magistrate. Thus, it would have been difficult for the Supreme Court to ignore a request for investigation of the president presented by the Prosecutor General. The rejection to act on the request would not only damage the already low respect for the Supreme Court, but also could prompt the Prosecutor General to seek legal action against the Supreme Court. Fortunately for the Supreme Court, Prosecutor Generals did not present any requests for investigation of a president until 1993, when a far more independent-minded Prosecutor General presented his request that the Supreme Court investigate President Carlos Andrés Pérez.

Information Flow and Its Impact on the Impeachment Process

Whether a legislator might bargain with a president is also dependent upon that legislator's assessment of the guilt of the president, as well as his or her constituents' pressure for or against impeachment. Constituent pressure, as well as personal assessment of the president's guilt, is contingent upon available information about the president's alleged wrong-doing. The availability and credibility of incriminating information depends on the performance of the investigative body. Given the multi-party system and power-sharing arrangements in Congress, investigative committees in Brazil are highly decentralized. Both the president's supporters and his opponents are likely to be active on investigative committees, and no single party is likely to dominate. Regular committee members can actively participate in an investigation, both in producing and authenticating information and in transmitting that information outside the committee. Because the committee is unlikely to be dominated by either the president's supporters or his opponents, the committee's informational product will enjoy high credibility both among legislators and the populace.

If the committee fails to produce and transmit incriminating information about the president, the president is likely to survive, given his vast distributional power and legislators' need for patronage for electoral purposes. In the absence of authenticated information that suggests the president's wrong-doing, public opinion is unlikely to shift radically to demand impeachment. If, on the other hand, the investigative committee produces a report that suggests that the president is guilty of a serious crime, the president's bargaining power is weakened, especially if the information transmitted by the committee prompts public outrage.

In Venezuela, an impeachment investigation is conducted by the Supreme Court, and no information is allowed to become public until the investigation is concluded. The Chief Justice appoints one of the Supreme Court justices as the sole investigator, and in fact can appoint himself to be that investigator. Thus, investigative authority is highly concentrated, potentially in the hands of a single individual, the Chief Justice. Whether the Chief Justice is a supporter of the president or not, therefore, may have a strong impact on how an impeachment investigation will be carried out. Unlike in Brazil, where the investigative committee enjoys relative credibility because of its multi-party and decentralized nature, in Venezuela investigations suffer from possible (and highly likely) bias either in favor of or opposed to the president, because of its concentration of investigative authority and because of the strong partisan connections the majority of justices maintain.

Unlike Brazil, where the public has immediate access to investigative information through legislators and leaks to the media, in Venezuela, because of the secretive nature of judicial investigation, neither legislators nor the general public have access to the investigative information until the Court transmits it to the Senate. Before the information becomes available to the public, the Supreme Court conducts the initial evaluation of this information, by voting on whether to approve the justice-investigator's report to the Court. If the report recommends a trial, the Court's approval means that its majority considers the report to contain credible information about the president's guilt. The Court's approval would make it very difficult for the Senate to turn down the request to hold trial, since rejecting the request would mean its distrust of the Supreme Court's ability to judge right from wrong. Thus, if the full Supreme Court approves the justice-investigator's report recommending a trial, it is highly likely that the president will be impeached.

BRAZIL: THE IMPEACHMENT AND REMOVAL OF PRESIDENT COLLOR

Fernando Affonso Collor de Mello (hereafter Collor) was elected president of Brazil in December 1989 in the first direct presidential election after two decades of military rule. Voters were attracted to Collor, who promised to modernize the economy and the bureaucracy and denounced corrupt politicians. On his second day in office, Collor revealed his economic plan, which included a complete freeze on the withdrawal from any bank account surpassing C$50,000 (approximately U.S. $1,000 at the time) for one and a half years. The measure did not provoke any violent reaction, however, since only a small segment of the population had savings of more than that amount.[13] Hopes for the new government fighting inflation were still very high, and drastic measures in the economic plan were accepted as necessary. Inflation indeed slowed down, but Collor's approval rate also dropped from around 70 percent at the beginning of his term to less than 40 percent within three months; it continued to slide throughout his term.[14]

Accusations of corruption in the federal government were abundant during the first two years of the Collor administration; according to one expert, "at least thirteen different cases of alleged corruption arose."[15] None directly involved President Collor, however, and he reshuffled the cabinet, trying, quite successfully, to make it appear that his government was now cleared of corrupt elements.[16] Nevertheless, allegations of corruption continued to taunt the government, until finally the core of the government was affected. In May 1992, the president faced the most serious challenge against his government and his person. Pedro Collor, the president's younger brother, accused a friend of the president, Paulo Cesar "PC" Farias, of extortion, and charged that his brother, the president, was benefitting from PC Farias's shady deals.[17]

In response to Pedro Collor's accusation, Congress decided to form an investigative committee, ostensibly to find out whether PC Farias had committed serious crimes.[18] Reflecting the practice of power-sharing in congressional committees, the principal investigator was selected from the largest opposition party. The committee chair was from the largest party in the governing coalition; the president's party was too small to claim this post. The opposition had a thin, one vote majority in the committee, but however thin the margin was, holding a majority enabled opposition members to play important roles within the committee.[19] It voted to establish subcommittees to conduct an in-depth investigation on the activities of PC Farias. Given that the opposition held the majority in the committee, opposition members headed these subcommittees and conducted the investigation with vigor. Because many of PC Farias's activities involved the president and his family, information about the relationship between he and the president soon become an integral part of the investigation. The committee chair sought to restrict investigative activities by committee members to shield the president, but opposition members complained to the media of the allegedly obstructive moves by the chair, and such moves were soon reversed.

As the investigation progressed, more and more information was made public, which indicated that not only did PC Farias use his close link to the president for undue influence in government, but that the president also appeared to have benefited from his friend's shady deals; Farias showered the president and his family with gifts and cash. The investigative committee obtained evidence that showed that PC Farias had paid for the remodeling of the president's private residence, purchased an expensive car for the president's children, and paid miscellaneous expenses of the president, his wife, and other family members. Particularly damaging to the president was the revelation that the president's secretary and PC Farias were not affected by the bank account freeze that the president had imposed on the general populace. Knowingly or not, Brazil's widest-circulating newspaper had published, just days before the revelation, an article showing that the savings that had been frozen had lost up to 50 percent of their value.[20] Members of the congressional investigative committee obtained bank records that showed that the president's secretary, who regularly received checks from PC Farias for the president's personal expenses, had withdrawn most of the money from her bank account the day before the freeze took effect. It was not clear whether the president had known about (or ordered) the transaction, but the news angered many Brazilians, including legislators.[21]

Although in late May no one imagined that the president would face impeachment, by August public opinion demanded the president's exit, and talk of possible impeachment began to circulate in Congress as well. Street demonstrations against the president took place in major cities around Brazil. The principal investigator of the investigative committee completed his report suggesting that the president had benefited from PC Farias's illicit activities, defying pressure from the governing coalition and party leaders not to mention the president in the report. After the report was made public, the voices demanding impeachment grew even louder, both inside and outside Congress. The date for voting on impeachment was set for September 29; representatives were under pressure from many sides. With municipal elections fast approaching (scheduled for October 3), candidates for municipal offices expressed their support for impeachment and urged House representatives to do so as well. The president's friends publicly promised rewards from the administration if representatives voted against impeachment. Major newspapers began to publish a list of representatives who were in favor of, against, or undecided about the impeachment, making it easy for voters to see whether their representatives were being responsive to their demands for impeachment.

On September 29, the House voted to impeach President Collor by a landslide majority (441 to 38, with 23 absent and 1 abstention; see Table 7-1). The president was temporarily suspended. Exactly three months later, on December 29, the Senate convicted him of crime of responsibility, again by a wide margin (76 to 3; Table 7-2).[22] The president was permanently removed from office and banned from running for electoral office for eight years, the maximum punishment that can be imposed on a Brazilian president for a crime of responsibility in an impeachment case.

But the process was not yet over for Collor, for he was then tried on criminal charges by the Supreme Court. This trial lasted for almost two years. On December 12, 1994, the Supreme Court ruled, by a vote of 5 to 3, that there was insufficient evidence to convict the ex-president of passive corruption. Evidence of gifts that PC Farias gave to Collor, which included two ranches, expenses for the renovation of the president's private residence and apartment in Maceió, a Fiat Elba, and an apartment in Paris, were still not enough to prove that Collor was personally involved in corruption.

The ruling was disappointing to many Brazilians but not unexpected by legal experts. Brazilian prosecutors argued at the time of the trial that since concrete evidence is required to convict a suspect under the current penal (and penal procedural) codes, and since white-collar criminals rarely leave any physical evidence or commit the crime in front of witnesses, it is extremely difficult to convict someone for passive corruption.[23] Collor's case was no exception. Despite all the evidence that indicated the president had received gifts from PC Farias, the Prosecutor General failed to prove that the president had used his position as president to return the favors. Collor swiftly began a campaign to return to the political scene, while PC Farias remained in prison, in part for financial fraud committed during Collor's presidential term.[24]

VENEZUELA: THE IMPEACHMENT AND REMOVAL OF PRESIDENT PÉREZ

Carlos Andrés Pérez was president of Venezuela during the oil boom of 1974–1979. When the country found itself in economic distress in 1988, the

Table 7-1.
Impeachment Vote, Brazilian House of Deputies, 1992

Party/Coalition	Yes	No	Absent	Total
Governing Coalition *Bloco* (PFL, PRN, PSC; conservative)	79	24	11	114
Brazilian Labor Party (populist)	25	4	1*	30
Brazilian Socialist Party (leftist)	11	0	0	11
Christian Democratic Party (centrist)	16	0	2	18
Community Party of Brazil (leftist)	5	0	0	5
Democratic Labor Party (center left)	37	0	3	40
Democratic Social Party (conservative)	35	8	3	46
Liberal Party (conservative)	15	0	2	17
Party of the Brazilian Democratic Movement (centrist)	99	0	0	99
Party of Brazilian Social Democracy (center left)	40	0	0	40
Popular Socialist party (leftist)	3	0	0	3
Renovating Workers' Party (populist)	15	1	1	17
Social Labor Party (populist)	8	0	0	8
Workers' Party (leftist)	35	0	0	35
Former *Bloco* members (PFL & PRN representatives in Rio de Janeiro)	8	0	0	8
Other small parties	7	0	0	7
No party	3	1	1	5
Total	*441*	*38*	*24*	*503*

*This member was present but abstained.

electorate turned to Pérez again. He became president for the second time in 1989, becoming the first Venezuelan to do so under democratic rule. His popularity quickly dwindled, however, as he began to implement an economic austerity policy. Demands for his exit grew stronger as living standards continued to fall for the majority of Venezuelans, and a coup attempt took place in February 1992. Although public opinion did not support a military takeover, the coup organizers' criticism of the government

Table 7-2.
Indictment Vote, Brazilian Senate, 1992

Party/Coalition	Yes	No	Absent	Total
Brazilian Labor Party (populist)	7	0	1	8
Brazilian Socialist Party (leftist)	1	0	0	1
Christian Democratic Party (centrist)	3	0	0	3
Democratic Social Party (conservative)	2	1	1	4
Democratic Labor Party (center left)	4	0	1	5
Party of the Brazilian Democratic Movement (centrist)	22	0	4	26
Party of Brazilian Social Democracy (center left)	9	0	0	9
Party of the Liberal Front (conservative)	13	0	3	16
Party of National Reconstruction (conservative)	2	2	1	5
Workers' Party (leftist)	1	0	0	1
No Party	3	0	0	3
Total	*67*	*3*	*11*	*81*

resonated with the public; according to one poll, 40 percent of those polled attributed the coup attempt to "corruption, bad government in general."[25]

In November 1992, a critic of President Pérez, José Vicente Rangel, accused him of using public funds for private purposes. Curiously, his accusation sounded vaguely familiar to what Collor was most criticized for, that is, not suffering the consequences of a policy that he himself had imposed. In Collor's case, it had to do with the bank account freeze; in Pérez's case, it involved changes in the exchange rate regime. Rangel alleged that Pérez took out 250 million bolivars (Venezuelan local currency) of public funds and converted the funds into dollars just before issuing a decree to devalue the bolivar by over 60 percent. Rangel alleged that the president converted the dollars back to bolivars but returned only 250 million bolivars to public coffers, pocketing the difference generated by this operation. Another coup attempt occurred at the end of the month. In January 1993, Rangel filed his accusation against the president with the Prosecutor General, and on March 11, 1993, the Prosecutor General requested that the Supreme Court evaluate the charge.

Supreme Court president Gonzalo Rodríguez Corro, known as a Christian Democrat sympathizer and close friend of a Christian Democrat ex-president, assigned himself as presenter of the case.[26] The full court was to decide, based on his study, whether there was sufficient evidence to bring the president to trial. The study was completed on May 5, 1993. President Pérez requested the Supreme Court to make their decision immediately, arguing that the waiting period would exacerbate political instability, but the Court refused his request and took until May 20 to make its decision.[27] Opposition members of Congress circulated rumors that the Supreme Court president had recommended a trial, although the court's 15 magistrates kept complete silence on the decision until it was final.[28] The leaders of the Christian Democrats and the Movement Toward Socialism also made public comments urging, if not threatening, the Supreme Court to rule in favor of a trial.[29]

The 15 days before the Supreme Court decision saw heightened political instability and tension. On May 12, a group of army personnel linked to February 1992 coup leader Hugo Chávez (as of this writing, the beleaguered current president of Venezuela) threatened to resort to violence against Supreme Court magistrates if they voted against sending Pérez's case to trial. The group also suggested a plan to form a joint civilian-military transition government headed by Chávez once Pérez was removed from office. The president's side, on the other hand, tried to convince the populace that attempts to weaken the government and aggravate the political crisis were taking place, citing three states where subversive violence was reported to have occurred. Unfortunately for the president, the governors of these states refuted those claims, prompting criticism that the Pérez administration was trying to obscure the secret fund scandal by scaring people.[30]

On May 20, the Supreme Court voted on the merits of the trial of President Pérez on charges of malfeasance and embezzlement of $17 million in secret security funds. Nine magistrates voted in favor of trial, while six abstained. The next day the Senate voted unanimously to strip Pérez of presidential immunity, which meant that he was temporarily removed from office. Even the president's party, Democratic Action, supported the decision, arguing that it respected the Supreme Court's judgment. In fact the president himself had requested that the party do so before the Court's decision was known, believing that the decision would be in his favor.[31] Although critical of the Court's decision, the president complied with it and left the palace on temporary leave. He did not resign, however, refusing to give in to critics' demands to do so.

The 1961 constitution (Article 188) allowed presidents temporary leave for up to 90 continuous days.[32] After 90 days, tι.e Congress, in a joint session, could decide whether that leave should be characterized as permanent, and, if it did so, choose a new president to complete the term. As the trial of President Pérez was nowhere near an end after 90 days had passed, the congressional majority decided to put this constitutional clause to use. The Congress, in joint session, voted on August 31, 1993, to declare the permanent leave of the president.[33] Pérez's party (Democratic Action) voted against permanent removal, but did not have enough votes to prevent the decision, a decision which required only a simple majority (Democratic Action held less than 50 percent of the votes). Pérez called the decision a "coup against the Venezuelan constitution." He insisted that he was still the constitutional president and would return to the office once absolved of the corruption charges by the Supreme Court.[34] He attempted to challenge the congressional decision by asking the Supreme Court to judge on its constitutionality, but the Court refused to take the case.

In the Supreme Court trial that finally came to a close in May 1996, President Pérez was found guilty of mismanagement of public funds and sentenced to a 28-month prison term.[35] The magistrates convicted the president of mismanagement of the secret funds, but the charge of embezzlement was dropped. Eleven magistrates voted in favor, while four abstained. The Court also ordered him to "restitute, repair or indemnify the damage to the public patrimony once the corresponding sum was established."[36] Since there were no receipts or documents to identify how the funds were spent, it was unclear how the "corresponding sum" could be calculated.[37]

The ruling was considered unsatisfactory by critics of the ex-president, his defense team, and even less passionate observers. For enemies of the ex-president, the ruling was too soft; for the defense, the ruling should have been absolution of the defendant, since, in its view, no crime had been proven. Less passionate observers lamented that the trial did not lead to thorough investigation into the use of the secret funds, nor did it produce a convincing legal argument for convicting the ex-president of mismanagement of funds.[38] According to one analyst, if the law upon which the Supreme Court had based its decision to convict Pérez was applied to all public servants, the "immense majority" would have to be charged with the same crime.[39] Ironically, the legislature approved a bill to amend this law toward the end of Pérez's term (although by then the presidency was held by Ramón J. Velásquez). The bill did not go into effect, however, as Christian Democrat leaders, realizing that it might benefit Pérez, urged Velásquez not to sign it.[40]

WHY WERE THESE PRESIDENTS IMPEACHED AND REMOVED?

Accusations of corruption against presidents and legislators are commonplace in Latin America. Collor was not the first president to be accused of corruption in Brazil, and Pérez's first administration (1974–79) was widely perceived as corrupt. Yet it was only in 1992 in Brazil, and 1993 in

Venezuela, that a popularly elected president was impeached and removed from office for charges of corruption. What did these two presidents have in common that led them to be the first in their countries (and the first two in Latin America) to be removed by the legislature for corruption?

First, both presidents were elected by a public hoping for change, and accusations of corruption greatly damaged the trust voters had given to them. Both presidents had implemented economic policies that, while deemed necessary, negatively affected the middle and lower classes in the short term. In each case, accusations that the president was benefitting from corrupt behavior angered the populace, all the more so because the public faced economic hardship as a result of those economic policies and because it expected the president to be the agent of positive change, not of too-familiar corrupt politics. The sense that the president deceived his nation became especially strong in Brazil, after the revelation that he did not suffer from the bank account freeze he imposed. Similarly, the initial charge against Venezuela's President Pérez angered many Venezuelans because of the allegation that he took advantage of changes in the exchange rate regime that he implemented. In short, both presidents were viewed as taking advantage of their position for private gain at a time when the rest of the country was suffering economic pain.

Second, both presidents faced an opposition that felt it had nothing to lose and everything to gain from the removal of the president and that found the means to accomplish that objective. It is important to recognize that the fact that these presidents were minority presidents (whose parties did not hold a majority of seats in the legislature) is by itself not a sufficient explanation for why they were removed. Many minority presidents have been accused of corruption without being impeached, let alone removed. The difference between the two cases studied here and other cases of presidents being accused of corruption is that in Brazil and Venezuela in the early 1990s, the opposition acted strategically in order to achieve its goal. In Brazil, this meant that the opposition had to produce enough information and poplar pressure to convince a majority that was skeptical or even critical of the suggestion that the president should be impeached and removed. In Venezuela, it meant that the opposition had to shift the decision-making arena from the judiciary to the legislature.

In Brazil, the opposition—especially leftist parties that had long opposed the president's economic policy—assigned investigative experts to the investigative committee; these experts unearthed (and leaked) information suggesting that the president was indeed corrupt. The accumulated information and popular reaction to it forced most of the president's supporters to turn their backs on him and support his impeachment and removal. The Speaker of the House, also from an opposition party, strategically set the date of impeachment vote to be days before municipal elections. This increased the effectiveness of popular pressure, since those candidates associated with representatives who voted against impeachment could expect to lose many votes; thus, candidates pressured representatives to vote in favor of impeachment.

In Venezuela, the legislature had no formal role in investigation; judicial investigation, predictably, took a long time. However, the opposition found another way to remove the immensely unpopular president without having to wait for the conclusion of the judicial investigation: the declaration of permanent absence of the president. Under the 1961 constitution, it was surprisingly easy to remove a president using this clause, requiring only an absolute majority approval of the House and the Senate. If it had required two-thirds majority, as is the case with the Brazilian Senate's vote to convict, Democratic Action (the president's party) could have prevented the approval, but as it was, the party commanded less than half the votes and the declaration was approved.

Third, both presidents seem to have miscalculated how legislators and justices would act during the impeachment and removal proceedings. Since there was no precedent for a president being impeached in either country, it would perhaps be unfair to criticize them for their lack of foresight. Many congressional investigative committees had been constituted in Brazil prior to the one that investigated PC Farias (and indirectly the president), but none had led to the arrest or removal of a politician. Accusations against presidents were nothing new in Venezuela either, but none had actually led to the recommendation of a trial of a sitting president. In addition, both presidents seem to have believed that the law was on their side.

In Brazil, President Collor did not try to influence the investigation to prevent the collection of information. He focused rather on first trying to persuade enough legislators to vote against impeachment and removal with promises of rewards (such as government posts and favorable distribution of budget), and then on buying time through repeated appeals to the Supreme Court.[41] The president's apparent calm seems to have stemmed from his confidence that he could persuade enough legislators to vote in his favor, first in the House and then in the Senate. Such confidence, in turn, was based on his belief that the Supreme Court would rule as he expected it to. Regarding the House's decision on impeachment, the president also believed that the Court would rule against a roll-call voting procedure. At the time, two laws conflicted with each other regarding voting procedure for impeachment. One law (Law 1079, of 1950) stated that the voting had to be roll call, while the House's internal code as of 1992 stated that the voting procedure for impeachment (for a common crime) was secret voting. Collor and his allies argued that Law 1079 was revoked when the constitution of 1988 went into effect, and they were confident that their argument would win in court. As it turned out, the Supreme Court ruled otherwise.

In the case of the vote in the Senate to convict the president, Collor had hoped to postpone the process until the new year by appealing to the Supreme Court for more time for the defense, or by requesting the appearance of witnesses who were not in Brazil at the time (which would further delay the trial). He even went so far as to fire his defense lawyers on the day that voting was scheduled in the Senate. This last move did not, however, produce as much delay as the president had hoped. Instead of postponing the trial until the new year, the Supreme Court endorsed the Senate's timetable to hold the trial after Christmas break; senators now had to come back to the capital from their states after Christmas to cast their votes. Instead of helping the president gain more votes, his last attempt to delay the trial irritated even some of the president's sympathizers, pushing them to the other side of the fence. The president, nevertheless, clung to his belief that he could escape conviction until the very last moment, refusing to resign until it was too late.

In Venezuela, the president's first and most costly miscalculation took place in the early stage of the impeachment process. He simply did not believe that the accusation against him would lead to the Supreme Court's recommendation to hold a trial. To be sure, the Supreme Court had recommended a trial for no president before him (or after him, for that matter), and the only known part of the accusation—that the president had transferred public funds from one government organ to another—was such a common practice across administrations that President Pérez did not believe it could constitute the foundation for recommending a trial. So confident was the president that he would not be recommended for trial that he asked his party to respect the Court's ruling. He was simply not worried about the possibility of impeachment, thinking that the Court would rule against the need for a trial. Rather, he was worried about opponents within his own party who were increasingly voicing their demand for him to step down and who might criticize a Court ruling that the president was innocent.

As it turned out, the president played right into the hands of his opponents. Since he himself had asked the party to respect the Court's decision, he could not afford to criticize the decision after it was made. Because he was confident that the Court would not recommend a trial, the president did not even have a defense lawyer to consult with after the Court's decision to recommend a trial was made public. If the president had set up a defense team, he could have delegated the task of defending him to his lawyers, lawyers who would also have had the legal expertise to point out the lack of credible evidence of corruption and demand that the Senate debate the Court's decision. (In fact, the president began to consult with legal counsel some days before the ruling was due, but did not have a defense team in place.) Given the highly violent political climate, it might not have been possible to assemble the defense team before the Supreme Court's decision (since even Supreme Court justices were targets of letter bombs at the time). Nevertheless, the lack of preparation on the part of the president would not have been so complete had he foreseen impeachment and trial.

The president continued to believe that he would be absolved of the charges and would return to the main stage of Venezuelan politics, a belief that was repeatedly proven wrong. He certainly did not anticipate Congress' declaration of his absolute absence while he was on trial. If he or his defense team had, the constitutionality of such a declaration while he was on trial might have been challenged before Congress made its move. Whether the Court would have ruled in the president's favor is doubtful, however, given the pressure under which the Court was operating during that period. Even after the Supreme Court ignored the president's request to rule on the constitutionality of the declaration that effectively removed him from office, he still believed that the Court would not convict him of any crime. He expected to return to his party as its savior after he was absolved, but instead found himself expelled from the party after the Court convicted him.

DIFFERENCES BETWEEN THE TWO CASES OF IMPEACHMENT AND REMOVAL

While the end result of the impeachment process was the same for both Collor and Pérez in that they were both removed from office, the processes by which they were removed, as well as the final assessment of their guilt, differ greatly. To begin with, while Brazilian President Collor was removed as a result of the impeachment trial by the Senate, Venezuelan President Pérez was not removed as the result of conviction by the Supreme Court. The Venezuelan legislators did not wait for the impeachment and removal process to run its normal course, but instead opted for a more speedy removal process (i.e., declaration of absolute absence) that was legally available to them; however, using this mechanism while the president was on trial certainly begs the question of its constitutionality.

Secondly, the impeachment and removal process in Brazil proceeded with no violence; pressure was expressed in the form of peaceful marches, and no military officer threatened or predicted the use of violence. In sharp contrast, the Venezuelan process was preceded by two attempts of military coup, and during the process threats of and actual use of violence cast a dark shadow on the Supreme Court. Coup leaders openly suggested that they might resort to violence if the Supreme Court did not rule in favor of opening a trial of the president. Letter bombs were sent to some of the Supreme Court magistrates, and one bomb actually struck the Supreme Court building, permanently injuring a Court employee.

Third, while the impeachment process in both countries began with a vague accusation of corruption, the investigation in Brazil led to an accumulation of information that increasingly convinced the legislators as well as the public of the president's guilt, while the investigation in Venezuela failed to produce any hard evidence (such as bank records or purchases of luxury goods) to prove that the president had privately benefited from an alleged transfer of funds. Indeed, the Venezuelan Supreme Court dropped the charge of embezzlement in its final sentence for lack of evidence. The only crime the ex-president was convicted of was that he diverted a fund earmarked for internal security to the Secretariat of Presidency (which had no responsibility for internal security matters), and that the fund was allegedly used to send security personnel for the newly elected president of Nicaragua (Violeta Chamorro) to help safeguard that new democracy.

Fourth, the Brazilian president was given every opportunity to contest congressional actions in the Supreme Court, while the Venezuelan president was given no such opportunity. Collor appealed to the Federal Supreme Court to request more time for the defense at every stage of the impeachment and removal process, and he also challenged the House Speaker's authority to set the voting rule. The Supreme Court duly responded every time the president took his case to the Court. The president was given more time for his defense as a result, although his challenge to the House Speaker failed.

In contrast, because the Supreme Court is deeply involved in the impeachment and removal process in Venezuela, President Pérez had little chance of success in challenging the process. Unlike Brazil, for example, under the 1961 constitution, Venezuela had no constitutional court or other legal institution that would have the authority to assess the constitutionality of the legislature's and the Supreme Court's actions during the impeachment and removal process. The president's appeals to the Supreme Court fell on deaf ears. The Court's refusal to respond to the president extended beyond the impeachment and removal process. After the Congress declared the president to be permanently absent and removed him, Pérez appealed to the Supreme Court, being the only organ with authority to decide on such a matter. The Court never responded to the president's appeal.

In sum, although both presidents were removed as a result of an impeachment process, the conditions under which this occurred differed greatly. The Brazilian process followed every step of the impeachment and removal process as prescribed, and accumulated evidence proving presidential corruption; there was no use or even threat of violence; and there were ample opportunities for the president to defend himself and contest congressional decisions. The process in Venezuela was characterized by the use and threat of violence; a shortage of evidence proving presidential corruption; the removal of the president prior to the conclusion of the trial; and a distinct lack of opportunity for the president to strike back.

ISSUES IN USING PRESIDENTIAL IMPEACHMENT AS A MECHANISM TO CHECK THE EXECUTIVE

In the beginning of this chapter I discussed the possible use of impeachment and removal as a mechanism to check one particular type of abuse of power by the executive, namely, corruption. This account of two presidents demonstrates both the potential and the limits of presidential impeachment as an effective means to check corrupt executives. While both presidents were removed from office, and although the impeachment processes in both countries began with accusations of corruption, neither president was convicted of corruption in the trial by the Supreme Court. One could argue that the presidents were punished for their abuse of power since the legislature in both countries removed them from office, but was removal indeed a punishment for abuse of power?

In the case of President Collor, the Supreme Court's ruling that he was innocent allowed him to argue that his removal was politically motivated, although few Brazilians accorded this argument any credibility. Because the president was absolved, none of the gifts from PC Farias were subject to confiscation, even though the money that PC Farias used for the gifts was believed to have been obtained from illicit activities. The alleged gains from corruption remained in the hands of the ex-president. The legislature did all it could do to check the abuse of power by the executive by impeaching and then convicting the president of the crime of responsibility. The extent of legislative check on the president is, however, limited to his political responsibility, and therefore, punishment is also limited to his political rights (i.e., removal and suspension of the right to run for electoral office). In other words, a legislative check on the executive is not effective in cases of abuse of power that involve corruption, since the legislature cannot take away the material gains the executive might obtain through corrupt behavior.

In the case of President Pérez, removal occurred not as a result of a conviction that the president was corrupt, but as a result of a congressional declaration of the absolute absence of the president. Therefore, his removal cannot be considered as punishment for corruption, or for any other type of abuse of power. In addition, the Supreme Court, especially in the early stage of the impeachment process, was heavily pressured by the threat of and actual violence. In other words, the Supreme Court's decisions were influenced by an abuse of power by a segment of the military and supported by some prominent political leaders, not by the president.

The 1961 constitution gave the legislature a very small role to play in the impeachment and removal process in Venezuela, and removal as a result of impeachment could happen only when the Supreme Court convicted the president of a crime. In other words, a legislative check on the executive was virtually nonexistent under the 1961 constitution. In 1993 the Congress found a constitutional way to remove the president, but not based on a judgment that the president had abused his power; Congress did not have the authority to make such a judgment under the 1961 constitution. By removing the president in this way, the legislature left room for the president to argue that the Congress had overstepped its jurisdiction and that the removal was therefore unconstitutional, although at the time no one was listening to the then-unpopular president.

The Venezuelan Supreme Court's final sentence did convict the president of a crime, but not of embezzlement, as had been alleged. The only crime the president was convicted of was that of mismanagement of public funds that were used for purposes for which they were not intended. In other words, the Court admitted that there was not enough evidence to prove that the president had used the funds for private purposes. Despite this ruling, the Court demanded that the president repay the nation for damages he caused. Given that the Court determined that the funds had been used for public purposes, however, it was not clear what the Court expected the president to pay for.[42] Just as Collor saw his absolution as a victory, Pérez saw the Court's ruling as a victory, for he was finally absolved of the corruption (embezzlement) charge. He could now fall back on the Court's ruling to argue that the corruption charge was a politically motivated, baseless charge his opponents made up to discredit him. His removal did not symbolize the triumph of anti-corruption forces. If anything, it lowered the credibility of accusations of corruption against a president, as it exemplified, perhaps too well, how such accusations can quickly become political tools to bring down a president.

In sum, it is too naive to view the removal of these presidents as an example of how the legislature can effectively punish a president for abuse of power. The Brazilian case shows that a president can indeed be punished for abuse of power, but it also shows the limitations of a legislative check on executive corruption. The limitation is that legislative punishment cannot go beyond suspension of political rights. In order to provide punishment that goes beyond removal from office and suspension of political rights, adequate laws need to be established to deal with the substance of the president's crime. The Venezuelan case shows the problems associated with a system where the legislature is given a very limited role in which to check the executive. The Supreme Court was forced to make many politically sensitive decisions while the legislature forced its way, so to speak, into the impeachment and removal process, by way of a constitutionally sanctioned declaration of permanent absence of the president.

The cases of presidential removal in Brazil and Venezuela demonstrate both the potential and the limitations of a legislative check on the executive as a control mechanism against corruption. A legislative check can lead to removal of a president where a legislature-dominant impeachment and removal process is used; thus it has real potential to control executive abuse of power. However, its effectiveness against corruption is limited, for the legislature cannot take the material gains of corruption away from the executive. A legislature without the authority to check executive power can still manage to remove a president, as the Venezuelan Congress did in 1993. However, such removal by the legislature is not a part of the judiciary-dominant impeachment and removal process, and thus can undermine the effectiveness of judicial check of the executive, since it means that the president can be removed without a final judgment by the judiciary concerning presidential abuse of power. These cases show that presidential removals are far from being an effective tool to fight corruption. It is perhaps more likely that accusations of corruption are used by a president's opponents as justification for their attempts at removing, or at least humiliating, the president. Just as we should be wary of abuse of power by the chief executive, the above account calls for caution in using an impeachment and removal process for such a purpose, for this process can easily become a tool for abuse of power by the opponents of the chief executive.

CHAPTER 8

Comparative Presidential Impeachment: Conclusions

Naoko Kada

INTRODUCTION

As we have demonstrated in previous chapters, impeachment is an inherently political process. Yet studies of impeachment have largely been the exclusive realm of legal scholars. This is partly because, until the last decade of the twentieth century, no country other than the United States had effectively impeached a sitting president. In other countries with presidential systems, presidents were either too strong or too weak to give constitutional mechanisms of impeachment a chance. Strong presidents held control of the government using a vast array of constitutional and political powers, and in many cases, authoritarian measures, making it virtually impossible to oppose them without risking political suicide or worse. Weak presidents were easily removed by force. In many countries presidents were both too strong and too weak; because they were too powerful for a democratic opposition to remove them from office, violence became the only means to remove them.

By the end of the twentieth century, however, authoritarian regimes were increasingly less common and democratic regimes emerged in all corners of the globe. A large number of these new democracies have presidential or semi-presidential systems of government. We have identified 93 democracies that have constitutions with explicit provisions for presidential impeachment and removal by impeachment. Yet, as of the end of 2002, only twelve countries have thus far attempted to impeach their president; three of these are countries that have practiced democratic politics for at least 30 years. Only the U.S. has seen more than one impeachment of a president in a history of over 200 years. The relative infrequency of impeachment proceedings in the new democracies is puzzling considering the following.

First, in countries that have had strong chief executives, the presidency, even after a transition to democracy, is often imbued with formal and informal powers to control the government and its policies.[1] Presidents are likely to use these powers to their maximum advantage. On the other hand, a democratically elected legislature, once it does not need to fear repression for opposing the president, is likely to try to maximize its own influence in government and policy-making. Thus, the institutional setting is theoretically ripe for intense conflict between the president and the legislature, and the legislature, unable to constrain the president, is therefore likely to be tempted to impeach and possibly remove the president.

Second, in countries where presidents have been historically weak (e.g., where military coups were a common means of removing them), there is no established custom to respect the fixed tenure of a presidency. But military coups have become increasingly unpopular in international public opinion as well as among military leaders,[2] and as nations adapt to democratic rules of the game, the likelihood of removal of presidents by force diminishes. At the same time, however, the electorate expects democratically elected politicians to respond to popular demands and deliver on their campaign promises. If the government cannot meet these expectations, a frustrated public will blame the government, and the president in particular, insisting that leadership pay for its failure. The president is the prime target of this criticism because he personifies the government. If public demands for the punishment of its political leaders become louder, threatening regime instability, the legislature might be willing to sacrifice the president.

Unlike in parliamentary systems, where a cabinet is subject to a vote of confidence (positive or negative) by the parliament and thus can be changed when the majority of legislators no longer support it, presidential systems are built on the principle of separation of powers, and, by extension, greater executive stability. No matter how unpopular an administration becomes, there is no possibility of change in government by a vote of confidence in the legislature. In other words, legislators cannot sacrifice a president in the same manner or with the same (relative) ease as they do a prime minister (and his or her cabinet) in parliamentary systems. The only way the legislature can force a change of chief executive in a presidential system is by impeachment. This is why some legislators may be tempted to use it in an attempt to remove a president whose popularity is declining, even when presidential wrongdoing is debatable.

IMPEACHMENT PROCEDURES IN CONSTITUTIONAL ENGINEERING

Given this historical and theoretical background, it is not surprising that recently democratized countries have experimented with impeachment procedures in the last decade. What might be surprising is that only a small number of countries have done so. There are several possible reasons for the relative infrequency of presidential impeachment (successful or otherwise), but one important reason is that the crafters of most constitutions have designed impeachment and/or removal of the president to be fairly difficult. Again, this is not surprising given the goal of greater executive stability in adopting a presidential system.

As Tables 8-1 to 8-3 demonstrate, impeachment and removal procedures differ greatly between democratic countries with independent presidencies.[3]

Table 8-1.
Constitutional Impeachment and Removal Provisions by Country: Legislative (Bicameral and Unicameral) Impeachment*

Country (Year of Constitution)	Impeachment by (Majority Required)	Trial by (Majority Required)	High court involved?
BICAMERAL			
Argentina (1994)	LH ($^2/_3$ present)	UH ($^2/_3$ present)	No
Brazil (1988)	LH ($^2/_3$ members)	UH ($^2/_3$ members)	No
Chile (1980)	LH ($^1/_2$ members)	UH ($^2/_3$ members)	No
Colombia (1991)	LH ($^1/_2$ present)	UH ($^2/_3$ present)	No
Comoros (2001)	LH ($^2/_3$ members)	UH (not specified)	No
Dominican Rep. (1994)	LH ($^3/_4$ members)	UH ($^3/_4$ members)	No
Haiti (1987)	LH ($^2/_3$ members)	UH ($^2/_3$ members)	No
India (1950)	LH or UH ($^2/_3$ members)	LH or UH ($^2/_3$ members)	No
Ireland (1937)	LH or UH ($^2/_3$ members)	LH or UH ($^2/_3$ members)	No
Israel (1948)	Comm. in LH ($^3/_4$ members)	UL ($^3/_4$ members)	No
Italy (1948)	LH & UH ($^1/_2$ members)	LH & UH ($^1/_2$ members)	No
Liberia (1986)	LH (not specified)	UH ($^2/_3$ members)	No
Malawi (1994)	LH ($^2/_3$ members)	LH & UH ($^2/_3$ members)	No
Mexico (1917)	LH ($^1/_2$ present)	UH ($^2/_3$ present)	No
Nigeria (1999)	UH & LH ($^2/_3$ members)	UH & LH ($^2/_3$ members)	Yes
Palau (1991)	UH & LH ($^2/_3$ members)	UH & LH ($^2/_3$ members)	No
Paraguay (1992)	LH ($^2/_3$ present)	UH ($^2/_3$ members)	No

(*continues*)

Table 8-1. (*continued*)
Constitutional Impeachment and Removal Provisions by Country: Legislative (Bicameral and Unicameral) Impeachment*

Country (Year of Constitution)	Impeachment by (Majority Required)	Trial by (Majority Required)	High court involved?
Philippines (1986)	LH ($^1/_3$ members)	UH ($^2/_3$ members)	No
Russia (1993)	LH ($^2/_3$ members)	UH ($^2/_3$ members)	Yes
Trinidad & Tobago (1976)	LH & UH (JS, $^2/_3$ members)	LH & UH (JS, $^2/_3$ members)	Yes
Uruguay (1966)	LH (not specified)	UH ($^2/_3$ members)	No
United States (1789)	LH ($^1/_2$ present)	UH ($^2/_3$ present)	No
Yugoslavia (1992)	LH (not specified)	LH (not specified)	No
UNICAMERAL			
Armenia (1995)	UL ($^1/_2$ members)	UL ($^2/_3$ members)	Yes
Bangladesh (1986)	UL ($^1/_2$ members)	UL ($^2/_3$ members)	Optional
Dominica (1978)	UL ($^2/_3$ members)	UL ($^2/_3$ members)	Yes
Ecuador (1998)	UL ($^2/_3$ members)	UL ($^2/_3$ members)	Yes
Georgia (1991)	UL ($^2/_3$ members)	UL ($^2/_3$ members)	Yes
Guatemala (1985)	UL ($^2/_3$ members)	(Not specified)	No
Guyana (1980)	UL ($^2/_3$ members)	UL ($^3/_4$ members)	Yes
Kiribati (1979)	(Not specified)	UL ($^1/_2$ members)	No
Latvia (1922; 1998)	UL ($^1/_2$ members)	UL ($^2/_3$ members)	No
Lithuania (1992)	(Not specified)	UL ($^3/_5$ members)	No
Malta (1964)	UL (not specified)	UL (not specified)	No
Mauritius (1968)	UL ($^2/_3$ members)	UL ($^1/_2$ members)	Yes
Panama (1972)	UL (not specified)	UL (not specified)	No
Peru (1993)	Committee in UL (not specified)	UL (not specified)	No
Seychelles (1993)	UL ($^2/_3$ members)	UL ($^2/_3$ members)	Yes
Sierra Leone (1991)	UL ($^2/_3$ members)	UL ($^2/_3$ members)	Yes
Singapore (1963)	UL ($^1/_2$ members)	UL ($^3/_4$ members)	Yes
Slovakia (1992)	(Not specified)	UL ($^3/_5$ members)	No
Sri Lanka (1978)	(Not specified)	UL ($^2/_3$ members)	No
Tanzania (1977)	UL ($^2/_3$ members)	UL ($^2/_3$ members)	Yes
Turkey (1982)	UL ($^1/_3$ members)	UL ($^3/_4$ members)	No
Ukraine (1996)	UL ($^2/_3$ members)	UL ($^3/_4$ members)	Yes
Zimbabwe (1979)	UL ($^1/_3$ members)	UL ($^2/_3$ of $^2/_3$ members)	No

* Key for Tables 8-1 through 8-3: Lower house of a bicameral legislature (*LH*); upper house of a bicameral legislature (*UH*); joint session (*JS*); unicameral legislature (*UL*). A "high court" could include a Supreme Court (*SC*), Constitutional Court (*CC*), High Court of Justice (*HCJ*), or a special judicial tribunal convened for the impeachment process; involvement of the court could include verification that the president has committed a crime or violated the constitution, or that the impeachment and/or trial was processed according to the constitution and can occur prior to the vote on impeachment, between the impeachment and trial phases, or after the trial phase.

Table 8-2.
Constitutional Impeachment and Removal Provisions by Country: Mixed
(Legislative and Judicial) Impeachment*

Country (Year of Constitution)	Impeachment by (Majority Required)	Trial by (Majority Required)
Albania (1998)	UL ($^2/_3$ members)	CC (not specified)
Azerbaijan (1995)	CC & SC (not specified)	UL ($^{95}/_{125}$ members), CC
Benin (1990)	UL ($^2/_3$ members)	HCJ (not specified)
Bolivia (1967)	LH & UH (JS, $^2/_3$ members)	SC (not specified)
Bulgaria (1991)	UL ($^2/_3$ members)	CC (not specified)
Burkina Faso (1991)	UL ($^4/_5$ members)	HCJ (not specified)
Cape Verde (1999)	UL ($^2/_3$ members)	SC (not specified)
Central African Rep. (1995)	UL ($^2/_3$ members)	HCJ (not specified)
Congo-Brazzaville (1992)	LH ($^2/_3$ members)	HCJ (not specified)
Costa Rica (1949)	UL ($^2/_3$ members)	SC (not specified)
Cote D'Ivoire (1960)	UL ($^2/_3$ members)	HC (not specified)
Croatia (1990)	UL ($^2/_3$ members)	CC ($^2/_3$)
Cyprus (1960)	UL ($^3/_4$ members)	HCJ (not specified)
Czech Rep. (1992)	UH (not specified)	CC (not specified)
Djibouti (1992)	UL ($^2/_3$ members)	HCJ (not specified)
East Timor (2002; draft)	UL ($^2/_3$ members)	SCJ (not specified)
El Salvador (1983)	UL ($^1/_2$ members)	SC (not specified)
Finland (2000)	UL ($^3/_4$ members)	HC Impeachment (not specified)
France (1958)	LH & UH ($^1/_2$ members)	HCJ (not specified)
Gabon (1991)	LH ($^2/_3$ members)	HCJ (not specified)
Germany (1949)	LH or UH ($^2/_3$ members)	CC (not specified)
Ghana (1992)	UL ($^1/_3$ members) & Special Tribunal	UL ($^2/_3$ members)
Greece (1975)	UL ($^2/_3$ members)	Ad Hoc Court (not specified)
Honduras (1982)	UL (not specified)	SC (not specified)
Hungary (1949)	UL ($^2/_3$ members)	CC (not specified)
Kyrgyzstan (1993)	LH ($^2/_3$ members)	CC (not specified)
Macedonia (1991)	UL ($^2/_3$ members)	CC ($^2/_3$)
Madagascar (1992)*	LH & UH ($^2/_3$ members)	SC (not specified)
Mali (1992)	UL ($^2/_3$ members)	HCJ (not specified)
Mauritania (1991)	LH & UH (JS, $^1/_2$ members)	HCJ (not specified)

(*continues*)

Table 8-2. (*continued*)
Constitutional Impeachment and Removal Provisions by Country: Mixed
(Legislative and Judicial) Impeachment

Country (Year of Constitution)	Impeachment by (Majority Required)	Trial by (Majority Required)
Moldova (1994)	UL ($^2/_3$ members)	SC (not specified)
Mongolia (1992)	CC (not specified)	UL (majority present and voting)
Nicaragua (1986)	UL ($^1/_2$ members)	SC (not specified)
Poland (1997)	LH ($^2/_3$ members)	Tribunal of State
Portugal (1976)	UH ($^2/_3$ members)	SC Justice (not specified)
Romania (1991)	LH & UH (JS, $^2/_3$ members)	SC Justice (not specified)
Senegal (2001)	UL ($^3/_4$ members)	HCJ (not specified)
Slovenia (1991)	UL (not specified)	CC ($^2/_3$)
South Korea (1987)	UL ($^2/_3$ members)	CC ($^2/_3$)
Venezuela (1961–99)	UH ($^1/_2$ members)	SC (not specified)

* During the 1996 impeachment of Albert Zafy, the Madagascar senate had not yet been constituted.

In some countries (Table 8-1) only the legislature is involved in the impeachment process; these can be thought of as "legislature-dominant" systems. In others (Table 8-2), a judicial body as well as the legislature participates; these we refer to as "mixed" systems. In still others (Table 8-3), mechanisms of direct democracy (plebiscite, referendum) and other means are used. Among legislature-dominant countries, in virtually no country (the exception is Italy) can the fate of the president be decided by a simple majority (50 percent plus one vote) of the decision-makers involved. In all other legislature-dominant countries, at least one decision (impeachment or removal) requires that a super-majority, such as two-thirds or three-quarters of the decision-makers, must agree that the president should be impeached or removed. The mixed systems and those that require direct democracy, on the other hand, guard against abuse of the impeachment process by the legislature by involving other powers, i.e., those of the judiciary and the people themselves.

Why are impeachment procedures designed the way they are, making it difficult to remove sitting presidents? After reading this book, the reader should have no difficulty answering this question: impeachment is fundamentally a political process, prone to abuse. As seen in Tables 8-1 to 8-3, in virtually every country that specifies impeachment rules, presidential impeachment is a decision taken by the legislature. To be sure,

Table 8-3.
Constitutional Impeachment and Removal Provisions by Country: Other

Country (Year of Constitution)	Impeachment by (Majority Required)	Trial by (Majority Required)
Austria (1929)	LH ($^2/_3$ of at least $^1/_2$ members present)	Referendum
Estonia (1992)	(Not specified)	(Not specified)
Ethiopia (1995)	(Not specified)	(Not specified)
Fiji (1990)	Special Tribunal (not specified)	Great Council of Chiefs (not specified)
Guinea-Bissau (1984)	(Not specified)	(Not specified)
Iceland (1944)	UL ($^3/_4$ members)	Plebiscite
Mozambique (1990)	(Not specified)	(Not specified)
Sao Tome and Principe (1990)	(Not specified)	(Not specified)
Taiwan (1947)	Control Yuan (special, Senate-like body) ($^2/_3$ members)	UL ($^2/_3$ members)
Togo (1992)	(Not specified)	(Not specified)
Vanuatu (1980)	(Not specified)	Special Legislative Body ($^2/_3$ of $^3/_4$ members present, including $^3/_4$ of Chairs of Local Government Councils)

impeachment is a judicial, not legislative, function, but it is nonetheless performed by legislators or elected politicians. Hence, impeachment is a political process, and in many countries the trial that follows impeachment is also handled by the legislature, making the process more political than in cases where the judiciary handles the trial. If we accept the fact that impeachment is a political process (as the U.S. founding fathers certainly did), it is little wonder that constitutions are written to prevent the abuse of the procedure.

Table 8-4 is a rough measure of the difficulty imposed by constitutions in impeaching and removing presidents. Drawing on data presented in Tables 8-1 through 8-3, this table is a matrix measuring the voting rule required to impeach and remove the president (the X-axis) by the number

Table 8-4.
Constitutional Impeachment and Removal Provisions: Institutions by Majorities Required*

	Minority, Simple or Super Majority	Simple Majority, Simple Majority	Simple Majority, Super Majority (or converse)	Super Majority, Super Majority
One Institution	3	3	5	0
Two Institutions	3	8	39	20
> Two Institutions	0	2	4	4

* N=91: Cases were dropped if there were no constitutional provisions for impeachment. "Referendum" or "plebiscite" were coded as one institution. A joint session of a bicameral legislature was coded as two institutions. If no majority was specified the case was coded as simple majority. If there is only one phase specified, the "one institution" row is used. India and Ireland could be coded as one or two institutions; it is coded as two.

of institutions involved in the impeachment and removal process (the Y-axis). As one moves down the rows and to the right, veto points (places at which the process may be halted) increase as does the voting threshold required to move the process forward; thus, impeachment becomes increasingly more difficult.

Despite constitutional hurdles, however, seven presidents faced a serious threat of impeachment in the past decade. Some were impeached, some were removed, and others survived—some of these with impunity. What led to these different results? Two closely related factors exerted strong influence on every case studied in this book: legislative support for the president and public opinion.

LEGISLATURES AND PRESIDENTS

The legislature is the single most important actor in deciding the fate of the president. Even in cases where presidents were removed by means other than impeachment (the Philippines and Venezuela), the legislature prompted popular protest that resulted in the removal of the president (Philippines) or used its constitutional authority to declare the presidency vacant (Venezuela). In every country it is the legislature that decides whether the president will be impeached or not. Without the consent of the legislature, no attempt to impeach a president can go beyond accusing the president of an impeachable offense. As Victor Hinojosa and

Aníbal Pérez-Liñán aptly describe, a legislature that tries to protect a president from impeachment and removal constitutes a "legislative shield" for the president. On the other hand, a legislature eager to be rid of a president functions quite the opposite, placing the president *in front* of that shield while hiding behind it, in hopes that the angry masses will stone the president, not noticing or caring who put him in such a position.

The authors in this book are interested precisely in this shield, or particularly, the legislators who decide whether or not to form the shield. Why do some presidents succeed in gaining support from enough legislators to prevent impeachment (or removal by impeachment), while others fail to do so? How do legislators decide whether or not to support the president? We have provided answers for specific cases, taking into account country-specific factors, but there are some factors common to all. These include (1) the voting threshold for impeachment (and removal); (2) the partisan composition of the legislative body that decides impeachment (and removal); (3) presidential patronage; and (4) public opinion.

Voting Threshold

The voting threshold for impeachment and removal differ greatly among the cases presented. The most unique is in the Philippines, where the votes of a mere one-third of the members of the House can impeach the president. Such a low threshold was unthinkable for framers of constitutions who were concerned about weak presidents, but it was a reasonable threshold for framers of the Philippine constitution, who were concerned, after 15 years of dictatorship, about strong presidents. This voting rule was crucial in bringing about the fall of President Estrada; recall that only 87 out of 220 legislators signed the petition for impeachment. If impeachment required even a simple majority, it would not have passed the House, the president would not have been investigated, and it is highly unlikely that he would have been removed from office. In virtually all other cases, impeachment requires at least a simple majority vote, and sometimes a super-majority vote. Needless to say, the more votes needed to impeach, the harder to impeach, but the partisan composition of the legislature is equally if not more important in deciding the fate of the president.

The Partisan Composition of the Legislature

If the president's party holds enough seats in the legislature, impeachment and removal become highly unlikely, although not impossible if evidence of grave offenses exists and has been brought to light. Conversely, if his party is not in control of the legislature, there are fewer incentives to shield the president, other things being equal. This argument is best supported by the U.S. cases (and least supported by the Russian case, since Yeltsin had no formal relation with any party in legislature). As Bill Perkins demonstrates in his survey of impeachment attempts throughout U.S. history, presidents whose party controlled the House have never been subjected to an impeachment vote. In other words, only presidents whose party did not control the House of Representatives faced serious threats of impeachment. None of the other countries analyzed in this book has a two-party system like the U.S., but Colombia was almost a two-party system when the narco-dollar scandal hit President Samper. Here, too, the president was not subjected to an impeachment vote. In fact, the Colombian House went even further, preventing future investigation on the subject.

As Hinojosa and Pérez-Liñán point out, however, Samper could not count on the unconditional support of all of his copartisans. In the Philippines, too, some of the president's copartisans supported impeachment. Without their support, impeachment of Estrada would not have happened. Similarly, Zafy in Madagascar and Collor in Brazil were impeached, even though it takes two-thirds of legislators' votes in each country, and even though each president had, at the time of parliamentary elections, a majority supporting him; in both cases, a president was impeached because a substantial portion of the governing coalition turned against him. These instances suggest that, at least in the analysis of non-U.S. cases, partisan composition of the legislature by itself does not serve well as a predictor of impeachment. We need to look beyond the number of legislators per party and look at individual legislators' incentives in order to fully understand the impeachment process. One factor, of course, is how parties can constrain individual legislators. Perhaps due to ideological cohesion, the U.S. cases show that members of each party generally oppose each other in voting. In Venezuela, too, party discipline was quite strong, so strong that even the vote on impeachment was not roll call: the leader of each party spoke as the representative of all other party members.

In the rest of the countries studied, parties do not have as strong a hold on legislators as the U.S. or Venezuelan parties seem to have. Where the party system is less institutionalized and remains fluid, as is the case in the Philippines, Russia, Madagascar, and Brazil, most parties lack ideological cohesion, disciplinary measures, or both. Parties cannot effectively punish legislators for defying the party line or defecting to another party. In Colombia, party switching between the two major parties is unheard of, but the two parties lack ideological cohesion and disciplinary measures. Given that parties have little if any influence on legislators' decisions on impeachment, what, then, does? Presidential patronage is one answer common among the case studies of the Philippines, Colombia, and, perhaps to a lesser extent, Russia and Brazil.

Presidential Patronage

Throughout the case studies, it has become clear that presidential patronage is one of the key elements in legislators' decisions to shield or to impeach the president. Presidential patronage can range from funding for pork barrel projects to cabinet posts and other positions at the national or local levels of government. How much patronage a president can distribute differs across countries and across constitutions; some constitutions give presidents more control over budgets and appointments than others. But a constitution is not the only factor that determines the patronage power of a president; the power balance between a president and the legislature influences actual (as opposed to theoretical) presidential patronage power. Patronage is an important political tool for a president in any political system, but in countries where political parties lack cohesion and discipline, it is perhaps the single most important tool a president has. Unable to rely on party leaders to deliver votes to prevent impeachment (and/or removal), presidents must cultivate loyalty from individual legislators. Patronage is the most direct and immediate way of securing loyalty in the midst of an impeachment crisis, and the country analyses provide ample evidence of the use of, or consideration of, presidential patronage during such crises.

Yuko Kasuya, in her analysis of the Philippines case, and Hinojosa and Pérez-Liñán in the Colombian case, demonstrate that presidential patronage was a major consideration for a significant number of legislators when deciding whether or not to support the president. Kasuya shows that among legislators who belonged to the president's party, those who had belonged the longest (and thus, by inference, had received more patronage from the president) and those who did not face their term limitation (and thus expected to receive more patronage in the future) tended to vote against impeachment. Hinojosa and Pérez-Liñán show that legislators who had received above-average pork barrel funding tended to vote in favor of the president. They add, however, that this tendency was not always observed among the president's party members. Jody Baumgartner, in his analysis of the Russian case, and Naoko Kada, in the Brazilian case, also recognize the importance of presidential patronage as a potential tool to gain support from legislators. Baumgartner suggests that both the pro-government party Our Home is Russia, and the Liberal Democratic Party that originally supported impeachment, voted against it, likely because of expected presidential patronage. In Brazil, on the other hand, Kada argues that promises of presidential patronage were not sufficient to reverse the tide demanding impeachment of the president.

Aside from the analysis of Colombian pork barrel funding, the case studies do not draw a direct link between patronage and legislators' votes during the impeachment crises. This is due mainly to the fact that it is difficult to determine what constitutes presidential patronage, how much

influence the president has on decisions of pork barrel funding and government appointments, and how much of legislators' support for the
president is attributable to patronage. True, it is difficult to quantify the
influence of presidential patronage on legislators pondering presidential
impeachment. Despite this difficulty, the importance of patronage in politics in these countries has been documented by numerous studies by
country experts, and it is highly likely that patronage played an important
role in impeachment crises as well.

This said, in studying Brazil's impeachment and removal of Collor,
Kada argued (both here and elsewhere) that expectations of patronage did
not prove effective in obtaining legislative support, and instead promises
of presidential patronage became a risk for some legislators.[4] This was primarily because public opinion had turned so overwhelmingly against
Collor that any association with him became a negative asset for politicians in Brazil. Yet scholars of Brazilian politics have long recognized the
power of patronage in that country. How did public opinion manage to
influence Brazilian politics in this instance?

PUBLIC OPINION AND PRESIDENTS

The Preconditioning Effect of Public Opinion

Generally speaking, public opinion matters in two ways. First, it might
alter the willingness of legislators to attack a president. This may be called
the preconditioning effect of public opinion *prior to impeachment proceedings*, in that it preconditions legislators' willingness to pursue impeachment. For example, in Venezuela, President Pérez suffered a rapid decline
in popularity, and, after two coup attempts, the voices demanding presidential exit grew increasingly louder, even within the president's own
party. Faced with a president who steadfastly rejected the idea of resignation, and given the high popularity of coup leaders (and fearing the possibility of another coup attempt), supporting presidential impeachment
became a political asset for legislators. In general, we can say that the
lower the popularity of a president, the greater the incentives for legislators to strike at him.

Conversely, a popular president is much less likely to be the subject of
impeachment proceedings. Of course, as the case of President Clinton in
the U.S. illustrates, public opinion cannot shield a president from
impeachment. As the case of President Samper in Colombia demonstrates, however, politicians are reluctant to run the risk of losing electoral
support by trying to impeach a popular president. This reluctance is war-
ranted; some U.S. Representatives who voted for Clinton's impeachment
lost their re-election bids after his impeachment, in part due to citizen
groups (who had opposed impeachment) who mobilized voters to vote
against them.[5]

The Resolution Effect of Public Opinion

Second, public opinion may change the end result of impeachment proceedings. This may be called the resolution effect, for public opinion at the time of deciding the president's fate greatly influences actions by legislators. This differs from the preconditioning effect in that there is real potential for change in public opinion during impeachment proceedings. If the public becomes convinced that a previously popular president has committed a grave offense, then it is possible that they will begin to demand impeachment. The cases of Philippine's President Estrada and Brazil's President Collor illustrate this point well. As Kasuya reports, the Senate investigation of Estrada gathered enough evidence to convince the public of his wrong-doing before it decided not to seek more information. Even though Estrada was still popular in the countryside, urban masses began to demand his ouster, and in the end achieved it. In Brazil, too, it was shown that public opinion began to support impeachment only after the legislative investigation uncovered evidence of presidential corruption and the media reported this information.

Conversely, if investigation of an unpopular president yields no evidence of an impeachable offense, public opinion in favor of impeachment might decline, as Yeltsin's case in Russia demonstrates. According to Baumgartner, although Yeltsin's popularity was already quite low (around 20 percent) at the start of impeachment proceedings, public opinion was never mobilized to support impeachment. This is because the investigation of the president did not lead to any proof of wrong-doing that could trigger an unfavorable public response, in stark contrast to the investigations of Estrada and Collor. It can probably be concluded that the resolution effect of public opinion is conditioned by the availability of information that mobilizes the public toward impeachment.

The Relative Importance of Public Opinion

The degree to which both the preconditioning and resolution effects of public opinion can affect legislative behavior is limited, however, by the timing of the impeachment process and by the degree of influence of factors other than public opinion. Of particular importance seems to be the timing of elections. All other things being equal, if legislators must vote on impeachment immediately prior to an election (whether at the national or local level), the weight of public opinion is felt much more strongly than if the vote happens just after an election. This is why Brazilian legislators, with municipal elections held days after the impeachment vote, paid so much attention to public opinion. Conversely, in the U.S., the impeachment vote against the popular President Clinton occurred after the mid-term election, thus granting legislators some measure of electoral immunity.

Aside from the timing of elections, the effect of public opinion on legislators also depends on what other factors influence legislative behavior. While party and president are the two main sources of influence over legislators, other sources, such as regional bosses and family members, may also come into play. The influence of each source in relation to others varies between countries, political systems, and individuals within a political system. For example, Kasuya argues that what matters for the re-election of legislators in the Philippines is pork, not public opinion. If voter turnout is low and only the votes of party loyalists matter, public opinion will have less effect than where voter turnout is high, and where public opinion is better reflected in election results. Whatever the reasons for politicians' lack of responsiveness to public opinion, its effect is destabilizing when the distance grows between what the public wants and what politicians deliver. When public opinion seems to have little effect on the behavior of legislators, as Kasuya illustrates in her analysis of the Philippines, the masses might (and did) resort to extra-parliamentary means to remove a president.

THE LIMITATIONS OF IMPEACHMENT AS A CHECK ON THE EXECUTIVE

Kada's chapter assesses the effectiveness of impeachment mechanisms as a check against a particular type of presidential abuse of power: corruption. Both Collor in Brazil and Pérez in Venezuela were accused of corruption and removed from office, but, Kada points out, neither was required to return their ill-gotten gains. In Collor's case, the Supreme Court determined that prosecutors failed to present proof of a direct link between Collor's sudden wealth and his corrupt behavior. In Pérez's case, the president was removed without being convicted, and when the trial finally came to an end, the Supreme Court dropped the charge of embezzlement for lack of proof. Although the political costs of impeachment and removal should not be underestimated, these cases cast doubt on the effectiveness of impeachment mechanisms in preventing future corruption by presidents. If the only punishment imposed is loss of office (as was the case for Collor, and in most other countries as well), individuals seeking presidential office for personal enrichment may not be deterred. Conversely, if a president may be subjected to impeachment and removal even when solid proof of an abuse of power is lacking (as was the case for Pérez), presidents may be tempted to accumulate personal wealth in office while the opportunity exists.

The effect of impeachment proceedings on other presidents studied is also limited. While Estrada was removed from office, the extra-constitutional manner of his removal left room for him to question the new government's constitutionality and to retain popularity among his supporters.

President Samper survived in office, but his presidency after the impeachment crisis is regarded as a weak one, relying on patronage distribution and marked by a failure to revive the Colombian economy. In Russia, opposition legislators supported impeachment attempts not so much to remove the president but rather to protest Yeltsin's reform efforts, and, in the 1998–99 case, to protect themselves from dissolution of the lower house.

Despite these limitations and possible negative consequences, impeachment remains the single mechanism by which a president who abuses power may be constitutionally removed from office. To be sure, in some countries presidents can be removed using other means: as Kada explains, Venezuelan president Pérez was not removed because his impeachment was confirmed, but because the Senate declared the presidency vacant. Many other constitutions have provisions regarding the absence and illnesses of the chief executive that might lead to removal from office. However, by attributing removal to factors beyond the control of the president in question, these provisions do not allow, strictly speaking, for the punishment of an abuse of power. Furthermore, not all constitutions have these provisions, and without them, impeachment remains the only constitutional means of presidential removal. Considering that many of the new presidential democracies are still in their infancy, and that in many, military coups were a standard method for the removal of presidents, it could be argued that we should welcome impeachment attempts as the expression of efforts to maintain democratic regimes.

It is precisely because impeachment might replace coups that we need to pay closer attention to how these processes are being carried out. While it is undeniable that impeachment is far more preferable to coups because the latter too often carries the use of violence, impeachment carries the risk of being used to impose the will of a momentary majority, much as coups frequently are. Already, as the title of Philip Allen's chapter indicates, the notion of impeachment as a replacement for coups is spreading: in Madagascar the impeached president criticized his impeachment (perhaps naturally) as a "parliamentary coup." Three years earlier, Pérez in Venezuela voiced the same criticism regarding his removal. In both of these cases a legislative majority opposing the president formed over a period of about three years as disillusionment with the president grew. Zafy's incompetence in economic management and his high-handed style alienated him from the parliament; Pérez's imposition of an economic austerity program and its lack of immediate and positive results led to his fall.

The problem with impeachment becoming a constitutional coup is that impeachment in these cases undermines not only individual presidents, but the institution of the presidency as well. For example, a legislative majority that opposes the president may rapidly emerge if a president tries to implement policies that are unpopular, simply because they bring short-term pain for long-term gain. If a president does not implement such policies for fear of impeachment, or if a president is impeached because he tried to implement such policies, then the meaning of an independent presidency is lost. One could even argue that impeachment is worse than coups in that while coups are clearly counter to democratic principles, impeachment is not, but lends a legal cloak to the protagonists who attempt to topple a president. This volume is an attempt to reveal what lies beneath the legal cloak.

AREAS FOR FURTHER RESEARCH

The collective message here is that impeachment processes are inherently political, and thus merit more scholarly attention than political scientists have traditionally been willing to spare. The effectiveness of impeachment mechanisms as a check on executive power is limited. This will not, however, prevent future attempts at impeaching chief executives. This final section suggests some exciting and intriguing areas for further research into presidential impeachment.

Presidents as Actors

Throughout this volume the authors focus on legislators as the prime actors in impeachment processes, based on the common belief that impeachment is a political process. In so doing, however, presidents were in most cases relegated to a minor role, as the subject (or victim?) of impeachment efforts. Exceptions are Baumgartner's analysis of Russia, where the president gave a twist to the impeachment proceedings by linking it to possible dissolution of the parliament, and Allen's analysis of Madagascar, which vividly portrays the interaction between a president and the assembly. But it is difficult to imagine that presidents in other cases simply waited passively for the legislature to make its decisions. Far more likely is that they tried to influence the impeachment proceedings in many ways, via legal action, political negotiations with legislators and party leaders, and so on.[6] The analysis of presidential patronage sheds some light on presidents as actors during the impeachment crises, but even here, we lack clear proof of active engagement on the part of the presidents in question.

The importance of conceptualizing presidents as actors in impeachment processes is best shown in a game tree (see Figure 8-1).

The impeachment process is described here as a game between the president and the legislature and/or the judiciary. Our description of the impeachment process in the introductory chapter shows only the stages where the legislature or the judiciary makes decisions about the president's fate, but at every stage the president has a choice between resignation and

Figure 8-1. Presidential Impeachment as a Multi-stage Game

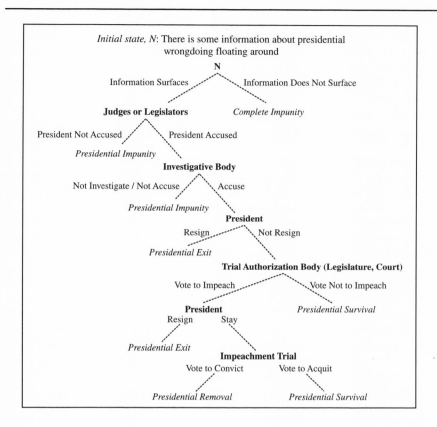

staying in office. A president who decides to stay in office can fight the legislative decision (by challenging it in the courts, by pressuring legislators to change their votes in the next stage, or even self-coup), or be inactive (by simply following legislative decisions). Even though the tree is simplified and does not show the results of challenges to impeachment processes, in reality these challenges can alter the course of the impeachment process. For this reason, in order to obtain a comprehensive understanding of impeachment processes, scholars need to look at presidents as actors, not only as the subject, of these processes.

The game tree is also useful in understanding presidential decision-making during an impeachment crisis. By assigning subjective probabilities and payoffs to each possible end result in the game, it helps us understand why presidents choose a certain option at a certain stage of the process. For example, given that impeachment and even removal was highly likely, and given that he could have become the first president to be removed by Congress for an impeachable offense, it is easy to understand why Nixon preferred resignation at an early stage. Conversely, Pérez of Venezuela did not resign, and instead urged his copartisans to respect the Supreme Court decision, based on his prior belief that the Court would rule against impeachment.

Presidential Patronage

Patronage is a fascinating subject of study for political scientists, but a rigorous analysis requires a greater amount of fine-tuning of the concept. For example, as Kasuya points out, patronage considerations may be retrospective (what *has* the president done for me?) or prospective (what *will* the president do for me?). Which considerations weigh more heavily in legislators' minds? Patronage takes different forms: is pork barrel funding more effective than appointments to government posts in securing legislators' support? Legislators would also need to calculate how much patronage they could receive from the next president and take this into consideration in their decision to impeach (and remove) the president. Will the next president have an equal or greater amount of patronage powers as the current president? Will he modify who gets presidential patronage, and by how much? Will he give more to me than the current president does?

The chapters in this volume focus on the current president and his relationship with the legislators, but it is quite plausible that the consideration of "who comes next?" affected legislators' decisions whether to support the president and presidents' resolve to fight impeachment (this is very likely true of earlier cases in the U.S. as well, during the era of the political party machine). Kada has observed elsewhere that these considerations indeed prompted some presidents and legislators to fiercely oppose impeachment.[7] Where the current president has a distant relationship with the next president (such as when the vice president is from an opposition party), impeachment and removal of the president is likely to lead to a dramatic change in patronage distribution. In order to assess the influence of patronage, then, future studies would benefit from not only the analysis of patronage by the current president, but also of what and how much patronage the next-in-line might distribute.

The Role of Information

As discussed in the section on pubic opinion, the availability of credible information that a president committed a grave offense is crucial in moving public opinion in favor of impeachment. In the Philippines, the Senate's decision not to seek additional evidence of presidential wrong-doing after enough evidence had been collected to strongly suggest grave offenses on Estrada's part triggered the People Power II Movement that led to his ouster. In Brazil, public opinion shifted in favor of impeaching Collor after a congressional investigation unearthed evidence that he had received financial and material benefits from a friend who had (allegedly) extorted businesses based on his ties to the president. In Russia, on the other hand, a congressional investigation was unable to uncover new and shocking information to convince the public of the need for impeaching President Yeltsin. In Colombia, the investigation was criticized for lack of rigor, and the House voted to prohibit any future investigation to prevent further incriminating evidence from surfacing and affecting pubic opinion. Thus, availability of information seems to work in favor of those who seek impeachment; its unavailability generally seems to favor a president in the midst of an impeachment crisis.

This survey also illustrates that the availability of information is neither necessary nor sufficient to bring about impeachment in every case. In the cases of Clinton, Zafy, and Pérez, presidential foes accomplished impeachment without convincing the public that the presidents in question had committed impeachable offenses. In these cases, Perkins' argument that impeachment is a purely political, and not legal, process resonates most strongly. In the other four countries, however, there is strong evidence that information did matter.

If we accept the notion that information does matter in impeachment processes, a question naturally arises: where does this information come from? Who provides it, and when is information credible and when is it not? Hinojosa and Pérez-Liñán, and Baumgartner to a lesser extent, point to the crucial role of the media in impeachment processes; also, Kada has demonstrated that congressional investigative bodies control the flow of information to the public, generating or transmitting information in some cases while preventing information from being made public in others.[8] Of course, the media and the legislature are not the only generators or transmitters of information (see especially Kasuya's compelling account of the role of cellular telephones in the transmittal of information in the Philippines), nor do they necessarily produce the most important evidence against presidents, but they create the stages on which important information can be presented to the public. Therefore, to deepen our knowledge of impeachment processes, we need to understand how and why these actors decide to seek and present certain information to the public and withhold other information; this is probably a political question, and again reinforces the idea that presidential impeachment is a political process. On a different level, how different political systems and institutions create different propensities for generating and presenting information for or against presidents is another area that is ripe for research.

This list of areas for further research testifies to the fact that impeachment processes have indeed been understudied. It also means that there are opportunities for presidential scholars, that there are many interesting questions waiting to be investigated. We hope that we have made a modest beginning with this book.

Endnotes

ENDNOTES FOR CHAPTER 1

1. Richard A. Posner, *An Affair of State: The Investigation, Impeachment, and Trial of President Clinton* (Cambridge, MA: Harvard University, 2000, Chapter 6).

2. Matthew Soberg Shugart and John M. Carey, *Presidents and Assemblies: Constitutional Design and Electoral Dynamics* (Cambridge, UK: Cambridge University, 1992, p. 29); this is referred to, per Juan Linz, as the problem of "temporal rigidity"—(Juan J. Linz and Arturo Valenzuela, *The Failure of Presidential Democracy*, (Baltimore: Johns Hopkins University, 1994). In most countries presidents can be declared incapacitated, but this procedure is even rarer— less "institutionalized"—than impeachment.

3. Thirty-two of 46 countries in Europe now have some form of a presidency, as do many in Latin America (Kaare Strøm and Octavio Amorim Neto, "Duverger Revisited: Presidential Power in European Parliamentary Democracies," paper presented at the Annual Meeting of the American Political Science Association, Atlanta, GA, September 2–5, 1999); all countries of the former Soviet Union have displayed a "preference for presidentialism" as well (Gerald Easter, "Preference for Presidentialism: Postcommunist Regime Change in Russia and the NIS," *World Politics*, 1997, 49:184–211). See Shugart and Carey, *Presidents and Assemblies*, for a discussion of regime types.

4. This speaks to Juan Linz's argument that presidentialism is inherently a less stable regime form than parliamentarianism; see Linz and Valenzuela, *The Failure of Presidential Democracy*. Others take issue with this argument; see Shugart and Carey, *Presidents and Assemblies*.

5. This is a point well made by Aníbal Pérez Liñán ("Presidential Crises and Political Accountability in Latin America (1990–1997)," paper presented at the Annual Meeting of the Latin American Studies Association, September, 1998).

6. Ronald E. Pynn, ed., *Watergate and the American Political Process* (New York: Praeger, 1975).

7.   Mark J. Rozell and Clyde Wilcox, eds., *The Clinton Scandal and the Future of American Government* (Washington, DC: Georgetown University, 2000); Irwin L. Morris, *Votes, Money, and the Clinton Impeachment* (Boulder, CO: Westview, 2002).

8.   David J. Lanoue and Craig F. Emmert, "Voting in the Glare of the Spotlight: Representatives' Votes on the Impeachment of President Clinton" (*Polity*, 1999, 32(2):253–269) and Lawrence Rothenburg and Mitchell S. Sanders, "Lame-Duck Politics: Impending Departure and the Vote on Impeachment" (*Political Research Quarterly*, 2000, 53(3):523–536).

9.   Diane J. Heith, "*The Polls*: Polling for the Defense: The White House Public Opinion Apparatus and the Clinton Impeachment" (*Presidential Studies Quarterly*, 2000, 30(4):783–790) and Stanley A. Renshon, "*The Polls*: The Public's Response to the Clinton Scandals, Part 1: Inconsistent Theories, Contradictory Evidence" (*Presidential Studies Quarterly*, 2002, 32(1):169–184).

10. Lee Sigelman, Christopher J. Deering, and Burdett A. Loomis, "'Wading Knee Deep in Words, Words, Words': Senatorial Rhetoric in the Johnson and Clinton Impeachment Trials" (*Congress & The Presidency*, 2001, 28(2):120–139).

11. Terry Sullivan, "Impeachment Practice in the Era of Partisan Conflict" (*Congress & The Presidency*, 1998, 25(2):117–128).

12. For the Johnson impeachment, see David Miller Dewitt, *The Impeachment and Trial of Andrew Johnson, Seventeenth President of the United States* (New York: Macmillan, 1903); Milton Lomask, *Andrew Johnson: President on Trial* (New York: Farrar, Straus, 1960); Noel B. Gerson, *The Trial of Andrew Johnson* (Nashville: T. Nelson, 1977); Michael Les Benedict, "From Our Archives: A New Look at the Impeachment of Andrew Johnson" (*Political Science Quarterly*, 1998, 113(3):493–511); Michael Les Benedict, *The Impeachment and Trial of Andrew Johnson* (New York: Norton, 1999); and Chester G. Hearn, *The Impeachment of Andrew Johnson* (Jefferson, NC: McFarland & Co., 2000).

13. For Nixon's travails, see Bob Woodward and Carl Bernstein, *All the President's Men* (New York: Simon and Schuster, 1974); Bob Woodward and Carl Bernstein, *The Final Days* (New York: Simon and Schuster, 1976); Theodore H. White, *Breach of Faith: The Fall of Richard Nixon* (New York: Atheneum, 1975); J. Anthony Lukas, *Nightmare: The Underside of the Nixon Years* (New York: Viking Press, 1976); a more recent account, and one that is not uncontroversial can be found in Len Colodny and Robert Gettlin, *Silent Coup: The Removal of a President* (New York: St. Martin, 1991).

On the Clinton impeachment, see Nathan Aaseng, *The Impeachment of Bill Clinton* (San Diego, CA: Lucent Books, 2000); Peter Baker, *The Breach: Inside the Impeachment and Trial of William Jefferson Clinton* (New York: Scribner, 2000); David P. Schippers and Alan P. Henry, *Sellout: The Inside Story of President Clinton's Impeachment* (Washington, DC: Regnery, 2000); and Jeffrey Toobin, *A Vast Conspiracy: The Real Story of the Sex Scandal That Nearly Brought Down a President* (New York: Random House, 1999).

14. Michael J. Gerhardt, *The Federal Impeachment Process: A Constitutional and Historical Analysis*, 2nd edition (Chicago: University of Chicago, 2000) is considered a standard text; see also Posner, *An Affair of State*; Charles L. Black, Jr.,

Impeachment: A Handbook (New Haven, Yale University, 1974); and Emily Field Van Tassel and Paul Finkelman, *Impeachable Offenses: A Documentary History from 1787 to the Present* (Washington, D.C.: *Congressional Quarterly*, 1998).

15. Thanks to William Perkins for his contributions to this section.

16. Gerhardt, *The Federal Impeachment Process*, p. xii; emphasis added.

17. James Wilson, *The Works of James Wilson*, edited by James D. Andrews (Chicago: Callaghan and Company, 1896), p. 408, quoted in Gerhardt, *The Federal Impeachment Process*, p. 21.

18. The Kelley Memorandum was written by two constitutional lawyers, Bethel B. Kelley and Daniel G. Wylie, at Ford's request. *Legal Materials on Impeachment, House Committee Print*, Committee on the Judiciary, House of Representatives, 91st Congress, 2nd Session, August 11, 1970 (Washington, D.C., 1970). See Raoul Berger, *Impeachment: The Constitutional Problems* (Cambridge: Harvard University, 1973, p. 91). Thanks to Bill Perkins for this information.

19. Exceptions to this are mainly restricted to the contributors to this volume.

20. This section draws on Posner, *An Affair of State*, p. 96.

21. Black, *Impeachment*, p. 5.

22. See Peter Charles Hoffer and N. E. H. Hull, *Impeachment in America, 1635–1805*. Parts One and Two (New Haven, Yale University, 1984).

23. The impeachment of other public officials is beyond the scope of this work.

24. For a discussion of regime types and variations on institutional balance of power, see Shugart and Carey, *Presidents and Assemblies*.

25. The notion of the political effectiveness of a presidential scandal draws on Victor Hinojosa and Aníbal Pérez Liñán, "Presidential Survival and the Impeachment Process: Colombia in Comparative Perspective" (paper presented at the Annual Meeting of the Midwest Political Science Association, April 2002), pp. 6–8.

ENDNOTES FOR CHAPTER 2

* I wish to acknowledge the invaluable assistance of Garry Young whose contributions I regularly sought, particularly with revisions to the manuscript.

1. Alvin M. Josephy, Jr., *The Congress of the United States* (New York: American Heritage Publishing Co., 1975, p. 405).

2. *Congressional Quarterly*, (Washington, D.C., 1974, p. 16).

3. Alexander Hamilton, *Federalist 65*, in Alexander Hamilton, James Madison, and John Jay, *The Federalist* (New York: Barnes and Noble, 1961).

4. In 1952, impeachment petitions were sent to Congress and President Truman in regard to the Korean War (without a declaration by Congress), the dismissal of General Douglas MacArthur as Supreme Commander Far East, and the president's seizure of the steel mills. *Truman Papers*, Central Files OF 101 J, Harry S. Truman Library.

5. Michael Rubner, "The Reagan Administration, the 1973 War Powers Resolution, and the Invasion of Grenada," (*Political Science Quarterly* 100, 1986, p. 627). Congressman Theodore S. Weiss (D-NY) introduced a resolution calling for the impeachment of Reagan for "the high crime or misdemeanor of ordering the invasion of Grenada in violation of the Constitution of the United States, and other high crimes and misdemeanors ancillary thereto." U.S. Congress, House, 98th Cong., 1st sess., 27 October (*Congressional Record* 129:8779). Four years later, Congressman Henry B. Gonzalez (D-TX) sought to impeach Reagan for the president's involvement in the Iran-Contra affair. Gonzalez also wanted to remove George Bush in 1991 for United States involvement in the Persian Gulf War.

6. Wilson was charged with a "gross betrayal of public interest" for his advocacy of American entry into the League of Nations, Eisenhower for "tyrannical abuse" and "reckless exercise of discretionary power" for sending troops to Little Rock in 1957, and Lyndon Johnson for a perversion of the "public welfare" by pushing through his Great Society programs. No action was taken by Congress in any of these cases. Walter Ehrlich, *Presidential Impeachment: An American Dilemma* (Saint Charles, MO: Forum Press, 1974, p. 70).

7. During the 1795 House debate over funds needed to implement Jay's Treaty of Amity, Commerce, and Navigation with Great Britain, Edward Livingston (R-NY) requested from President Washington copies of all papers, documents, and instructions relating to the treaty. Uriah Tracey (F-CT) sarcastically asked Livingston if he wanted the papers for the impeachment of Washington or Jay, to which Livingston replied that would depend upon what the papers revealed. Josephy, *The Congress of the United States*, p. 104. Washington himself, however, noted in his refusal response to the House that he was not obliged to turn over information about the treaty but that he would be if the documents were needed for impeachment proceedings. John R. Labovitz, *Presidential Impeachment* (New Haven: Yale University, 1978, p. 211). Annals 4th Cong., 1st Sess., 760–762, 1796.

8. Gary C. Jacobson, "Impeachment Politics in the 1998 Congressional Elections," (*Political Science Quarterly* 114, 1999).

9. Jacobson, "Impeachment Politics." David Y. Thomas, "The Law of Impeachment in the United States," (*American Political Science Review* 2, May 1908, pp. 378–395).

10. Gerhardt, *The Federal Impeachment Process; Congressional Quarterly* (Washington, D.C., 1974, p.16).

11. These individuals included Randolph, James Madison, George Mason, William Paterson, Hugh Williamson, James Wilson, Benjamin Franklin, Elbridge Gerry, Rufus King, Gouverneur Morris, Alexander Hamilton, and Charles Pickney. Gerhardt, *The Federal Impeachment Process*, p. 4.

12. Benedict, *The Impeachment and Trial of Andrew Johnson*; Benedict, "A New Look at the Impeachment of Andrew Johnson."

13. Gerhardt, *The Federal Impeachment Process*, p. 7.

14. ibid., p. 8.

15. Max Ferrand, ed., *The Records of the Federal Convention of 1787* (New Haven: Yale University, 1911:2:61, 69; 493; 545; 545, respectively); quoted in Gerhardt, *The Federal Impeachment Process*, pp. 8–9.

16. Thomas, "The Law of Impeachment in the United States," p. 381. Swayne was charged with obtaining money from the United States by a false pretense, using without compensation the property of a railroad that was in the hands of a receiver appointed by himself, not residing within his district as required by law, and maliciously and unlawfully fining for contempt of court. The Senate acquitted Swayne on all 12 articles of impeachment.

17. Gerhardt, *The Federal Impeachment Process*, p. 103.

18. Leonard Lurie, *The Impeachment of Richard Nixon* (New York: Berkley Medallion Books, 1973, p. 9).

19. Berger, *Impeachment*, p. 91. Kelly and Wylie, *Legal Materials on Impeachment*.

20. Berger, *Impeachment*, p. 87. Cannon, Clarence, *Cannon's Precedents of the House of Representatives* (Washington D.C.: Government Printing Office, 1935).

21. Berger, *Impeachment*, p. 91. Kelly and Wylie, *Legal Materials on Impeachment*.

22. Thomas, "The Law of Impeachment," p. 393.

23. The Whig party was still being formed in 1834 and included National Republicans, bank men, state's righters, nullifiers, high tariff advocates, friends of internal improvements, and those who "abominated Jackson or his policies." Robert V. Remini, *Andrew Jackson and the Course of American Democracy, 1833–1845*. Vol. II. (New York: Harper and Row, 1984, p. 13). Another not insignificant difference between the Whigs and Jackson was institutional. "The one [the president] would rule by executive fiat, the other [Congress] by legislative mandate." Remini, *Andrew Jackson*, p. 138. Jackson's fifth and sixth years were not unified years. "In the House, on a test question, the administration could rely on a majority. In the Senate the opposition could command a majority, which was small, but safe and sufficient." A. S. Colyer, *Life and Times of Andrew Jackson* (Nashville, TN: Press of Marshall and Bruce Company, 1904, p. 672). It was this opposition that censured Jackson. In the House, one member did draw up a resolution proposing the impeachment of Jackson (Remini, *Andrew Jackson*, p. 150).

24. Josephy, *The Congress of the United States*, p. 184.

25. Interestingly, Senator Tyler had supported Andrew Jackson in 1828 and in 1832. He broke with Jackson over nullification and even voted for Jackson's censure in 1834. Tyler had then sided with the newly forming Whigs, who only a few years later attempted to impeach and remove him from the presidency.

26. "There was no excitement and little debate," reported Senator David Gardiner who witnessed the vote, "and this . . . foolish attempt will only result in increasing the number of the President's friends." Robert Seager II, *And Tyler Too* (New York: McGraw-Hill Book Company, Inc., 1963, p. 169).

27. "The fact that there was a movement to impeach Tyler simply for exercising the veto power demonstrated the Whigs' passionate commitment to curtailing the

powers of the executive and their frustration at failing to implement their plans even after having won a presidential election." Michael Nelson, ed., *Guide to the Presidency* 2nd ed., Vol. 1 (Washington, D.C.: *Congressional Quarterly*, 1996, p. 82).

28. The House particularly had problems with presidential influence in the passage of certain laws regarding states or territories, and abuses at certain public buildings and works. It was also concerned about the safety of federal installations given the recent attack upon Harper's Ferry by John Brown. *Congressional Globe*, 1860.

29. *New York Times*, March 6, 1860, p. 1.

30. Johnson is treated herein as a Democrat, as indeed he had always been. Abraham Lincoln chose the Union-devoted and thus politically attractive Civil War governor of eastern Tennessee to be his running mate in 1864 in his effort to stave off the seriously troubling candidacy of former Union General (and Democrat) George B. McClellan.

31. See Benedict, *The Impeachment and Trial of Andrew Johnson*, and Benedict, "A New Look at the Impeachment of Andrew Johnson."

32. The House had passed a resolution (84–47, again strictly partisan) on July 11, 1867, telling the Judiciary Committee to "take charge of testimony taken by the committee of the last Congress" (ICPSR, 40th House).

33. Louis W. Koenig, *The Chief Executive* (New York: Harcourt, Brace, Jovanovich, Inc., 1975).

34. Benedict, *The Impeachment and Trial of Andrew Johnson*.

35. Josephy, *The Congress of the United States*, p. 245.

36. Berger, *Impeachment*, p. 264.

37. The literature betrays a major discrepancy in the Democrat and Republican counts. It almost unanimously refers to seven Republicans joining the 12 Democrats in voting to acquit Johnson. Van Tassel and Finkelman, *Impeachable Offenses*; James E. Sefton, *Andrew Johnson and the Uses of Constitutional Power* (Boston: Little, Brown and Company, 1980); Labovitz, *Presidential Impeachment*; Josephy, *The Congress of the United States*; *Congressional Quarterly*, 1974; Ralph J. Roske, "The Seven Martyrs," *American Historical Review* (January 1959); Edmund G. Ross, *History of the Impeachment of Andrew Johnson* (New York: Ben Franklin, 1896). Benedict focuses upon the "seven recusants," but also classifies Republicans James Dixon (CT), James R. Doolittle (WI), and Daniel S. Norton (MN) as "Johnson Conservatives." Benedict, *The Impeachment and Trial of Andrew Johnson*. Keith Poole and Howard Rosenthal also identify them as Republicans even though their DW-NOMINATE scores are more in line with the Democrats (see *http://voteview.uh.edu/default_nomdata.htm*; also see Keith Poole and Howard Rosenthal, *Congress: A Political-Economic History of Roll Call Voting*, New York and Oxford: Oxford University, 1997). The seven Republicans who voted for acquittal, in addition to Dixon, Doolittle, and Norton, were Edmund G. Ross (KS), William P. Fessenden (ME), Joseph Fowler (TN), James W. Grimes (IA), John B. Henderson (MO), Lyman Trumbull (IL), and Peter G. Van Winkle (WV).

38. Nelson, *Guide to the Presidency*, p. 42.

39. *Congressional Quarterly* (1974), p. 6.

40. Gerhardt, *The Federal Impeachment Process*; *Congressional Quarterly* (1974).

41. Julian Hawthorne, *The History of the United States: From 1492 to 1920* (New York: P. F. Collier and Sons, 1920).

42. Johnson did ask for Senate approval of the removal, which was rejected.

43. See Benedict, *The Impeachment and Trial of Andrew Johnson*, and Benedict, "A New Look at the Impeachment of Andrew Johnson." See also Labovitz, *Presidential Impeachment*.

44. In the words of John R. Labovitz, Johnson's defense attorneys "all but turned the noncriminal definition of grounds for impeachment upside down: the president cannot be impeached except for a statutory crime, but that crime is not sufficient cause for his removal unless it involves conduct subversive of constitutional government and highly prejudicial to the public interest" (Labovitz, *Presidential Impeachment*, p. 89).

45. In approving an inquiry, the House also provided the committee with subpoena powers. *Washington Post*, February 7, 1974, p. 1.

46. Van Tassel and Finkelman, *Impeachable Offenses*, p. 259.

47. Nixon subsequently paid nearly a half million dollars to overcome tax liabilities after his lawyers conceded that the deed on the donation of his Vice Presidential papers to the National Archives had been backdated to circumvent a new law barring such deductions. Koenig, *The Chief Executive*.

48. In 1884 Democrat Grover Cleveland was first elected, but he brought only the House with him; the Senate remained in Republican hands. In 1968 Richard Nixon did not bring either body with him. The last time that had happened was in 1848, when Zachary Taylor (a Whig) won the presidency while the Democrats took both the House and the Senate.

49. Regression analysis proved to be problematic. Logit models incorporating "yes" or "no" impeachment votes by individual members of Congress as the dependent variable, and party and preference measures as independent variables, provided results that were not unexpected. Party measures were specified by identifying members and non-members of the president's party. Preference measures were specified by using DW-NOMINATE scores for every member during the given year of the vote (Poole and Rosenthal, *Congress*). In nearly every case the perfect and near-perfect separation in the sample points meant that maximum likelihood estimates could not even be computed. Because so many impeachment votes have resulted in partisan outcomes, it was also impossible to determine measures for correctly predicting outcomes. Furthermore, it was almost always impossible to disentangle party from preferences. In essence, Logit models performed poorly *exactly* because party and member preferences explain congressional voting behavior in cases of presidential impeachment.

50. The charges against Republican President Herbert Hoover were initiated by a Republican. In early 1933, the new Democratic House allowed two floor votes

on the impeachment of Hoover even though Hoover was a lame duck. Both votes were overwhelmingly against proceeding with impeachment of the beleaguered president.

51. This tabulation does not include House voting on each of the 11 articles of impeachment against President Johnson. Of the 11 votes, ten were completely partisan. To include them would inflate the percentage of 100%/100% voting and corrupt the table in favor of the Johnson scenario.

52. In the 410–4 vote against Nixon, all four "no" votes were cast by Republicans. *Washington Post*, February 7, 1974, p. 1.

53. Van Tassel and Finkelman, *Impeachable Offenses*, p. 226.

54. In addition to the perfect partisanship of the initial House Judiciary Committee vote against Clinton, on October 8, 1998, the House formally voted to proceed with impeachment. "House In A Partisan 258–176 Vote, Approves A Broad, Open-Ended Impeachment Inquiry," headlined the *New York Times* the next day. Thirty-one Democrats defected, joining the block-voting Republicans (*New York Times*, October 9, 1998, p. 1).

55. *Washington Post*, February 13, 1999, A29.

56. Poole and Rosenthal, *Congress*.

57. In the original House vote, Gary C. Jacobson has found that "opposition to impeachment among Democrats and independents in the electorate allowed most House Democrats to vote against holding impeachment hearings; only thirty-one sided with the unanimous Republicans in the 8 October vote to go forward. Most Democrats who did vote for hearings were, whatever their primary motives, acting prudently. . . . Support for the hearings was very high among Democrats seeking reelection in districts won by Bob Dole in 1996 but almost nonexistent in districts won by Clinton with a comfortable margin." (Jacobson, "Impeachment Politics," p. 48.) This was before the 1998 election. In the post-election votes on the four articles, however, "all but four Republicans voted for at least one article" and "only five Democrats voted for any of them" (ibid., p. 51). The election itself appears to have removed Democratic jitters in the ensuing House *and* Senate votes. For the first time since 1934, the president's party had actually gained seats in the House.

58. The Poole and Rosenthal scores place Collins, Abraham, Dewine, Roth, and Warner consecutively.

59. Kerry would not run for reelection in 2000, which perhaps explains why he felt that he could vote right along with his party in defense of Clinton.

60. The 1996 margin of victory variable was significant ($p<.05$), but only because of the natural connection between Democrats-no votes-Clinton states and Republicans-yes votes-non-Clinton states. That is, the lower the 1996 margin, the more likely the senator was a Republican and likely to vote for removal. Forty-one of the 55 "no" votes came from the 31 states Clinton had won in 1996, while 24 of the 45 "yes" votes came from the other 19 states. The ratios between no-yes votes in Clinton states (1.95) and between no-yes votes in non-Clinton states (.58) indicates that senators in the former were nearly twice as likely to vote for acquittal while those in the latter were nearly twice as

likely to vote for removal. Also, all 14 Democrats up for reelection in 2000 voted for acquittal while 15 of 19 Republicans up for reelection in 2000 voted for removal. The only relationship between party and margin of 1996 vote in the second Clinton Senate vote is that Democrats tended to come from states the president had won by an average of 11% and Republicans tended to come from states the president had *won* by an average of 6%—though they still largely voted against him in trial. (The four who voted for him came from states with an average 1996 margin of 22.25%, while the other 15 came from states with an average 1996 margin of 1.67%).

Reelection concerns were also not significant in the Johnson Senate case, although the test is dramatically different in that senators at that time were elected by state legislatures. For various reasons, 15 members of the 40th Senate would not be present in the 41st Senate. Non-returners would include three of the Republican defectors (Dixon, Henderson, and Van Winkle), four Democrats (Hendricks, Johnson, Buckalow, and Patterson), and five Republicans—including Benjamin Wade himself, whose candidacy for renomination was unsuccessful in the Ohio legislature. The irony is extraordinary; Wade, who was one lone senator's vote away from becoming president, did not even return to the Senate. In addition, in 1874 the Tennessee legislature sent Johnson to the Senate where he gave just one speech in which he vilified those who had tried to remove him from office six years before. He died shortly thereafter. David C. Whitney, *The American Presidents*, 4th edition (Garden City, NY: Doubleday, 1978).

61. Posner, *An Affair of State*, pp. 101–102.

62. *Congressional Quarterly*, 1974, p. 20.

63. Gerson, *The Trial of Andrew Johnson*.

64. Ehrlich, *Presidential Impeachment*, p. 67.

ENDNOTES FOR CHAPTER 3

1. For example, the *Time* magazine correspondent reported the People Power II as "mob rule." See Anthony Spaeth, "Oops, We Did It Again" (*Time*, January 29, 2001).

2. For example, former presidents Corazon Aquino and Fidel Ramos both cautioned during the 16th anniversary of People Power I that Filipinos "should refrain from taking to the streets too often to topple unpopular leaders" (*Philippine Daily Inquirer*, February 25, 2002).

3. Journalistic accounts of Estrada's removal include Cecilio T. Arillo, *Power Grab! The Story Behind the Jan. 20, 2001 EDSA People Power 2 Conspiracy that Swept Vice President Gloria Macapagal Arroyo to Power* (Metro Manila: CTA Research & Publishing, 2001), Amando Doronila, *The Fall of Joseph Estrada: The Inside Story* (Pasig and Makati: Anvil Publishing and *Philippine Daily Inquirer*, 2001), Greg Hutchinson and Ellen Tordesillas, *Hot Money, Warm Bodies: The Downfall of President Joseph Estrada* (Manila: Anvil, 2001), Oscar S. Villadolid and Alice Colet Villadolid, *The Impeachment of A President* (Metro Manila: Jose

Antonio Pavia, Art Angel Printshop, 2001). Among these, Doronila's is the most comprehensive and informative.

4. Constitutional Convention, *The Record of the Constitutional Convention: Volume II* (Manila: Government Printing Office, 1986, p. 279).

5. See Article 9, Section 2 of the 1935 Constitution. Under the 1973 Constitution, only one-fifth of the National Assembly (*Batasang Pambansa*) members' support was needed to initiate impeachment (see The 1973 Constitution, Article 13, Section 3). I have been unable to find any literature that mentions why the requirement was set so low, but my speculation is that the 1973 Constitution was practically written by Marcos himself. By setting the low impeach requirement, he may have wanted, on the one hand, to claim that his martial law regime was "democratic," as he repeated in many of his political discourses. On the other hand, he included a countermeasure so that he could avoid being impeached in practice. The 1973 Constitution adopts a semi-presidential form of government, in which the president had the power to resolve the *Batasang*. Thus Marcos, as the president, could influence the *Batasang* members by the threat of dissolution, because legislators usually loathe another costly election. Marcos in reality faced an impeachment move in 1984 but it did not go through.

6. Constitutional Convention, *The Record of the Constitutional Convention*, p. 374.

7. Arturo M. Tolentino, *Voice of Dissent* (Quezon City: Phoenix Publishing, 1990, p. 325).

8. See Solita Monsod, "Mediocre by Empirical Findings," in Thelma Sison San Juan, ed., *People Power II: Lessons and Hopes* (Manila: ABS-CBN Publishing, 2001).

9. They were the Bishops-Businessmen's Conference, the Financial Executives Institute of the Philippines, the Makati Business Club, and the Management Association of the Philippines.

10. Metro Manila is the colloquial of the official term, the National Capital Region, which includes the following cities and municipalities; Caloocan, Las Piñas, Makati, Malabon, Mandaluyong, Manila, Marikina, Muntinlupa, Navotas, Parañaque, Pasay, Pasig, Pateros, San Juan, Taguig, and Valenzuela. According to the 2000 national census, it had 9.9 million inhabitants while the total national population was 76.5 million.

11. The three House members were Heherson Alvarez of *Lakas*, the main opposition party, Ernesto Herrera of Estrada's party LAMP, and Michael Defensor of the Liberal Party.

12. The 1987 Constitution provides that 20 percent of House seats should be elected in proportion to the votes received by parties. The rest are elected from single-member legislative districts by plurality vote (Article 6, Sections 7 and 8).

13. Isagani de Castro, "Congress Impeachment" in Thelma Sison San Juan, ed., *People Power II*, p. 23.

14. Doronila, *The Fall of Joseph Estrada*, p. 98.

15. The House of the Representatives, "Minutes of the Committee on Justice" (November 6, 2000). The House rule on impeachment says that "Impeachment shall be initiated only by a verified complaint for impeachment filed by any member of the House of Representatives or by any citizen upon a resolution of endorsement by any Member thereof or by a verified complaint or resolution of impeachment filed by at least one-third of all the Members of the House" (see "Rules of Procedure in Impeachment Proceedings of the House of Representatives of the Philippines," Rule 2, Section 2, 1995). During the committee meeting, 87 copies of the Resolution of Endorsement signed by House members were submitted together with the Complaint of Impeachment, and these copies were considered sufficient to fulfill the required procedure.

16. House of Representatives, *Journal of the House of Representatives: Journal No. 36* (November 13, 2000). Later, some House members questioned the legitimacy of Villar's handling of the situation, but no legal action to repeal the House's impeachment decision followed.

17. See, for example, Carl H. Landé, *Leaders, Factions and Parties: The Structure of Philippine Politics, Monograph Series No. 6* (New Haven: Yale University Southeast Asian Studies Program, 1965), and Yuko Kasuya, *The Presidential Connection: Parties and Party Systems in the Philippines* (unpublished doctoral dissertation, La Jolla, CA: University of California, n.d.).

18. For example, Manuel Villar, who became the Speaker of the 11th Congress, was elected under Lakas' banner and switched to LAMP shortly after the 1998 election. Villar, a newcomer to LAMP, was elected as Speaker largely because Estrada exhibited his support for Villar in front of other House members in various occasions after the election (author's interview with Representative Rolex Suplico, November 16, 1999).

19. In the unwritten practice of the Philippine House of Representatives, the "majority" refers to those members who voted for the winning Speaker candidate regardless of party affiliation. Thus, even a member of the "opposition party," namely one who does not belong to the incumbent president's party, can become a majority member as long as he votes for the winning candidate for Speaker (author's interview with Representative Rodolfo Bacani, November 26, 1999).

20. *Philippine Daily Inquirer*, (October 20, 2000), and *Philippine Free Press* (October 28, 2000, p. 29).

21. David Mayhew, *Congress: The Electoral Connection* (New Haven: Yale University, 1974).

22. For the influence of constituency preference over the members of the U.S. House of Representatives, see Marvin Overby, "Assessing Constituency Influence: Congressional Voting on the Nuclear Freezone, 1982–83" (*Legislative Studies Quarterly*, 1991, 16:297–312), and Eileen Lorenzi McDonagh, "Constituency Influence on House Roll-Call Votes in the Progressive Era 1913–1915 (*Legislative Studies Quarterly*, 1993, 18:185–210). For Clinton impeachment case, see Lanoue and Emmert, "Voting in the Glare of the Spotlight."

23. Yuko Kasuya, "Patronage of the Past and Future: Legislators' Decision to Impeach President Estrada of the Philippines" (paper presented at the Midwest Political Science Association National Annual Conference, Chicago, April 25–28, 2002).

24. I counted candidates who were nominated from LAMMP, and from the parties that composed LAMMP, as those who run under LAMMP. There were 68 LAMMP candidates who won the 1998 House election, but three later changed their party affiliation: Representatives Arroyo and Jalosjos became independent members, and Herrera switched to *Lakas*.

25. Kasuya, "Patronage of the Past and Future," p. 23.

26. Those departing House LAMP members who run for other levels of offices (e.g., senatorial, gubernatorial, mayoral positions) may value the future presidential patronage as important as continuing members, thus this argument does not apply for this type of departing members.

27. Kasuya, "Patronage of the Past and Future," p. 23.

28. The Philippine Senate has 24 seats. There were two vacancies at the time of trial.

29. They were Senators Rodolfo Biazon, Nikki Coseteng, Franklin Drilon, and Ramon Magsaysay, Jr.

30. Senator Robert Barbers was absent; thus only 21 votes were counted.

31. The prosecution panel was composed of 11 House members headed by the minority floor leader Feliciano Belmonte, Jr. They were appointed by the House of Representatives during the November 13 session that approved the impeachment of Estrada.

32. Transparent and Accountable Government, "Estrada on Trial: Chronology of Events" (online at *http://tag.org.ph/whatsnew/2000/impeachupd_chronology_oct00.htm*).

33. See Doronila, *The Fall of Joseph Estrada*, Chapter 14, and Manuel Mogato, "At 4 P.M. the President Falls," in Thelma Sison San Juan, ed., *People Power II*.

34. Doronila, *The Fall of Joseph Estrada*, p. 212.

35. For a detailed account of the Supreme Court decision-making process and Arroyo's dealing with the Supreme Court, see Doronila, *The Fall of Joseph Estrada*, Chapter 16.

36. Estrada brought the issue of Arroyo government's legitimacy to the Supreme Court immediately after the People Power II. His petition can be summarized as follows. The 1987 Constitution provides that "In case of death, permanent disability, removal from office or resignation of the President, the Vice President shall become the President to serve the un-expired term" (Article 7, Section 8). Yet the manner in which he left the presidential palace on January 20 did not qualify as any of the four cases where the vice president could assume the office of the president. Thus Estrada claimed that Arroyo was only an acting president. Two months later, on March 2, the Supreme Court judges dismissed the Estrada petition by the vote of 13 to 0. To summarize the Supreme Court's opinion, Estrada's resignation was "implied" through the

circumstantial evidence of January 20. For the Supreme Court ruling, see "Decision: JOSEPH E. ESTRADA, petitioner, vs. GLORIA MACAPACAL-ARROYO, respondent. [G.R. No. 146738. March 2, 2001]."

37. "ABS-CBN/SWS Survey, February 2–7, 2001," in Social Weather Station, *From Juetenggate to People Power 2: The SWS Surveys of Public Opinion Presentation Material* (Metro Manila: Social Weather Station, 2001).

38. For the classification of Philippine social classes, see Cynthia B. Bautista, "Images of the Middle Class in Metro Manila" (*Public Policy: A University of the Philippines Quarterly*, (1999, 3–4: 1–37, p. 9).

39. In the survey conducted two months before the May 1998 election, 22% of the ABC (upper and middle) class respondents answered that they would vote for Lim, 17% for Roco, and 15% for Estrada. As for the D (lower) class, 28% would vote for Estrada, 12% each for Lim, Osmeña, and de Venecia. The E (lowest) class answered 35% for Estrada, 14% for Lim, and 12% for De Venecia and Osmeña respectively. See Social Weather Station, *The Social Weather Station Survey, June–July, 1998* (Metro Manila: Social Weather Station, 1998, p. 35).

40. I calculated this percentage based on the report in Social Weather Station, *The Social Weather Station Survey, June–July 1998*, p. 124. The base figures of my calculation are as follows: the sample population of this exit poll survey was composed of 9% from ABC (upper and middle) class, 71% from D (lower) class, and 26% from E (lowest) class. Among the ABC group, 26% voted for Roco, 23% for Estrada, and 20% for Lim. In the D class, 38% voted for Estrada, 16% for de Venecia, and 13% for Roco. In the E class, 48% voted for Estrada, 18% for de Venecia, and 14% for Osmeña.

41. *Philippine Free Press*, November 11, 2000, p. 8.

42. See "SWS Survey October 26–30, 2000" in Social Weather Station, *From Juetenggate to People Power 2*. I calculated the lower class's net agreement ratio of minus 20% by taking the average between the class D's minus 11% and the class E's minus 34% net agreement ratio.

43. However, it should be noted that the middle class's dislike of Estrada did not mean that they trusted Vice President Arroyo, who was the Constitutional heir in the event of Estrada's removal. The upper and middle class's evaluation of Arroyo was as low as that of the lower classes. About 66% of upper- and middle-class respondents answered that Arroyo's capability as the president would be the same as or worse than Estrada's, while the figure was about 70% for the lower classes. See "SWS Survey October 26–30, 2000," in Social Weather Station, *From Juetenggate to People Power 2*.

44. See "ABS-CBN/SWS Survey December 8–11, 2000, and January 6–9, 2001" in Social Weather Station, *From Juetenggate to People Power 2*. Details on the class breakdown are not available from the data source.

45. See the "ABS-CBN/SWS survey, January 6-9, 2001," in Social Weather Station, *From Juetenggate to People Power 2*.

46. See Cynthia B. Bautista, "The Middle Classes and People Power 2," in Thelma Sison San Juan, ed., *People Power II*, p. 189.

47. Other religious groups also joined the Catholic Church's lead. The National Council of Churches of the Philippines, the biggest alliance of non-Catholic churches in the country, and the Philippine Independent Church (*Iglesia Filipino Independente*), commonly known as the *Aglipayan* church, also directed their followers to street demonstrations. The religious groups that supported Estrada were *El Shaddai, Iglesia ni Cristo*, and the Jesus Miracle Crusade. For the political involvement of the Catholic Church, see Joselito B. Zulueta, "A Divided Hierarchy, Yet a Successful Revolution," in Thelma Sison San Juan, ed., *People Power II*.

48. Peachy Yamsuan, "The Church: A Moral Battle," in Thelma Sison San Juan, ed., *People Power II*, p. 41.

49. Yamsuan, "The Church," p. 51.

50. Transparent and Accountable Government, "Estrada on Trial: Chronology of Events."

51. Ging Deles, "Learning Along the Way," in Thelma Sison San Juan, ed., *People Power II*, p. 197. The ERM was composed of organizations that belong to the Sison block of the Community Party of the Philippines, and its leading organization was the New Nationalist Alliance (*Bagong Alyansang Makabayan* or BAYAN). Other organizations that were under ERM include the May First Movement (*Kilusang Mayo Uno* or KMU), and the Philippine Peasant Movement (*Kilusang Mangbubukid ng Pilipinas* or KMP). SANLAKAS is a breakaway group of the Sison-founded Communist Party, launched by Felimon Lagman. The non-communist Left and various community-work oriented NGOs formed the umbrella organization KOMPIL II. The original KOMPIL was formed in 1985 as the umbrella group for all anti-Marcos dictatorship forces. Among the three, SANLAKAS had the most left-leaning ideological position, and KOMPIL was the most moderate. During People Power II, these Leftist groups provided logistical support to the mass action, including secretarial work, marshal duties, and food solicitation and distribution.

52. They include, aside from MBC, the Bishops-Businessmen's Conference, the Financial Executives Institute of the Philippines, and the Management Association of the Philippines. For the involvement of these groups in the anti-Estrada movement, see Guillermo M Luz, "People Power 2: A Business Perspective," in Amando Doronila, ed., *Between Fires: Fifteen Perspectives on the Estrada Crisis* (Pasig and Makati: Anvil Publishing and *Philippine Daily Inquirer*, 2001).

53. See Satur Ocampo, "The Left Sensed It Early" in Thelma Sison San Juan, ed., *People Power II*.

54. "ABS-CBN/SWS Survey February 2–7, 2001" in Social Weather Station, *From Juetenggate to People Power 2*. It should be noted that there were other sources of information regarding the impeachment trial, such as radio and newspapers. However, their role was far less important than that of TV. In the same survey, 89% of respondents answered that the main source of information on the impeachment trial was TV, while 38% answered radio, and 13% newspapers.

55. "ABS-CBN/SWS Survey February 2–7, 2001" in Social Weather Station, *From Juetenggate to People Power 2*. Among the Metro Manila residents, 90% of ABC

(upper and middle) class answered unjust, while 77% of D (lower) class and 70% of E (lowest) class answered unjust.

56. As of mid-2001, there were 6.8 million cellular phone subscribers, and the majority of cellular users live in Metro Manila (*Philippine Daily Inquirer*, July 3, 2001). Metro Manila had a population of 9.9 million according to the 2000 census. These two in combination suggest that almost one in two Filipinos who lived in Metro Manila owned a cell phone around 2001. Furthermore, the upper- and middle-class population was about 30% to 40% in Metro Manila in the late 1990s (Bautista, "Images of the Middle Class in Metro Manila," p. 9). Considering the affordability of cellular phones, it is reasonable to assume that almost everyone in the upper and middle class in Metro Manila owned a cell phone.

57. Bautista, "The Middle Classes and People Power 2," p. 189. Data sources I consulted do not specify who the senders of such messages were.

58. Bautista, "The Middle Classes and People Power 2," p. 189.

59. Hutchinson and Tordesillas, *Hot Money, Warm Bodies*, p. 167.

60. "SWS Survey January 27, 2001" in Social Weather Station, *From Juetenggate to People Power 2*. This source states that 39% of AB class and 20% of C class personally joined any anti-Estrada rally during January 16 to 20.

61. "SWS January 27, 2001 Survey" in Social Weather Station, *From Juetenggate to People Power 2.*

62. According to University of the Philippines sociology professor Randolph David, during the anti-Marcos movements, the most "revolutionary" media were the videotapes sent from overseas Filipinos that recorded CNN's news coverage on the Philippines (*Business World*, January 30, 2001).

63. About the relationship between Philippine mass media and the government, see Luis V. Teodoro, "An Opportunity for Renewal," in Thelma Sison San Juan, ed., *People Power II*.

ENDNOTES FOR CHAPTER 4

* Authors' names are in alphabetical order. We are indebted to Jaime Bermúdez, Gustavo Gallón, Arlene Tickner, the Comisión Colombiana de Juristas, and the Universidad de los Andes for their support of our research in Bogotá. The Pastrana administration authorized the use of survey data collected by Napoleón Franco y Asociados for the Colombian government during 1994–98. Jorge Londoño (Gallup) and Javier Restrepo P. (Napoleón Franco) provided valuable data on presidential approval. Former President Ernesto Samper gave the authors two extensive interviews in May of 2000 and made available detailed information on regional investment for representatives. Research for this paper was supported with funds from the Helen Kellogg Institute for International Studies and the Social Science Research Council.

1. David Bushnell, *The Making of Modern Colombia: A Nation in Spite of Itself.* (University of California, 1993, pg. vii).

2. Jonathan Hartlyn, *The Politics of Coalition Rule in Colombia* (New York: Cambridge University, 1988).

3. M. S. Shugart and John M. Carey, "Incentives to Cultivate a Personal Vote: A Rank Ordering of Electoral Formulas" (*Electoral Studies*, 1995, 14(4):417–39). Eduardo Pizarro Leongómez, "La Atomización Partidista en Colombia: el Fenómeno de las Micro-Empresas Electorales" (University of Notre Dame, IN: Kellogg Institute for International Studies—Working Paper #292, 2002).

4. Matthew S. Shugart and Scott Mainwaring, "Presidentialism and Democracy in Latin America: Rethinking the Terms of the Debate," in Scott Mainwaring and Matthew S. Shugart, eds., *Presidentialism and Democracy in Latin America* (Cambridge: Cambridge University, 1997). Shugart and Carey, *Presidents and Assemblies*.

5. Olga Behar and Ricardo Villa S., *Penumbra en el Capitolio* (Santafé de Bogotá: Planeta, 1991, pp. 139–143).

6. Timothy P. Wickham-Crowley, *Guerillas and Revolution in Latin America* (Princeton, NJ: Princeton University, 1992, pp. 45–46).

7. There was a pause in Escobar's violence against the state. He negotiated a plea bargain with the Gaviria government and surrendered to authorities (exchanging his freedom for a lenient prison sentence and guarantees that he would not be extradited to the U.S.). The agreement broke down when Gaviria received word of Escobar's opulent lifestyle behind bars and his continued running of his narcotics operation. When word reached Escobar that the government planned to move him to a new prison and change his living conditions, he escaped and renewed his violent campaign against the state. For a detailed account of these events and of Escobar's negotiation with the Gaviria administration, see Harvey F. Kline, *State Building and Conflict Resolution in Colombia, 1986–1994* (Tuscaloosa and London: The University of Alabama, 1999, Chapter 7).

8. Russell Crandall, *Driven By Drugs: U.S. Policy Toward Colombia* (Boulder and London: Lynne Rienner Publishers, 2002, pg. 82).

9. Douglas Farah, "The Crack Up," *Washington Post*, July 21, 1996.

10. ibid.

11. National Security Decision Directive 221

12. Alvaro Camacho Guizado, "Drug Trafficking and Society in Colombia" in Bruce M. Bagley and William O. Walker III, eds., *Drug Trafficking in the Americas* (Miami: University of Miami and Transaction Publishers, 1994, pg. 100).

13. Crandall, *Driven By Drugs*, 102.

14. Crandall, *Driven By Drugs*, 101.

15. Confidential Interview, former senior U.S. State Department official, Washington, D.C., April 2001.

16. Confidential Interview, former U.S. Defense Department official, Washington, D.C. April 2001.

17. Farah, "The Crack Up."

18. Confidential Interview, former senior U.S. State Department Official, Washington, DC April 2001. U.S. officials strongly deny that they sought Samper's removal by extra-constitutional means (a coup).

19. Ernesto Samper Pizano, *Aqui Estoy y Aqui me Quedo: Testimonio de un Gobierno* (Bogotá: El Ancora Editores, 2000, p. 284).

20. The State Department's International Narcotics Control Strategy Report calls Colombia's counter-narcotics performance "inadequate" and finds that "Although the [Government of Colombia] has made important progress in some areas this year, the [United States Government] cannot certify Colombia as fully cooperating with the United States on drug control." Secretary of State Madeline Albright said at the press briefing announcing the decision, "Coming on the eve of that country's congressional and presidential elections, the wavier decision is intended to lay the groundwork for increased cooperation and support those in Colombia who are striving to strengthen the rule of law and buttress their embattled democracy." (State Department, On the Record Press Briefing, February 26, 1998.)

21. Samper Pizano, *Aquí Estoy y Aquí me Quedo*, pp. 19–20. For an interesting study of media influence on Samper's approval rates, see Jaime Bermúdez, "Battles for Public Opinion: Mass Media, Political Scandal, and Presidential Popularity in Colombia (1994–1996) and Venezuela (1989–1993)" (unpublished doctoral dissertation, University of Oxford, 1999).

22. Samper Pizano, *Aquí Estoy y Aquí me Quedo*, p. 15. For Medina's version of the events, see Santiago Medina Serna, *La Verdad Sobre las Mentiras* (Bogotá: Planeta, 1997).

23. Ingrid Betancourt Pulecio, *Sí Sabía—Viaje a Través del Expediente de Ernesto Samper* (Santa Fe de Bogotá: Ediciones Temas de Hoy, 1996). (At the time of this writing, Betancourt has been held hostage by the FARC since February 2002).

24. Comisión Ciudadana de Seguimiento, *Poder, Justicia e Indignidad. El Juicio al Presidente de la República Ernesto Samper Pizano* (Santafé de Bogotá: Comisión Ciudadana de Seguimiento, 1996). The Commission refers to its investigation of the Funds, but it does not present any detailed evidence. See also "Danza de Millones" (*Dinero*, March 1996, pp. 26–30).

25. The three Funds (for social policy, rural development, and highway infrastructure) were created by the Decree 2132 of 1992. On the previously used "auxilios parlamentarios," see Behar and Villa S., *Penumbra en el Capitolio.*, pp. 63–71.

26. The average exchange rate between 1995 and 1998 was 1,129 pesos per U.S. dollar (World Development Indicators, 2001), thus a billion pesos invested in a district during this period was roughly equivalent to 886,000 dollars. The office of former President Ernesto Samper provided the authors with the report on regional investment in May 2000.

27. Data for two representatives are missing. Because "suplentes" have some independence in the Colombian system, it is hard to know whether they direct their share of the funds to the same geographic region as the principal.

For analytical purposes, we assume that the principal and the "suplente" constitute a single recipient and share their commitments. To test this assumption we run the statistical model (Table 2), eliminating 20 cases in which the person voting on June 12 was not the main recipient listed in Samper's investment report. The results remained unchanged.

28. For a similar attempt to measure constituency support for the president, see Kasuya, "Patronage of the Past and Future."

29. The interaction terms are the product of the investment measure times the opposition dummy.

30. Samper has acknowledged that the party "was divided" at the time, and that Gaviria represented his "main rival" in the party (interview with the authors, May 2000).

31. The prediction corresponds to the title of an investigative book by Mauricio Vargas, Jorge Lesmes, and Edgar Téllez, *El Presidente que se Iba a Caer. Diario secreto de tres periodistas sobre el 8.000* (Santafé de Bogotá: Planeta, 1996).

ENDNOTES FOR CHAPTER 5

1. Article 50, Constitution of the Republic of Madagascar, 1992; French language version. Note that the official documentation of the case was expressed in French, one of the two official languages of the Republic, although most of the parliamentary debate took place in Malagasy.

2. Title VII of the Third Republic's constitution also allowed for development of a strong role by local communities (collectivities); conceivably opening a way for an idiomatic structure as in the short-lived vision of the slain Ratsimandrava, this provision has been used by the Ratsirakist advocates of a federal alternative controlled by a central party; it was virtually ignored by the Vital Forces, eager to consolidate their own roles in a centralized, unitary state. See Philip M. Allen, *Madagascar: Conflicts of Authority in the Great Island* (Boulder, CO: Westview, 1995, pp. 190–93, 234–36).

3. The Senate was not created until 2001, when it suited then President Ratsiraka's federalist convenience.

4. Economist Intelligence Unit, *Country Report: Madagascar* (2nd Quarter 1994, p. 24); *Marchés Tropicaux et Méditerranéens (MTM)*, June 10, 1994.

5. Zafy, interviewed in *UNESCO Courrier* (No. 156, March–April 1996, p. 21). For an excellent analysis of the referendum and its context, see Philippe Rajoelisoa, "Le Referendum Constitutionnel du 17 Septembre 1995 et Ses Suites" (*Afrique Contemporaine*, No. 181, Jan.–March 1997, pp. 50–58).

6. Rajoelisoa, "Le Referendum Constitutionnel," pp. 54–55.

7. ibid., p. 56. On the other hand, it may be that the Assembly had no choice in its August 3 confidence vote, for to repudiate Ratsirahonana at that time would have constituted a second ministerial crisis (censure of Rakotovahiny being the first), thus offering Zafy a constitutional pretext for dissolving parliament and organizing new elections before the impeachment verdict; see *Lettre de l'Océan Indien, Antananarivo*, July 13, 1996.

8. *L'Express de Madagascar*, August 30, 1996; summarized and excerpted in *Afrique Contemporaine*, pp. 58–61.

9. Note that this duty was substantially weakened by the referendum of the following month, and indeed represented one of the pretexts for Zafy's submission of the referendum to the public.

10. Décision No. 17-HCC/D3 du 4 septembre 1996 relative à l'empêchement définitif du Président de la République, *Journal Officiel de la République de Madagascar* (September 5, 1996); extracts in *Afrique Contemporaine*, pp. 61–67.

11. Zafy, interview with Yves Rocle, *Radio France Internationale (Paris)*, September 10, 1996; Jean Hélène, in *Le Monde (Paris)*, September 7, 1996; Honoré Razafintsalama, in *MTM*, August 30 and September 13, 1996.

12. Zafy, interviewed by Stephen Smith, in *Libération (Paris)*, September 10, 1996. Prophetically in that interview, Zafy predicted that his chief opponent would once again be Ratsiraka but (and here slightly less prophetically) that all democratic-minded people would reject the old tyrant.

13. *Libération*, September 10, 1996; *MTM*, September 13, 1996.

14. *Jeune Afrique*, January 15, 1997; see also Richard R. Marcus, "Madagascar: Legitimizing Autocracy" (*Current History*, 2001, 100(646)).

15. Zafy, interviewed in *Le Monde*, February 8, 2002; although no doubt determined to vindicate its impeachment decision, this court had after all been appointed by Zafy himself and would appear to have little reason to commit fraud for the sake of Didier Ratsiraka.

16. Marcus, "Madagascar: Legitimizing Autocracy," pp. 229–230.

17. Zafy's attempt at an opposition coalition was called the *Hery Miara-dia*, or Democratic Front.

18. For contemporary accounts of the mid-2002 resolution, see Malagasy press reports for July 5–8 (and other pertinent dates), collected on *http://www. wanadoo.mg*; also close coverage throughout late June and early July in *Le Monde (Paris)* (online at *http://www.lemonde.fr*).

ENDNOTES FOR CHAPTER 6

1. See Vera Tolz, "Drafting the New Russian Constitution" (*RFE/RL Research Report*, 1993, 2(29):1–12); David Lane and Cameron Ross, "The Changing Composition and Structure of the Political Elites," in David Lane, ed., *Russia in Transition: Politics, Privatization, and Inequality* (London: Longman, 1995); Stephen White, Richard Rose, and Ian McAllister, *How Russia Votes* (Chatham, NJ: Chatham House, 1997, pp. 98–106).

2. Stephen Holmes, "Superpresidentialism and its Problems" (*East European Constitutional Review*, 1993, 2(4)/3(1):123–126); Shugart and Carey (*Presidents and Assemblies*) classify Russia's system as "presidential-parliamentary."

3. The following section draws almost exclusively from the detailed description found in Oleg G. Rumyanstev, "'Impeachment,' Russian Style" (*Perspective*, 1998, 9(1), referenced online at *http://www.bu.edu/iscip/vol9/Rumyanstev.html* on

March 14, 2002). Other statutory requirements are found in "The Statute on the Special Commission of the State Duma"(ratified by a resolution of the Duma on June 19, 1998), which outlines the process of evaluating both the procedural aspects and legal grounds of an impeachment attempt.

4. Joel M. Ostrow, *Comparing Post-Soviet Legislatures: A Theory of Institutional Design and Political Conflict* (Columbus, OH: Ohio University, 2000).

5. "Impeachment: Day One" (*Current Digest of the Post-Soviet Press*, June 6, 1999, 51(19):9).

6. In this case, since Russia has no vice president, the prime minister assumes the office of the presidency for a period of no longer than three months, when new elections must be held.

7. Stephen White, *Russia's New Politics: The Management of a Postcommunist Society* (Cambridge, UK: Cambridge University, 2000, pp. 40–50).

8. Duma deputies are elected to four-year terms, half from plurality winner, single-member districts, the other half from party lists (with a five percent hurdle for entry into the Duma).

9. See Thomas F. Remingtom and Steven S. Smith, "The Development of Parliamentary Parties in Russia" (*Legislative Studies Quarterly*, 1995, 20:457–489) for a detailed discussion of the origins of Russian legislative organization.

10. Ostrow, *Comparing Post-Soviet Legislatures*, p. 101.

11. Thomas Remington reports mean unity scores for 11 groups and factions in the 1994–95 Duma which range from .69 to .82 ("Political Conflict and Institutional Design: Paths of Party Development in Russia," in John Löwenhardt, ed., *Party Politics in Postcommunist Russia*. London: Frank. Cass, 1998, pp. 205–206).

12. Michael McFaul, "Parliamentary Parties and Presidential Coalitions" (Carnegie Endowment for International Peace, 2000, online at *http://www.ceip. org*).

13. William Mishler and John P. Willerton, "The Dynamics of Presidential Popularity in Post-Communist Russia: How Exceptional is Russian Politics?" (Centre for the Study of Public Policy, University of Strathclyde: Studies in Public Policy Number 335, 2000, p. 10).

14. It was also understood that one of the many reasons for forcefully disbanding the legislature in October 1993 was that talk of impeachment was in the air once again.

15. Russia's federal system is categorized as "asymmetrical federalism," meaning that the 89 constituent units enjoy different degrees of autonomy depending on their status. See Joan DeBardeleben, *Russian Politics in Transition*, 2nd edition (Boston: Houghton Mifflin, 1997, pp. 165–168), for a succinct summary.

16. Russia has no vice president.

17. *RFE/RL Newsline*, March 17 & 31, 1998, available online at *http://rferl.org*.

18. ibid., April 7, 1998.

19. ibid., May 21 & 25; June 9, 1998.

20. Lyudmila Aleksandrova, "Russian Communists To Switch to 'Genuine Confrontation'" (*Itar-Tass*, 1998, reprinted in *Johnson's Russia List*, Number 2193, May 25, 1998, online at *http://www.cdi.org/russia/johnson*).

21. ibid., June 22 & 30; "Duma Presses Ahead with Plan to Impeach the President" (*Jamestown Foundation Monitor*, June 10, 1998, reprinted in *Johnson's Russia List*, Number 2193, May 25, 1998, online at *http://www.cdi.org/russia/johnson*).

22. For a complete account of the collapse of the Soviet Union, see Jack F. Matlock, Jr., *Autopsy on an Empire: The American Ambassador's Account of the Collapse of the Soviet Union* (New York: Random House, 1995). A concise summary of the initiation of the first war in Chechnya can be found in John Colaruso, "Chechnya: The War Without Winners" (*Current History*, October, 1995:329–336). The disbanding of Parliament is covered in more detail in White, et al., *How Russia Votes*, pp. 92–94.

    A number of scholars have examined Russia's economic woes, and Stephen Fish summarizes much of this literature succinctly in "Russian Studies Without Studying" (*Post-Soviet Affairs*, 2001, 17(4):332–373). Finally, see Julie DaVanzo, *Dire Demographics: Population Trends in the Russian Federation* (Santa Monica, CA: Rand, 2001) for recent trends in Russian demographics.

23. "Communists Likely To Lose Impeachment Game" (*Itar-Tass*, 1998, reprinted in *Johnson's Russia List*, Number 2486, November 21, 1998, at *http://www.cdi.org/russia/johnson*).

24. For a summary, see Lilia Shevstova, *Yeltsin's Russia: Myths and Reality* (Washington, DC: Carnegie Endowment for International Peace, 1999, pp. 246–254).

25. ibid., pp. 179–194.

26. "Who Runs Russia: No Scandal, No Action." (online at *http://www.megastories.com/russia/power/impeach.htm*, N.D.)

27. "Impeachment Commission: Yeltsin Did Not Ruin Armed Forces" (*Interfax*, November 19, 1998, reprinted in *Johnson's Russia List*, Number 2847, November 22, 1998, online at *http://www.cdi.org/russia/johnson*).

28. *RFE/RL Newsline*, January 27, 1999. The plan also expanded Article 91 of the Constitution (on presidential immunity) to give ex-presidents full immunity from prosecution after leaving office, a seat on the Federation Council, and other privileges; see "Russia: Primakov Proposes A Yeltsin Retirement Plan" (*Center for Defense Information Russia Weekly*, Number 33, January 29, 1999, online at *http://www.cdi.org*).

29. *RFE/RL Newsline*, February 15, 1999.

30. *RFE/RL Newsline*, March 16, 18, 30, & 31; April 9, 14, 15, & 23, 1999.

31. David Hoffman, "Citing Economy, Yeltsin Fires Premier," *Washington Post*, May 13, 1999, p. A1.

32. "Communist Party Starts to Flounder After Yeltsin Duma Impeachment Fails" (*The Russian Journal*, May 17–23, 1999, 3(16), online at *http://russiajournal.com*); Michael Wines, "Drive to Impeach Russian President Dies in Parliament," *New York Times*, May 16, 1999, Section 1, p. 1.

33. Michael McFaul, *Russia's 1996 Presidential Election: The End of Polarized Politics* (Stanford, CA: Stanford University, 1997).

34. See *RFE/RL Newsline*, October 30, 1998; Anna Petrova, "Russians on the Duma's Accusations Against the President" (The Public Opinion Foundation, May 21, 1999, online at *http://english.fom.ru/reports*).

35. Boris Yeltsin, *Midnight Diaries*. Translated by Catherine A. Fitzpatrick. New York: Public Affairs, 2000, p. 133).

36. "Impeachment Becomes a Never-Ending Story" (*The Russia Journal*, April 19–25, 1999, online at *http://russiajournal.com*).

37. Paul Richardson and Mikhail Ivanov, "Doing It His Way: Russian President Boris Yeltsin" (*Russian Life*, 1999, 42(4):64).

38. See "Interest in Impeaching Yeltsin is Gone" (*Current Digest of the Post-Soviet Press*, February 10, 1999, 51(2):9); "War is Peace" (*Current Digest of the Post-Soviet Press*, April 28, 1999, 51(13): 18); Sergei Shelin, "Background of Confrontation" (*New Times*, June, 1999: 12–14).

39. Anna Petrova, "The Federation Council Will Not Vote for the President's Impeachment" (The Public Opinion Foundation, April 7, 1999, online at *http://english.fom.ru/reports*).

40. Anna Petrova, "The Federation Council."

41. John Helmer, "How Primakov Fell and Yeltsin Defeated Impeachment" (for *The Straits Times*, in *Johnson's Russia List*, Number 3288, May 16, 1999, online at *http://www.cdi.org/russia/johnson*).

42. Yeltsin, *Midnight Diaries*, p. 285.

43. "Impeachment Process Will Take Up to Three Months" (*Center for Defense Information Russia Weekly*, May 14, 1999, Number 48, online at *http://www.cdi.org*.) Accessed on August 20, 2001; *RFE/RL Newsline*, May 14, 1999.

44. Petrova, "The Federation Council."

45. "Russian Poll: Financial Crash Most Important Event of 1998" (*Interfax*, December 28, 1998, reprinted in *Johnson's Russia List*, Number 2539, December 31, 1998, online at *http://www.cdi.org/russia/johnson*).

46. *RFE/RL Newsline*, April 15, May 13, 1999.

47. The Duma does not have the power to compel witnesses to attend; see "Second Day" (*Current Digest of the Post-Soviet Press*, June 6, 1999, 51(19)):10.

48. "Who Runs Russia: No Scandal, No Action."

49. Michael Wines, "Impeachment Also Is Proceeding, in a Convoluted Way, in Russia" (*New York Times*, December 19, 1998, reprinted in *Johnson's Russia List*, Number 2526, December 19, 1998, online at *http://www.cdi.org/russia/johnson*).

50. "Zhirinovsky Pledges Backing to Anti-Yeltsin Resolution" (*FBIS-SOV-97-015 Daily Report*, January 22, 1997, online at *http://wnc.fedworld.gov*).

51. In some cases their support shifted during impeachment attempts; in 1997, for example, they switched sides, initially supporting and then opposing the medical impeachment attempt. "Zhirinovsky Favors Yeltsin's Removal"

(*FBIS-SOV-97-010 Daily Report,* January 15, 1997); "Zhirinovsky Pledges Backing to Anti-Yeltsin Resolution" (*FBIS-SOV-97-015 Daily Report*, January 22,
1997, online at *http://wnc.fedworld.gov*).

52. Daniel Treisman, "Dollars and Democratization: The Role of Money and
Power in Russia's Transitional Elections" (*Comparative Politics*, 1998,
31(1):1–21).

53. Fred Weir, "Fred Weir on Impeachment Voting" (*Johnson's Russia List*, Number 3288, May 16, 1999, online at *http://www.cdi.org/russia/johnson*).

54. *RFE/RL Newsline*, December 22, 1998; "Impeachment Becomes a Never-Ending Story."

55. Valeria Korchagina, "Impeachment Drive Backed by Yavlinski" (*Johnson's
Russia List*, Number 3279, May 11, 1999, online at *http://www.cdi.org
/russia/johnson*).

56. *RFE/RL Newsline*, May 13, 1999; John Thornhill, "Zyuganov Moves Against
Yeltsin" (*Johnson's Russia List*, Number 3278, May 10, 1999, online at
http://www.cdi.org/russia/johnson); "Yeltsin Dodges Impeachment" (*The Ten-
nessean Online*, May 16, 1999, online at *http://atimes.com*); "Game's Over" (*Current Digest of the Post-Soviet Press*, June 16, 1999, 51(20):1).

57. Subtle threats of retaliation against deputies had been made by the president's envoy to the hearings on the first day. See "Impeachment: Day One"
(*Current Digest of the Post-Soviet Press*).

58. "Yeltsin Dodges Impeachment"; "Survival of the Fittest," *Time* (May 24, 1999,
p. 36). Helmer, "How Primakov Fell and Yeltsin Defeated Impeachment."

59. "Game's Over," p. 1.

60. Leonid Radzikhovsky, "Speech by Grigory Yavlinsky on Impeachment."
Translated by Dmitri Glinski Vassiliev (*Johnson's Russia List*, Number 3284,
May 13, 1999, online at *http://www.cdi.org/russia/johnson*).

ENDNOTES FOR CHAPTER 7

1. See Naoko Kada, *Politics of Impeachment in Latin America* (Unpublished doctoral dissertation. San Diego: University of California, 2002).

2. The constitutionality of congressional investigation of the president has been
questioned, but the Congress has never directly investigated the president in
Brazil. The tactic has been to expose what appears to be an illicit act by the
president in the course of investigation that was initially intended to uncover
wrong-doing by others.

3. Even when a request is presented, the court might take (and in some cases has
taken) a long time before it actually takes action.

4. Alagerina Cheibub Figueiredo and Fernando Limongi, "Partidos Políticos na
Cámara dos Deputados: 1989–94" (*DADOS*, 1995, 38(3):497–525) argue, using
roll call vote data in the lower chamber in which at least 10% of members
opposed the bill, that parties vote more cohesively than had been assumed, but
Scott Mainwaring, "Multipartism, Robust Federalism, and Presidentialism: The

Case of Brazil" (in Mainwaring and Shugart, *Presidentialism and Democracy in Latin America*) points out that the level of cohesion is still low compared to most other democracies.

5. Regarding Brazilian catchall parties, see Scott Mainwaring, "Brazil: Weak Parties, Feckless Democracy," in Scott Mainwaring and Timothy R. Scully, *Building Democratic Institutions: Party Systems in Latin America* (Stanford, CA: Stanford University, 1995).

6. Mainwaring, "Brazil: Weak Parties, Feckless Democracy," p. 378.

7. Frances Hagopian, *Traditional Politics and Regime Change in Brazil* (Cambridge, UK: Cambridge University, 1996), and Mainwaring, "Multipartism, Robust Federalism, and Presidentialism," pp. 83–84.

8. Shugart and Carey, *Presidents and Assemblies*, p. 155. Chile, Korea, and Uruguay are in the same category. See also Scott Mainwaring, *Rethinking Party Systems in the Third Wave of Democratization: The Case of Brazil* (Stanford, CA: Stanford University, 1999).

9. For more details on early development of the party system, see Miriam Kornblith and Daniel H. Levine, "Venezuela: The Life and Times of the Party System," in Mainwaring and Scully, *Building Democratic Institutions*, especially pp. 39–48).

10. For more information on the Radical Cause party, see Margarita López Maya, "New Avenues for Popular Representation in Venezuela: La Causa-R and the Movimiento Bolivariano 2000," in Damarys Canache and Michael R. Kulisheck, *Reinventing Legitimacy: Democracy and Political Change in Venezuela* (Westport, CN: Greenwood, 1998, pp. 84–88).

11. Michael Coppedge, *Strong Parties and Lame Ducks: Presidential Partyarchy and Factionalism in Venezuela* (Stanford, CA: Stanford University, 1994); see, in particular, pp. 94–135.

12. See Shugart and Carey, *Presidents and Assemblies*, p. 155.

13. According to the president, only about ten percent of savings accounts contained more than C$50,000 (*New York Times*, March 20, 1990). According to one expert, however, the freeze affected $115 billion of $150 billion in the country's bank accounts; see Theotonio Dos Santos, "Brazil's Controlled Purge: The Impeachment of Fernando Collor" (*NACLA Report on the Americas*, 1993, 27(3):17–21, p. 19).

14. *O Dia*, September 30, 1992. The approval rating is based on opinion polls taken by Gallup.

15. Dos Santos, "Brazil's Controlled Purge," p. 19.

16. Collor did not take the initiative in investigating allegations of corruption in government, despite his credential as the "hunter of fat-cat bureaucrats," a reputation gained while he was the governor of Alagoas.

17. Pedro and PC had conflicting business interests. According to Pedro's memoir, he took the matter into his own hands when it became clear that his brother was not going to stop PC's ambitions. See Pedro Collor de Mello, *Passando a Limpo: A Trajetória de um Farsante* (Rio de Janeiro: Editora Record, 1993).

18. The parties in congress formed a "grand accord" where it was declared that the president was not the subject of investigation by this committee. Reality turned out to be otherwise, however.

19. The opposition came to hold majority because a party leader of a small party in government decided to give its seat to an opposition senator. See Kada, *Politics of Impeachment in Latin America.*

20. See *O Globo*, August 12, 1992.

21. Many legislators referred to this new finding when local newspapers asked why they were voting for impeachment.

22. Collor's defense lawyer read the president's letter of resignation after the session began, when it became obvious that he would be convicted. The Senate voted, nevertheless, to continue the trial of the president as if he had not resigned. The constitutionality of this act was challenged by Collor. The Supreme Court's vote was tied, and the constitutionality was upheld only by adding three votes from the Supreme Court of Justice (whose U.S. equivalent would be the Federal Circuit Court).

23. *Jornal do Brasil*, March 29, 1993.

24. Farias completed two years of his term, when he benefited from amnesty at Christmas and was paroled in December 1994. He was found shot dead in 1996.

25. See Juan Carlos Rey, "Corruption and Political Illegitimacy in Venezuelan Democracy," in Canache and Kulisheck, *Reinventing Legitimacy*, p. 125, originally from Andrew Templeton, "The Evolution of Public Opinion," in Louis W. Goodman, Johanna Mendelson Forman, Moises Naím, Joseph S. Tulchin, and Gary Bland, *Lessons of the Venezuelan Experience* (Baltimore: Johns Hopkins, 1995, p. 80).

26. William Ojeda, *Cuánto Vale Un Juez* (Valencia and Caracas: Vadell Hermanos, 1995, p. 96).

27. The Supreme Court was to make its decision in two weeks.

28. *Notisur*, May 14 & 21, 1993.

29. See, for example, Caldera's comment on May 17, 1993 and the prediction of "major crisis" by Freddy Muñoz, of the Movement toward Socialism, on May 18, 1993, both *in El Universal.*

30. These reports obtained from *Notisur*, May 21, 1993.

31. Author interview with President Pérez, December 20, 1999.

32. When the president takes a temporary leave he appoints a government minister to be interim president.

33. In the same session it voted to make the interim president the president for the rest of Pérez's term.

34. *Notisur*, September 10, 1993.

35. Because of his age, Pérez was not put in prison but served his term at home, in accordance with Venezuelan penal code.

36. The Chief Justice said this sum included the costs of the troops sent to Nicaragua (*El Universal*, May 31, 1996). As of 2002, the question of whether the former president must pay the costs of the trial was yet to be resolved; the defense team contends that since the president was absolved of the more serious crime he need not pay the costs of the trial.

37. The Court did not ask Pérez to account for how the funds were used, and instead decided to hire "experts" to calculate the alleged damage caused by the ex-president and government officials.

38. See, for example, Angel Bermúdez, "El Largo Proceso a Carlos Andrés Pérez" (*El Universal*, May 31, 1996); quoted in Cadi Martin, ed., *El Juicio a CAP: Inocente o Culpable?* (Caracas: Arte Fotolitográfico, 1996, pp. 206–209); also, Alberto Quirós Corrade, "La Razonable Insatisfacción," (*El Universal*, June 6, 1996), quoted in Martin, *El Juicio a CAP*, pp. 233–241.

39. Juan Carlos Rey, "La Crisis de Legitimidad en Venezuela y el Enjuiciamiento y Remoción de Carlos Andrés Pérez de la Presidencia de la República" (*Boletín Electoral Latinoamericano*, 1993, 9, p. 112).

40. Author interview with Juan Carlos Rey, November 15, 1999.

41. The president's friends carried out a plan to discredit the congressional investigation by offering an alternative explanation for why the president could afford a luxurious life that presidential salary alone would not pay for. It stirred the investigative committee for only a short while, as a witness appeared at the committee to discredit the president's friends' explanation.

42. The defense team quickly pointed out the Court's contradictory demand. The dispute over the fines has remained unresolved, but the Court has not raised the issue to public attention.

ENDNOTES FOR CHAPTER 8

1. For an extensive analysis of presidential power, see Shugart and Carey, *Presidents and Assemblies*.

2. Samuel Huntington, *The Third Wave: Democratization in the Late Twentieth Century* (Norman, OK: University of Oklahoma, 1991).

3. Included in the tables are those countries who, according to the Central Intelligence Agency's "World Fact Book" (online at *http://www.odci.gov/cia/publications/fact book/index.html*) are identified as having a president as "chief of state"; such presidents may be selected by the legislature, but if so, and the president is also the prime minister, the country is excluded; if, however, the president is directly elected and also serves as prime minister, the country is included. We have included only those countries with presidencies that received a score of "five" or lower on Freedom House's combined measure of freedom in 2001–02; excluded, in other words, are those countries that received a 5.5 or above (see *http://freedomhouse.org/research/free world/2002/combinedaverage.pdf*). Data on The Gambia (1997) and Niger (1993, 1999) are missing and not presented.

4. Kada, *Politics of Impeachment in Latin America*.

5. Jacobson, "Impeachment Politics in the 1998 Congressional Elections."

6. See, for example, the accounts of the Clinton affair referenced in Chapter One, Note 13.

7. Kada, *Politics of Impeachment in Latin America.*

8. On congressional investigation, see Naoko Kada, "The Role of Investigative Committees in Impeachment Processes in Brazil and Colombia" (*Legislative Studies Quarterly*, February 2003). For a detailed analysis of how information is generated during impeachment processes, see Kada, *Politics of Impeachment in Latin America.*

Recommended Readings

ON GENERAL IMPEACHMENT ISSUES AND IMPEACHMENT IN THE UNITED STATES

Benedict, Michael Les. 1973. *The Impeachment and Trial of Andrew Johnson*. New York: W. W. Norton.

Berger, Raoul. 1973. *Impeachment: The Constitutional Problems*. Cambridge, MA: Harvard University.

Ehrlich, Walter. 1974. *Presidential Impeachment: An American Dilemma*. Saint Charles, MO: Forum.

Gerson, Noel B. 1977. *The Trial of Andrew Johnson*. New York: Thomas Nelson.

Gerhardt, Michael J. 1996. *The Federal Impeachment Process*. Princeton: Princeton University.

Leonard Lurie. 1973. *The Impeachment of Richard Nixon*. New York: Berkley Medallion Books.

Posner, Richard A. 1999. *An Affair of State: The Investigation, Impeachment, and Trial of President Clinton*. Cambridge, MA: Harvard University.

Savage, James D. 1994. "Corruption and Virtue at the Constitutional Convention." *Journal of Politics* (56).

Shugart, Matthew S., and John M. Carey. 1992. *Presidents and Assemblies. Constitutional Design and Electoral Dynamics*. Cambridge, UK: Cambridge University.

Thomas, David Y. 1908. "The Law of Impeachment in the United States." *American Political Science Review* (2).

Van Tassel, Emily Field, and Paul Finkelman. 1999. *Impeachable Offenses*. Washington, D.C.: *Congressional Quarterly*.

ON THE IMPEACHMENT OF JOSEPH ESTRADA (THE PHILLIPPINES)

Doronila, Amando. 2001. *The Fall of Joseph Estrada: The Inside Story*. Manila: Pasig and Makati: Anvil Publishing and *Philippine Daily Inquirer*.
Doronila, Amando, ed. 2001. *Between Fires: Fifteen Perspectives on the Estrada Crisis*. Pasig: Anvil Publishing and *Philippine Daily Inquirer*.
San Juan, Thelma Sison, ed. 2001. *People Power II: Lessons and Hopes*. Manila: ABS-CBN Publishing.

ON THE IMPEACHMENT OF ERNESTO SAMPER (COLOMBIA)

Bushnell, David. 1993. *The Making of Modern Colombia: A Nation in Spite of Itself*. University of California.
Dugas, John C. 2001. "Drugs, Lies, and Audiotape: The Samper Crisis in Colombia." *Latin American Research Review*. 32(2).
Hartlyn, Jonathan. 1988. *The Politics of Coalition Rule in Colombia*. Cambridge, UK: Cambridge University.
Kline, Harvey F. 1999. *State Building and Conflict Resolution in Colombia, 1986–1994*. Tuscaloosa and London: The University of Alabama.
Mainwaring, Scott, and Matthew S. Shugart, eds. 1997. *Presidentialism and Democracy in Latin America*. Cambridge, UK: Cambridge University.

ON THE IMPEACHMENT OF ALBERT ZAFY (MADAGASCAR)

Allen, Philip M. 1995. *Madagascar: Conflicts of Authority in the Great Island*. Boulder, CO: Westview.
Brown, Mervyn. 1978. *Madagascar Rediscovered: A History from Early Times to Independence*. London: Tunnacliff.
Covell, Maureen. 1995. *Historical Dictionary of Madagascar*. Lanham, MD & London: Scarecrow Press.
Marcus, Richard R. 2001. "Madagascar: Legitimizing Autocracy." *Current History*. 100(646).

ON THE IMPEACHMENT OF BORIS YELTSIN (RUSSIA)

Huskey, Eugene. 1999. *Presidential Power in Russia*. Armonk, NY: M. E. Sharpe.
Shevstova, Lilia. 1999. *Yeltsin's Russia: Myths and Reality*. Washington, DC: Carnegie Endowment for International Peace.
White, Stephen. 2000. *Russia's New Politics: The Management of a Postcommunist Society*. Cambridge, UK: Cambridge University.
White, Stephen, Richard Rose, and Ian McAllister. 1997. *How Russia Votes*. Chatham, NJ: Chatham House.
Yeltsin, Boris. 2000. *Midnight Diaries*. Translated by Catherine A. Fitzpatrick. New York: Public Affairs.

ON THE IMPEACHMENT OF FERNANDO COLLOR DE MELLO (BRAZIL)

Dos Santos, Theotonio. 1993. "Brazil's Controlled Purge: The Impeachment of Fernando Collor." *NACLA Report on the Americas* 27(3):17–21.

Flynn, Peter. 1993. "Collor, Corruption, and Crisis: Time for Reflection." *Journal of Latin American Studies* 25: 351–371.

Geddes, Barbara. 1994. *Politician's Dilema: Building State Capacity in Latin America.* Berkeley: University of California.

Mainwaring, Scott P. 1999. *Rethinking Party Systems in the Third Wave of Democratization: The Case of Brazil.* Stanford, CA: Stanford University.

Weyland, Kurt. 1993. "The Rise and Fall of President Collor and Its Impact on Brazilian Democracy." *Journal of Interamerican Studies and World Affairs* 35(1): 1–37.

ON THE IMPEACHMENT OF CARLOS ANDRÉS PÉREZ (VENEZUELA)

Coppedge, Michael. 1994. *Strong Parties and Lame Ducks: Presidential Partyarchy and Factionalism in Venezuela.* Stanford, CA: Stanford University.

Damarys, Canache and Michael R. Kulisheck, eds., *Reinventing Legitimacy: Democracy and Political Change in Venezuela.* Westport, CN: Greenwood Press.

Ellner, Steve. 1993. "A Tolerance Worn Thin: Corruption in the Age of Austerity" *NACLA Report on the Americas* 27(3): 13–16.

Ewell, Judith. 1993. "Venezuela in Crisis," *Current History* 92(572) (March 1993):120–125.

Rey, Juan Carlos. 1998. "Corruption and Political Illegitimacy in Venezuelan Democracy." In Damarys Canache and Michael R. Kulisheck, *Reinventing Legitimacy: Democracy and Political Change in Venezuela* (Westport, CT: Greenwood, 1998).

Index

About the Contributors

PHILIP M. ALLEN is Distinguished University Professor and former Dean at Frostburg State University in Maryland, where he manages undergraduate majors in Liberal Studies and teaches both French and Philosophy. He was Foreign Service Officer in Madagascar during the 1960s and spent 1999–2000 there as Senior Fulbright Lecturer at the University of Antananarivo. His books include *Madagascar: Conflict of Authority in the Great Island* (Westview, 1995) and *Security and Nationalism in the Indian Ocean* (Westview, 1987). He has also written numerous essays, articles, and reviews on Madagascar, neighboring islands, and French-speaking Africa.

JODY C. BAUMGARTNER received his Ph.D. from Miami University of Ohio in 1998, specializing in American and Comparative Politics, and currently teaches Political Science at East Carolina University. His research interests include campaigns and elections, party politics, and presidential power. Previous publications include *Modern Presidential Electioneering* (Praeger, 2000), "Pardon Power" ("Politics and Policy," 2001, with Mark H. Morris), "Party Politics in Armenia" (2002, Center for Policy Analysis, American University of Armenia), and a forthcoming essay on White House Studies co-authored with Ryan Barilleaux comparing the impeachment of Presidents Bill Clinton and Boris Yeltsin.

VICTOR J. HINOJOSA completed his doctoral studies at the University of Notre Dame in 2003 and is an Assistant Professor of Political Science at Baylor University, where he teaches international relations and comparative politics. His research focuses on U.S.–Latin American relations and Latin American politics. His most recent work examines narcotics control in U.S. relations with Mexico and Colombia.

NAOKO KADA received her Ph.D. from the University of California, San Diego in 2002. Currently she is a Visiting Lecturer at the Department of Political Science, San Diego State University. Her research interests are the role of information in politics, executive-legislative relations and presidential power, and democratic governance and civil society in Latin America. She is working on a book that explores how information is generated and used in impeachment proceedings.

YUKO KASUYA is a Ph.D. candidate at the University of California, San Diego. She is currently completing her dissertation on party politics in the Philippines. Her research interests include party politics, electoral systems, and constitutional structures in the Philippines and other Southeast Asian countries. Her most recent publication (with Allen Hicken) is "A Guide to the Constitutional Structures and Electoral Systems of East, South, and Southeast Asia" in *Electoral Studies* (2003).

ANÍBAL PÉREZ-LIÑÁN is assistant professor of political science and core faculty of the Center for Latin American Studies at the University of Pittsburgh. His research focuses on political stability and institutional performance among Latin American democracies. Born in Argentina, Pérez-Liñán has conducted field research in Bolivia, Brazil, Colombia, Ecuador, Paraguay, and Venezuela. He is currently finishing a book titled *Crisis Without Breakdown: Presidential Impeachment in Latin America*.

WILLIAM B. PERKINS is a doctoral candidate at the University of Missouri, Columbia. His primary research has focused on the United States presidency, with secondary interests in public policy and electoral behavior. Pending publications include journal consideration of a paper on presidential agenda-setting (in the *Journal of Politics*, co-authored with Garry Young) and two papers as chapters in a book about the presidency of Harry Truman. He has also worked closely with John R. Petrocik on election studies. He is currently working on a dissertation about gubernatorial power.